TUMBLING WALLS

BY

WALTER E. JAMES

WITH

CHRISTY HAWES ZATKIN

A TRUE STORY OF ORDINARY PEOPLE
BRINGING RECONCILIATION IN
EXTRAORDINARY WAYS TO
AN ALIENATED WORLD

DIASPORA

THE DIASPORA FOUNDATION, INC.
LA JOLLA, CALIFORNIA

Now the story can be told without fear of reprisals
to East German Christians who have endured
more than four decades of governmental harassment
intended to suppress and isolate them,
to render their witness ineffective.
We salute these quiet heroes of the faith—
brothers and sisters in Christ—
by this telling of their authentic and moving record
now being revealed as the walls are tumbling.

Here is a story of barriers tumbling
before the power of God's love demonstrated in actions.
It points the way for committed Christians today,
encouraging them to follow the Spirit's lead,
to live out enthusiastically whatever is his call to them.
This book is written with a strong hope
it will be an inspirational and motivating witness
to the work of God's Spirit in lives
committed to his purposes and participating in his plans
for reconciling the world to himself.

Unless otherwise indicated, Scripture quotations are from *The New Testament in Modern English*, Revised Edition, J.B. Phillips. (Macmillan Publishing Company, Inc., New York: 1972).

Diligent effort has been made to locate all whose names and conversations have been included in this book.

FIRST FOUNDATION EDITION

First Printing 1990
Second Printing 1991
Library of Congress Catalog Card Number: 90-82802
ISBN 0-9627048-0-6

Cover Illustration: Jonathan Combs
Design: Michelle Eastburn Design

First Foundation Edition published and distributed by:
The Diaspora Foundation, Inc.
7504 Olivetas Avenue #C37
La Jolla, CA 92037.

*Copies available at cover price from
the publisher/distributor.
Please include $2.05 for shipping and handling.
California residents, please add state tax.*

I dedicate this book in grateful appreciation to

Marguerite Bolyard James

my beloved wife and partner,
who from the very beginning
has shared fully in my life's calling
and without whose loyal support
neither this mission nor my ministry
would have been possible.

TABLE OF CONTENTS

PHOTOGRAPHS

ACKNOWLEDGEMENTS

It was a great day when Christy Zatkin offered to help me with this book! Our joint efforts are reflected here in her skillfull reconstruction of my detailed journal account into a dynamic narrative. Hers was a wondrous labor of love. Our work was like alternate beats of one heart. Christy is a living example of what God can accomplish when one is available for his use. I am immensely grateful to Christy, to her husband Howard, their daughter Cynthia and son Geoffrey.

Joann Shira, my efficient and faithful secretary, served for thirty-six years as keeper of the archives—all the reports, tapes, publications, pictures and correspondence between the U.S. and Europe. And long after her services to my office ended, she continues to be a treasured aide, encourager and friend.

Jack and Mary Jane Patton added to my efforts their miracles of service, so essential as together we brought into being The Diaspora Foundation to facilitate the writing, publication and distribution of *Tumbling Walls*. Theirs, too, has been a labor of love, and I am deeply grateful.

A word of profound appreciation is due all who have served with me on the Foundation's Board of Directors: Kenneth Dickson, Dale H. Fearn, William Gibbs, Barbara and John Kott, Roy I. Madsen, Robert W. McClellan, John M. and Mary Jane Patton, Charles J. Peck, Jr. (deceased), Robert O. Price, Don W. Shaw and Kenneth Zinn.

And to the scores of friends who encouraged me in the five years of writing this book, and accompanied our efforts with their prayers, I express my heartfelt gratitude.

Again, let me say that the writing of *Tumbling Walls* has been entirely a labor of love, and the net proceeds will be used for continuing ministries of reconciliation in islands of need, such as those described in this story.

FOREWORD

Walt James was a staff member of the First Presbyterian Church of Hollywood, California, when I was invited by the senior minister, Dr. Louis H. Evans, Sr., to join the pastoral team. Walt had already earned a reputation with the authorities of the community—especially the police department—for his remarkable ministry to wayward, on-the-street kids. He had developed a program for these kids which caused many walls to tumble in the Southern California area.

Early in my experience as one of Walt's colleagues, I learned to appreciate his deep spirituality, his unconditional love for people and his gift of reconciliation which drew people together like a magnet.

In God's providence there came into our lives at that time a remarkable young man from Holland and of partly Jewish heritage named Ralph Hamburger, whom we learned to call "Cheesy." He carried a deep anger reflecting the emotional scars from his part in the Dutch underground during Holland's occupation by the Nazis.

Not long after Ralph's arrival in the United States, he became a regular participant in our church's college department. As he grew in Christ, Ralph became a conscience for many of us. Along with Walt James, Louis Evans, Jr. (son of the pastor), Twentieth Century Fox starlet Colleen Townsend (later to become Mrs. Evans, Jr.) and others, Ralph was drawn to become a member of a deputation team to post-World War II Europe.

This was the first of several subsequent teams from our church. Their goals were to earn the right to witness to the reconciling Gospel of Jesus Christ by helping a devastated Europe rebuild, and to serve as catalysts in helping enemies become reconciled. God uniquely enabled these deputation teams to build a strong, living bridge between people in Hollywood and Europe—especially Germany. I am sure that all the ongoing implications of this bridging ministry have yet to be revealed.

Though it may not be possible to trace the connections made by the living, caring, devoted ministries of Walt James, Ralph Hamburger and other members of those deputation teams, the story Walt James tells in this book clearly suggests that a connection was established, even in the early '50s, to the incredible ferment of the '90s in Eastern Europe, the freeing of East Germany from Soviet rule and the crashing down of the awful wall in Berlin.

Only eternity can reveal the chain reactions from Ralph Hamburger's commitment in Christ's name to Europe and particularly to Germany—a country and a people he once hated.

Also evident in *Tumbling Walls* is the amazing influence of Walt James' fatherly, brotherly, inspired Christian leadership that God has used for the reconciliation of minds, hands and hearts where once there had been only enmity. None but God himself knows how all the parts and pieces fit together, particularly those parts which Walt James has faithfully contributed.

This book is an historic record of committed Christians who helped to change our world; of hands, minds and hearts expressing the reconciling love of God through forty years of oppressive rule in East Germany. This, and much more, is a part of Walt's recounting of his unique experiences and observations of tumbling walls.

Richard C. Halverson
Chaplain, United States Senate
Washington, D.C.

BEFORE YOU READ THIS STORY...

The letters I'm receiving from Berlin and East Germany tell of events that I never dreamed would happen in my lifetime:

"The secret police—our producers of anxiety, the crew of horrors, torturers of the helpless, spies of the telephone, disappearers of mail, masters of the disadvantage from birth to grave—have lost their chains to bind us. Today their headquarters here in Greifswald like elsewhere are emptied, their papers sealed, their weapons taken, their jobs vanished. Now they look for work and nobody wants them.

"My soul is awash with tears, tears after so many years of hard tensions, tears of joy that our children will not be imprisoned any longer, tears of sorrow that the eyes of my parents could not see this day." (December 11, 1989)

"The Wall has fallen and at Christmas Eve we could walk for the first time since twenty-four years under the Brandenburg Gate, the emblem of Berlin. Fear is over, everyone breathes another way, the daily presence of the totalitarian regime is fading away." (January 12, 1990)

"I'm longing to sit down with you to share the unbelievable situation all over Eastern Europe. Every day again it is like a wonder that you can go into the East without fear, without any control. The VOPOS [police] are so friendly—our whole world seems to be changed.

"One thing is for sure: It was the Church, it was the Christians that helped the GDR [East Germany] not to have a bloody revolution." (January 26, 1990)

For years I've been greatly privileged to be part of a spiritual community which transcended the geographical and political barriers of the United States, Berlin and Eastern Europe, making the walls that separated us transparent through Jesus Christ. The people in this community have a zest for life, have all the things that make life sing, are joyous and full of enthusiasm because they decided to be Christ's people regardless of the cost. They have been lights shining in a dark world.

For those in what was the highly regimented and controlled atmosphere of Eastern Europe that cost has been high—even to forfeiting education and career. In America the cost hasn't looked as high because it's more subtle— the pervasive pull of status, lifestyle or of values coming up against ambition. The people I'm talking about, East and West, have reached the point where they acknowledge that they can't make it on their own...where they acknowledge that materialism, be they communists or capitalists, is no answer to the human spirit.

The youth of our nation and the world are hungering and thirsting for answers that satisfy the deep needs of the human spirit, for answers that give them a sense of direction and hope for the future. I submit that God and God alone has the answers both to the contemporary needs of the world and to the spiritual needs of the world's people.

Tumbling Walls is the story of people who have found that to be true in the rough and tumble of everyday life. It's the story of how God uses ordinary people in extraordinary ways when they make their lives available to Him. It's my recorded account of the actual experiences of people who decided to try the way of Jesus. They asked themselves, "What would be the result if I were to make myself wholly available to God? If I were to make myself expendable in the service of Jesus Christ?"

The story begins with World War II and moves through the post-war reconciliation period, the ideologically divided world of the Cold War and the Iron Curtain, the building of the Berlin Wall and finally into the present day of tumbling walls. As recorded through the years in my journals and correspondence, it's the unfolding of an experiment involving people on both sides of the Wall who have given their lives to God and to each other.

Recently some young people, realistically facing their own future in this challenging world, asked me some tough questions.

"Okay," they said, "We want to try God's way. How do we go about it? What principles can you and the people in your experiences pass on to guide us in our own attempts to be wholly available to God?"

Each one was asking, "Can God really use my talents? What is the cost if I make my life available to Him? Is it worth it?"

With these queries in mind, I invite you to join me as I reflect on some experiences and adventures which produced sterling, radical and life-transforming answers!   *The Author*

CHAPTER ONE
THE BOMB

During World War II the people of Kassel, Germany lived with a false sense of security. Day after day mighty armadas of Allied bombers would pass over their beautiful old city of 250,000 people for some six hours at a time, but not a bomb fell on Kassel. Located on the Fulda River at the base of the Habichtswald Mountains, Kassel was a pastoral area with green fields, grazing cattle, flowering trees, well-trimmed hedges and rural homes. There was little evidence that underneath the city thrived an industrial complex of gigantic proportions. Then on October 12, 1943, one thousand American B-17 bombers flew over, opened their bomb bays, dropped their deadly cargo, and flew on. In the twenty minutes it took this to happen, ninety-one percent of the heart of the city was destroyed, seventy-four percent of the city as a whole was ruined and 38,000 people were killed. There was still enough fight left in the city to put up stiff resistance when the U.S. Army swept through Germany in 1945. The ground bombardment in response to the resistance was devastating. Kassel was one of the most completely destroyed cities in all of Europe.

In the summer of 1950, just five years after Germany surrendered to the Allies ending the war in Europe, four college kids from Hollywood, California arrived in Kassel to take part in an international work camp sponsored by the Brethren Service Commission.

The town was still almost totally destroyed. People were living in the most primitive of conditions without running water, indoor plumbing, and often without even roofs over their heads. Prominently displayed in whatever assemblage of a home they could piece together were the pictures of family members killed in the war—husbands, fathers and brothers in the fighting; grandparents, wives, mothers, sisters and babies in the bombing. The daily battle was to find enough food to eat.

As the Hollywood four—Ralph Hamburger, Harriet Prichard, Duke Benson and John Grund—got off the train in the bomb damaged station, townspeople who heard the English-speaking voices were glowering at them and muttering to each other. By the time the four were driven to the bombed out barracks compound where the camp was located, more than two hundred people were following. They crowded into the area, milling around, shouting, shaking their fists and yelling. They were enraged that Americans, people from the country that had bombed out of existence their families, friends, city and livelihoods had the audacity to come here, even on a mission of reconstruction and reconciliation.

What were these four, young college-age Americans doing so far from home in a place where they so obviously weren't wanted? How could they be so audacious as to think they could be agents of reconciliation in the midst of such devastation?

The groundwork for their mission had been laid three years earlier with an urgent question: What if I were to count my life as 100 percent expendable for Jesus Christ? The question was asked by Louie Evans, Jr. in September 1947 at the First College Briefing Conference held high in the San Bernardino Mountains of Southern California at the Forest Home Conference Center. Twenty of us were assembled in a cabin working out the last minute details for the conference. Through the cabin's picture window, we saw Louie striding down the mountain, returning from a private time of prayer, his face full of glory and we knew something exceptional had occurred. He entered the cabin quietly trying to be unobtrusive. Seeing that was hopeless, he joined our circle and began sharing what had happened.

"I committed my life to the Lord's work at a conference up here three months ago. Along with some other guys, I put together some specific disciplines to guide that commitment. One of them was 'to live my life as an expendable for Christ.' But what does that really mean, to be expendable for Christ?"

"I was in the Navy stationed in the Pacific just as the war ended. I saw the beaches where so many thousands of our country's young men died. I saw the unending expanses of the Pacific where in the early years of the war, the small PT Boats were our country's only defense against the Japanese navy.

"As I agonized in prayer this afternoon, there suddenly came to my mind the name for the young sailors in those PT Boats. They were called the expendables[1]. They counted their own lives of no value for the sake of what they were fighting for. That's what being expendable means! What if I were to count my life as 100 percent expendable for Jesus Christ? What if I counted my life of no value for the sake of our Lord? Not just be a Christian, not just be a minister, but be an expendable in His service?"

Without conscious thought, we found ourselves kneeling on the smooth boards of that cabin floor praying together, "God, let me become an expendable in the service of Jesus Christ."

---

[1] From the book by W. L. White, *They Were Expendable* (New York: Harcourt Brace Jovanovich, 1942).

Expendability became the theme of the weekend. From that leaders' group the excitement infiltrated and infused every meeting, inspiring these young people who were leaders in their home churches with the same enthusiasm we felt. Harriet, Duke, John and Ralph, the four who would incur the wrath of the Kassel townspeople, had been a part of this conference.

So had Colleen Townsend, a young starlet on contract with Twentieth Century Fox. Colleen was dating Louie Evans and he'd invited her to come. She came because she wanted to know what had happened here three months ago to cause the dramatic change in Louie. She knew it wasn't just religion. She had that. She knew it wasn't just going to church. She did that. When he told her it was having a personal relationship with Christ, she backed off. She didn't understand that.

I sensed a special chemistry between Louie and "Coke," and wondered where their relationship was headed. On Monday morning, the last day of the conference, I saw Louie helping Coke put her suitcase in her car. It looked to me like the high pitch of this weekend was more than Coke could handle. Louie called me over.

Beaming at the world in general and Coke in particular, Louie asked, "Would you like to tell Walt what happened to you last night?" Coke, who because of her career, had just recently been featured in *Life Magazine*'s cover article, was a truly beautiful, young woman with her honey-blonde hair, big, blue eyes and a generous smile. Heads turned wherever she went. But as I looked at the radiance in her face this morning, I saw a refinement, a deepening of that beauty which was hard to describe.

Smiling at and with me, she said, "Remember I told you Saturday that I felt like I'd walked into the middle of a fireworks display?" I nodded. "Well, I really felt like someone on the outside looking in. My friends, one in particular," here she turned the full sunshine of her smile on Louie and I saw his knees buckle slightly, "kept challenging me. 'Look, Coke,' they'd say, 'if you're not sure about Jesus, just try this experiment. Ask him to show himself to you.' So after last night's meeting, I went out and sat on one of those big rocks at the edge of the forest and said, 'Lord, if you're real, show yourself to me.' And in a quiet way, that's just what he did.

"The excitement of the weekend was at its height that night at the concluding meeting. I wondered how Dr. Henrietta Mears, the conference leader and the Christian Education director at our church, was going to pin this weekend down, make it something to take home. I needn't have worried. She was a practical person and a genius at developing Christian leadership among students.

Seizing on the high level of motivation and commitment generated by the weekend, she placed a large map of the world on the front wall of the assembly hall. She said, "Young men, young women, there is no magic in small dreams. Go to the map and place a large 'X' where you propose to invest your life for Jesus Christ."

Silence filled that large room as people absorbed the full depth of her challenge. It was one thing in a spiritually high weekend to feel dedicated to the Lord's work. But Miss Mears was seeking from them a public commitment to the hopes and aspirations expressed in the rarefied air of the College Briefing Conference. For a few, long minutes, no one moved. Then slowly, some of the young people who had knelt with Louie earlier in the cabin began coming forward putting an "X" on the map and quietly stating where they felt called. Their commitments released others and a steady stream of glowing, young men and women followed them quietly stating their own calls.

My heart and spirit swelled with love and pride for these collegians and the way God was inspiring them. As I looked around the room, my eye was caught by a slender, young man sitting in the back intently watching each person who spoke. In the midst of all this human and spiritual warmth, he seemed isolated and alone. Leaning over to Duke Benson, I asked if he knew the man.

"Yeah, that's Ralph Hamburger." Duke replied. "He's a war refugee from Holland. Nice guy. Quiet."

Ralph's loneliness seemed so poignant, I rose to go speak to him. I was detained for a moment and when I turned, he had left. No quickening of my senses, no intuitive insight forewarned me of how involved Ralph and I would become in each other's lives.

For two years that commitment to expendability...to being wholly available to Christ...became a growing part of the lives of young people like Ralph, Louie Evans, Colleen Townsend, Duke Benson, Harriet Prichard, John Grund and others in the college department. And a part of my life too.

Since my job as the Minister of Weekday Activities at the First Presbyterian Church of Hollywood was to help members find ways to put their faith to work— or as our senior pastor, Dr. Evans, Sr. said, "to help the church flex its muscles,"—I was able to direct these young people to areas of service. The

Boys Clubs and the international students on the L.A. City College campus were two groups that benefited from their enthusiastic involvement.

My own ministry was going well. The initial concern from some segments of the church about reaching out and being a resource to the community had eased. We were finding the points of need and providing quality leadership at those points. Working through schools, PTAs and particularly the Ministerial Association, an ecumenical group, we were able to find kids in need and channel them into positive situations. Camps and conferences were a major part of this.

This type of ministry was similar to what I had been doing for the YMCA and it was what Dr. Evans had envisioned for his growing congregation. I loved it! But I had an inner conviction that being an expendable for Christ would involve something more...something I had yet to discover.

That "something more" hit me like a ton of bricks when Dr. Hugh Tiner, president of Pepperdine College spoke at the collegiate meeting in the fall of 1949.

"I would like to read to you excerpts from a letter college presidents across the nation recently received from Professor Albert Einstein," he said. "It contains some convictions which Dr. Einstein feels form a basic consensus among the ranking scientists of the world." He read: "The A-bomb will soon be manufactured inexpensively and in large numbers. There is not now, nor is there likely to be developed, any adequate defense against it. Only a few, short years remain in which to discover some spiritual basis for world brotherhood or civilization as we now know it will certainly destroy itself.

I challenged the college group. "What are you going to do about this?"

How could college kids, no matter how dedicated, meet this challenge of moving the world back a step from self-destruction? A group of them felt this might be where Christ was calling them to makes their lives expendable for him. They wanted to investigate this idea and I agreed to help. Meeting for three hours on Tuesday nights in the tower room of our church, we began studying the biblical basis for world brotherhood and outlining the guidelines found there. Enthusiasm and commitment were high as we looked for ways the Lord would use us as peacemakers in a world just four years removed from the horror of World War II.

We needed a specific focus. It came in the person of the young refugee from Holland, Ralph Hamburger. A student at Occidental College, Ralph had been a quiet member of the group since it began. As the weeks passed, I began to hear some of his story, how he had been part of the Dutch underground helping Jews and others escape from Nazi persecution. His deep hatred of the Nazis and the mentality of the underground were still consuming him in spite of his obvious, growing faith in Christ. One Tuesday night, at the conclusion of the meeting, he paced the floor like a tiger in a cage. His need outstripped his young faith.

"Walt," he said, "it's Christ or chaos for me. Either Jesus Christ can change my life, take away this hatred, or I am undone."

"Let's go to the mountains," I said. "That's where I do my best spiritual wrestling."

Getting in my car, we drove the ninety miles up into the mountains to Forest Home. It was winter and starting to snow. We quickly found a cabin and built a good fire in the huge, old fireplace. Kneeling beside the bed, we spent the night in a silent, soul-searching, unrelenting vigil of prayer. The fire was out and the cold was seeping in as the grey light of dawn slowly filled the room. Sensing something, I looked up. Ralph stood there—transformed—a great light in his face and being. The mattress where he had been kneeling was stained with his tears.

Without a word, we walked to the car in the clear, icy splendor of that early winter morning, shivering in our light-weight windbreakers, the only sound our shoes crunching in the snow.

Ralph broke the silence. "Walt, I am learning to forgive. I am learning the meaning, the reality of unconditional love. Christ is releasing me from the bondage of hatred. This is what Europe needs. I don't know a single person among all of my associates who doesn't hate as I have been hating. How do we tell them that Christ can end that? How do we make them understand?"

"Could you share this with the Tuesday night group?" I asked, knowing his reticence to talk about himself.

"Why?"

"We have been looking for ways to meet Dr. Einstein's challenge. Perhaps, somehow, taking the message of Christ's healing love to Europe is a way. But the group would have to understand the need."

He was thoughtful. "Yes,...I could talk to them. A little bit."

The terror began for Ralph in 1930 when he was seven years old. His father, Donald, a banker in Hamburg, Germany and a decorated World War I hero, was badly beaten, almost killed, by Hitler's Brown Shirts because he was Jewish. His mother, a Gentile, died the next year. It took Donald two years of watching conditions deteriorate in Germany to make the decision to abandon home, friends, work—everything. But in September 1932 he took a position with a bank in The Hague, Netherlands and moved there with his two sons and mother, an Englishwoman.

It was only from incidental comments over the years that I learned the sneering and ribbing hadn't ended for Ralph when the family left Germany. As a German and English-speaking outsider, he endured more of the same until he adjusted to a new culture and a new language.

His home life brightened when his father married Kathe Klindt from Hamburg. She was a pianist and encouraged Ralph's musical talent. The next years were good ones for the family, when they could ignore the clouds of war hanging over Europe. The dark note was that their request for citizenship in Holland was denied on political grounds.

All attempts at normalcy ended on May 10, 1940, when Ralph, now sixteen, was awakened in the soft, grey light of early dawn by swarms of aircraft flying low over The Hague. Quickly pulling on his clothes and running down the stairs and out into the street, he looked up at a sky filled with German military aircraft. Frightened, he retreated to the kitchen where the family, gathered around the radio, heard that Hitler's armies had invaded their place of refuge. No longer would the family, particularly his father Donald, be safe from the Nazis.

As the bombers droned overhead, Donald turned trembling to Ralph.

"You know what is happening to the Jews in Germany, don't you?"

"Yes.... Not here...! They couldn't...."

"It happens everywhere Nazis go. We must destroy anything we have which could conceivably incriminate us."

The two tore up political papers, old letters, anything that could even remotely be considered anti-Nazi. Late that night, shaking with fear, they threw it all into one of the canals near their home, hoping that no one had seen them.

In just five short days the valiant little country fell under Hitler's blitzkrieg, his lightening war.

The occupation forces, more or less gentle at first, became increasingly oppressive and ruthless. By the time Ralph finished high school in 1941, his father, along with all the Netherlands' Jews, had been forced to register and wear the yellow Star of David. Fear and tension deepened as Jews were forbidden to use public transportation, eat in restaurants, attend movies or go to concerts. Every time the doorbell rang after the 8:00 p.m. curfew the family froze in terror, thinking the Nazis were coming to take Donald away.

Ralph's family was forced in 1943, along with all of Holland's Jews, to move to Amsterdam, which was to be the Jewish ghetto of the Netherlands. Because his wife wasn't Jewish, Donald still had some freedom. The family didn't have to live in the ghetto and he no longer had to wear the Star. By this time Ralph was nineteen and had an office job, but his position was precarious because he wasn't racially "pure."

Ralph's rage grew as he saw Jewish people hauled away by the truckloads to concentration camps and extermination. One day a friend, catching a glimpse of Ralph's feelings on his face, asked casually, "You don't care much for the Nazis?"

"Seeing their oppression and terror enrages me!" he answered hotly.

Both glanced covertly at each other and then around them, startled by Ralph's incautious voice.

"Would you like to meet some others who feel the same way?" Ralph hesitated, understanding the meaning that lay behind the casual question. "Yes, but I wouldn't be good at violence."

His friend nodded and that evening took Ralph to meet members of the non-combatant part of the Dutch Resistance. He became part of a small team of people who worked with their hearts and minds and hands finding or making hiding places for the Jews and political refugees, helping to keep them fed and cared for and getting them out of the city when they could.

The work was extremely dangerous and nerve-wracking. It was a cause of great tension between Ralph and Katie. She was afraid for Pucci, as they called Donald.

"How can you do this?" she confronted Ralph. "Now, every time a shadow moves or a board creaks, I panic. With you in the Resistance, his danger will be even greater!"

"If you're that afraid for Pucci, you know what he can do." Ralph told her gently. "He can go into hiding. This work is something I have to do. Something I must do."

To avoid endangering his father, Ralph moved out and rented a room from a family. The father was an elder in the Dutch Reformed Church. The family's prayer before meals and Bible reading afterwards provided a place of peace, a counterpoint to his work. Intrigued by his first encounter with a living faith, Ralph joined the teen-age daughter and son when they began confirmation classes with their minister. Making as sincere a profession of faith in Christ as he knew how, he joined the church on Easter 1944 and became a regular churchgoer.

In the hectic fearsomeness of the times, the church and the family's times of prayer were like quenching water to his parched soul. But at the same time, the hurt and agony of seeing Jewish families torn apart, often knowing little or nothing about their loved ones, cooped up in small spaces and severely restricted in their movements, was a pain which wove itself into his young life.

One day the friend who had introduced him to the resistance movement asked, "You heard about William?"

Ralph stilled. "I heard he has started to carry a gun."

"Yesterday he was stopped while carrying sheets of an underground newspaper. When he tried to defend himself, he was killed on the spot."

The two walked on in silence as Ralph struggled to absorb the news of his friend's death. Finally, his companion spoke again.

"They need someone to take his place."

"What does it involve?"

"Putting the mimeographed copies of the newspaper in your briefcase, biking across town and delivering them to a 'safe' house."

"I won't carry a gun."

"That's best."

Late one rainy afternoon, Ralph had just finished his "paper route" and was biking home along a canal bank. In front of him he saw German troops lying on the bank of the canal, resting.

"Oh boy!" he thought. "That's not the direction I want to go."

He quickly turned but, seemingly out of nowhere, more troops materialized, all carrying submachine guns. There was no escaping. Along with four other men who had been biking along the canal, he was herded into a nearby gymnasium.

"What's happening?" he asked a young German soldier.

"Shut up!"

An officer paced the floor as more and more men were brought in and lined up against the wall. For at least an hour Ralph stood with the others, his tension increasing as the minutes dragged by. Uppermost in his thoughts was a scene he had witnessed the week before. A Nazi officer had been shot and killed. Twenty civilians were rounded up, taken to a nearby square and lined up against a wall. Ralph, passing through the square, was forced along with other townspeople to watch. The twenty were machine-gunned down, executed immediately to avenge the one officer's death. Was that about to happen to him?

Finally, the officer stopped pacing and looked over the group, seemingly counting them.

"You five," he snapped, pointing to Ralph and the four brought in with him. "Outside!"

They followed him while soldiers, guns at ready, followed them.

"Pucci and Katie won't know what happened for days," thought Ralph. "They may never know. I'll just be one more person who disappeared."

The sidewalk along the canal was lined with the bicycles of the men inside.

"Quickly now," said the officer. "Load these bicycles onto the barge."

Surprised, they did as they were told. When they finished, the officer looked them all over appraisingly, shrugged a shoulder, and motioned to the troops. They got onto the barge and left.

Weak with relief, Ralph realized that this time it was transportation, not revenge, that the Germans were seeking. His knees almost buckling, Ralph turned to the other four equally astonished men.

"Did you ever think you'd be grateful to the Germans for just stealing your bike?"

Ralph was apprehended several times and put into prison once. Eventually he became too recognizable and had to go into hiding. Along with some other members of the Resistance, he lived in an attic they had created under a roof.

An added danger was that Germany, critically short of man-power, was conscripting men of all ages and deporting them to Germany to work in forced labor camps. It wasn't safe to be on the streets, particularly if you were young and able-bodied.

His usefulness to the Resistance now limited, Ralph returned to live at home. To fill this desolate time of uncertainty, Ralph began voice lessons with a famous bass baritone from the Amsterdam music conservatory. In the midst of all that chaos, the man still took students. To Ralph, the music gave a calming focal point.

The last year of the war, 1945, was the worst. The Germans unleashed a reign of terror on the Dutch population. Thousands more men were deported to Germany to work in the factories. Warehouses and even farms were raided of their produce and livestock, hospitals and factories were dismantled and the equipment taken to Germany along with fire-engines, ambulances, farm equipment and even hearses. In the harbors floating docks, wharves, cranes, oil tankers and factories were blown up. Even the dikes, Holland's protection from the sea, were demolished, flooding whole towns and forcing mass evacuation.

The Nazis prevented food from reaching the western cities and starvation set in. In Amsterdam alone, approximately 500 people a week were dying from hunger. It became a daily occurrence to see people collapse in the streets. For some bit of paltry food Katie or another family member would stand in line four to eight hours a day. There was no electricity and only gas for cooking two hours a day. Deserted homes were demolished and the trees along the streets cut down to provide fuel for heating and food preparation. The winter was bitingly cold.

Finally, Ralph decided he must do something.

"I'm going on a hunger trek," he told Katie and Pucci.

"To the eastern part of the country to ask food from the farmers?" questioned Katie.

"Yes."

"No." Pucci shook his head. "I've talked to others who've done that. It's too dangerous. We'll survive."

"Maybe. But maybe not. I've got to go while I'm still strong enough to do it."

Ralph, Juliana, (a girlfriend's sister), and her uncle, Jan, left the next morning on bikes. Ralph's bike had no tires. He rode on the rims. It was January 1945, the middle of an extremely cold winter. Because of German checkpoints and patrols, they had to take indirect back roads often covered with snow. A day and a half later they were feeling smug about their ability to elude patrols.

"Oh, look!" Juliana cried pointing up in excitement. "It's an Allied fighter plane!" She waved joyously.

Ralph made a flying tackle from his bike to hers, grabbing her and rolling into the ditch with Jan right behind them as bullets strafed the road where they'd just been.

"Lie still!" Ralph commanded as the aircraft returned.

"But we're not Germans!" she sobbed.

"They don't know that. They shoot anything that moves."

Shaken, wet, numb with cold, they continued on, taking cover at the sound of any engine.

At the sight of their Dutch identification, farmers filled their sacks generously with everything from wheat to bacon. Then began the return trip, bikes laden with heavy sacks, weather still freezing. Getting back to Amsterdam was harder than leaving, checkpoints being even tougher to stop people from doing exactly what they had just done. They rode with eyes always searching for a quick hiding place, ears straining for warning of approaching aircraft or patrols.

Juliana stared at Ralph in amazement as they cautiously emerged from behind a wall as two jeeps disappeared around a turn.

"You're grinning!"

"It's such a joy to fool those no-goods!"

Finally they made it back into the city.

Pucci greeted Ralph with tears.

"I thought for sure this time I would never see you again!"

Twice more, Ralph made hunger treks. On the last, he was arrested by the Germans and drafted to go to work in the German factories. The officer put him on a boat across the IJssel Lake and told him he'd be met on the other side. As the boat docked, Ralph walked off with the rest of the passengers, not waiting for his reception committee.

In the last weeks of the war, trying to maintain their hope for survival, Ralph and his friends lived day to day by the advancement of the Allied troops. One friend rigged a short-wave radio using water glasses for power. Maps spread out on a table, they would listen to The Voice of America and the BBC for hours, trying to reconcile the varying reports and plot the Allied positions. One evening curfew slipped by unnoticed. Suddenly, Ralph realized the time.

"It's nine o'clock. I've got to go!"

"No! It's too dangerous to be out after curfew. Stay here."

"My parents will worry too much. I've got to go."

Slipping quietly through the streets, Ralph made it to within a few blocks of his home when a patrol suddenly rounded the corner coming toward him. He fled, bullets whining by, hitting the walls around him. He ducked into a doorway and pounded on the door. It opened and a hand reached out and jerked him in, closing the door quickly and quietly. Looking into an elderly couples' faces—strangers—Ralph listened as the patrol pounded on by.

"Thank you," he whispered gratefully, opening the door to leave.

"We're all in this together," was the quiet reply.

Finally, almost unbelievably, after five years of heart-rending oppression, the war was over. On May 5, 1945, the Canadian Army liberated Amsterdam. By then, about 275,000 Netherlanders had been killed or starved to death. Jews accounted for about 104,000 of that number, reducing by seventy-five percent The Netherlands' Jewish population.

The insensitivity, the cruelty and the destructiveness of the Germans had created a deep hatred, a revulsion of them in Ralph's heart. He and his friends jeered and jested as German prisoners-of-war were marched by.

"Beasts! You destroyed so many things. Now it's your turn!" Ralph's hatred could finally be expressed.

Dutch women who had fraternized with German soldiers had their hair shorn and were put in trucks and driven through the city to be publicly mocked and scorned. The feeling of being rid of the Germans was indescribable. Ralph celebrated with others, dancing in the streets for weeks on end. But in the midst of the elation, came the reality that the country was in shambles.

The devastating war years had put their mark on Ralph too. He tried several jobs, but would not hold on to any of them. Part of the time he just vegetated, much to the disgust of his parents. His young faith was not strong enough to give him direction.

His friend from the resistance appeared in the doorway one day.

"Come on. There are some people I want you to meet."

"Who?"

"Some Americans, part of a United Nations Relief and Rehabilitation team. They come in to the YMCA on weekends for recreation."

Ralph was deeply impressed by the Americans and the way they associated and dealt with each other. He moved into the "Y" with his friend and began to develop a friendship with the Americans, at their invitation going to see their work. Slowly the idea ripened in him that he would like to go to America. His parents didn't like the idea and had no money to help. His American relatives weren't particularly keen on acquiring a family refugee, but finally an uncle, twice-removed, in Beverly Hills agreed to be his sponsor, a requirement for immigrating to the United States. Ralph arrived in Los Angeles on Washington's Birthday, February 22, 1947.

Coming from war-torn Amsterdam to Beverly Hills was an indescribable shock. The Beverly Hills police picked Ralph up as he wandered the streets admiring the elegant homes. They thought he was a vagrant and escorted him back to his uncle's house to make sure he was supposed to be there. The uncle assured them that he was, but didn't sound too convinced himself. Ralph wrote home telling his parents in awe that he had been given a large room with two beds and had an entire bathroom to himself.

But what was really unbelievable was the amount of food people ate...and the amount they threw away.

After about six weeks, Ralph's uncle told him that it was time to do things the American way: get a job at the bottom and work his way up. He helped Ralph get a job as a bank messenger and find a room to rent. At first Ralph was offended that his uncle didn't work him into his business, the European way, but later he began to appreciate that decision.

What led to the most profound changes in Ralph's life was the discovery of a church home. He described the experience to me as we were coming down from the mountains after our all night prayer vigil that fall of 1949.

"It was by God's grace, Walt, that I found our church. I was literally knocked off my religious feet. The place was alive! The music was terrific. I met one of the pastors, Dick Halverson, and he became my mentor. I parked myself on the doorstep of his office, learning from him all that I could. He decided I should be in college, found a scholarship, and helped me to get started. After being out of school for seven years, I was suddenly a conditional freshman. All this was overwhelming!

"And the college group at church! They were so outgoing and joyful, they almost scared me off. Could they really be that interested in me? My cynicism made me question whether all this enthusiasm for Christ could be genuine. Yet they talked about and to God as if they really knew him. Do you know how skeptical I was, Walt?

"Still, the love and joy have just kept coming my way, like the prayers and love of the Christian family I rented a room from in Amsterdam, a balm upon my weary, wounded soul."

Christ's love was reaching out to Ralph through these people, healing him and transforming him. He was being prepared to help build a ministry that would take those California kids into Kassel and other areas of a war-torn and weary world, a world hungry for Christ's message of reconciling, unconditional love.

CHAPTER THREE

WORLD DEPUTATION

The Tuesday night after Ralph and I had gone to the mountain cabin, he told the college kids a little of his story, particularly his experiences during the war, so they could begin to comprehend the deep and bitter hatred he had harbored for the Nazis.

He ended by saying, "For the two years that I've been here, your love and joy have just kept coming my way. Christ is teaching me that he can deal with my hate. He is draining it out, healing the wounds, showing me the meaning of his unconditional love. This is what Europe needs! I don't know a single person among all my associates who doesn't hate as I've been hating. How can we show them Christ's redeeming, unconditional love? How can we make them understand that in spite of everything that has happened to them, they don't have to hate anymore?"

The gang got really fired up discussing Ralph's question. His story had moved, shaken and excited everyone. Was his challenge to take the message of Christ's redeeming, forgiving love to the war-weary students of Europe the specific goal for which we had been praying? Was this our way to meet Dr. Einstein's challenge? After much prayer and discussion, the group decided that yes, it was! The exaltation and inner peace we felt with the decision gave us the confirmation we needed.

There were two different directions we could go. One was to have gospel teams witness at European universities. The second was to go to work camps whose purpose was reconciling different nationalities through the process of living, working and worshipping together.

Being college students themselves, the group leaned toward the idea of witnessing at universities rather than going to the work camps. My inclination was toward the work camps, but we all agreed that the decision would be made through prayer. In every detail we looked for the confirmation of the Holy Spirit.

Ralph became the secretary and driving force in World Deputation, the name the group had adopted. I marveled at his ability to do this. Here he was, an unknown and stateless refugee, wielding an influence out of all proportion to what the world would have deemed his position or status. And he was doing it in Hollywood, the status capital of the world! He had sold his vision to that dynamic, high-powered group of college kids.

I suggested to Ralph that it was now time to consult with our senior pastor, Louie's dad, Dr. Louis H. Evans, Sr. Rated as one of America's ten outstanding preachers by *Time* and *Life* magazines, Dr. Evans was a tall, formidable-looking man with raven black hair, bushy eyebrows and blue eyes that looked right into your soul. I knew him to be a good judge of character and a master at knowing how to motivate each particular person. He played devil's advocate to Ralph's enthusiasm.

Ralph collapsed into a chair in my office immediately after the appointment and related the conversation:

"He listened to me without any comment, not even an 'uh' or an 'um,' his eyes boring into me, as I told him how the group had come together and how its commitment to witness abroad had been formed," Ralph told me. "Then I asked him for his support. Eventually, I ran out of words. Dr. Evans just kept staring at me, then asked tersely, 'Who do you and your group think you are? Missionaries? You're not even dry behind the ears yet!'

"A little shaken, I persisted. 'What do we have to do to qualify for this mission?'

"'Contact the youth department of our General Assembly and the youth department of the World Council of Churches and ask them this same question,' Dr. Evans replied. 'Remember, our church has a major mission budget still not underwritten. Show me this dramatic idea of yours will work without threatening that budget. You can't go around panhandling.'

"'We won't,' I agreed. Then, gathering my courage, I said, 'If God wants this, the money will come.'

"'Remember that!' he told me, a glimmer of a smile at last playing around his mouth."

With the goal set and the backing conditionally secured, Ralph began the tremendous amount of research and organization needed to make that goal a reality—finding places for involvement, making budgets, securing transportation, routing an itinerary, and working out time schedules.

The team established three rigorous disciplines to ready themselves for reconciliation. The first was study. We met for three hours one night a week. The first hour was for Bible study. I'd discovered a brand new translation of Paul's letters by an Englishman, J.B. Phillips, called *Letters to Young Churches*,[2] and it became "our Bible." We were committed to seeking out the biblical guidelines for reconciliation. The second hour we listened to speakers, often

---

[2] J. B. Phillips, *Letters to Young Churches* (New York: Macmillan, 1956).

missionaries, talking about Europe and its people and in the third hour we studied the German and French languages. Several of the group already had language background, a real asset.

The second discipline was prayer. We were committed to pray through every detail, using Romans 12 as our scriptural authority. Each member of the group agreed to set aside ten minutes a day for personal prayer. On Sunday mornings we met before church services for corporate prayer. Here were college students who loved to sleep late staggering out of bed in time to be at the church before 7:00 a.m. for a "starvation" breakfast and two hours of on-their-knees prayer!

The third discipline was field work. In our own community we found places where there were alienation, tension, pain and discrimination, and we worked to put into practice the principles and guidelines we were learning. Our ideals, and we ourselves, would be tested in experience. Did we have the personal integrity—the character—and the physical stamina for this type of mission?

Out of the nearly two hundred members of the college department, twenty-five to thirty felt called to this mission. For some that call was very clear. Harriet Prichard, a tall, auburn-haired young college student studying religion and music, had just returned from a two-month bike tour of Europe with Youth Hostels. The devastation of the European cities she had seen deeply affected her. She wanted to go back and do something about it, to make some kind of effort as a Christian to alleviate it.

Duke Benson, a blond, energetic engineering student with a knack for humor, and John Grund, also a student but serious and intense, were early members of the group.

Colleen Townsend firmly declared her intention to be part of the program.

For others, the call wasn't as clear. Louie Evans, president of the College Department, was graduating that fall semester of 1949. Although interested in Deputation, he was also eager to get started in seminary. Ralph felt strongly that Louie was the person to head World Deputation and I watched with awe and some amusement as these two dedicated young men lovingly battled out where Louie belonged.

"Time is pressing, Louie," Ralph said. "It may be right for you to go to seminary right away. Yet there is the other possibility. Maybe your experiences will bind you more firmly together with the foreign students at seminary. Maybe your experiences will be the foundation of a friendship and a bond in

Christ which might bind two or three nations together in their common quest to build the Kingdom. Lou, believe me, it is our responsibility; we may not get out from under it! We must find ways to share with the youth of other nations and conquer the barriers of prejudice and hate and ideologies!"

Louie started to answer, then hesitated, his focus going inward. The silence lengthened. Suddenly he smiled his wonderful smile and grabbed Ralph in an exuberant bear hug.

"You're one terrific recruiter. For better or for worse, you've convinced me."

Ralph adjusted his glasses, a bit flustered, but very pleased. Never one to miss a beat, he added, "And you will head the mission?"

"Head it!" Louie gasped.

"Well, of course. Instead of the College Department."

So Louie added his organizational skills to get this movement launched.

One of the first speakers at our weekly meetings shocked the group and shaped the mission. Corrie ten Boom, a white haired, grandmotherly Dutch Christian—a survivor of Hitler's death camps, who had worked as Ralph had in Holland during the war—was in town. (Years later she wrote about her experiences in *The Hiding Place*[3].) At Ralph's request, she came to meet with the group. She listened to the young people's enthusiasm for the gospel team ministry, smiling gently, then spoke.

"I wonder whether or not many of the students would ask why you Americans came to Europe to evangelize? Why you did not stay at home witnessing to Jesus Christ to the youth of your own country?"

Miss ten Boom continued. "As Ralph has said, the people of Europe do need to see the love and forgiveness of Christ. But the gospel team idea won't work. You have not suffered as the people in Europe have suffered, so what right have you to speak? If you want to make a vital witness to the power of your faith, go to a city destroyed by American bombs. Identify with the people. Work with them. Eat what they eat. Sleep where they sleep. Maybe if you do it well enough and long enough, without compensation, they will hear what you have to say."

She told us about her war experiences, hiding Jews because of her Christian convictions, being discovered and together with her sister put into a concentration camp where her sister died. The depth of suffering and unconscious courage she showed was humbling to us all. The room was silent when she finished, all of us mesmerized by her quiet story.

"We are such a privileged people," Harriet began haltingly. "After being in

---

[3] Corrie ten Boom, *The Hiding Place* (Washington Depot, Connecticut: Chosen Books, 1971).

Europe last summer I really felt I shouldn't go back without making some kind of a Christian witness. But maybe naive, inexperienced college students have no right going at all. What can we say in the face of all that pain and loss?"

"What I want to help you do is gain perspective, not discourage your vision," said Miss ten Boom. "Your faith and your vitality are needed in Europe."

"What you're saying," said Louie, "is we've got to work, not preach."

"That is crucial," she replied firmly. "Let me repeat myself. To make a vital witness to the power of your faith, you must identify with the pain and suffering of the people, work alongside them, eat what they eat, sleep where they sleep. And if you do it well enough and long enough, they may hear what you have to say. You must earn the right to be heard."

Taking to heart Corrie ten Boom's recommendations, the group chose work camps as the direction for its reconciliation ministry. Study, our first discipline, was taken even more seriously and individual and group prayer, the second discipline, practiced more deeply.

Field work, the third discipline, was designed to provide what Miss ten Boom had so clearly pointed out we needed: perspective. Team members took the abstract idea of reconciliation and made it concrete by becoming involved with alienated, disinherited and poverty stricken people. Many in the group, to their horrified amazement, found out for the first time the depth of degradation existing in their own communities. Watts, an area of Los Angeles with a very large concentration of ghetto Blacks; Cleland House, a neighborhood center in the Hispanic area of East L.A.; and Hicks Camp, a shanty town built on the banks of the Rio Hondo Wash, were three areas where team members became involved by starting recreation programs, tutoring and teaching Bible classes.

Group members were learning firsthand of pain, of being strangers in a strange land. I could see the growth in their compassion, in their ability to reach beyond their own limitations and most importantly, to be themselves, Christ's people, regardless of the circumstances. Coke Townsend pretty well summed up the situation.

"It's not enough to just have a personal walk with the Lord, is it Papa Walt?" she said to me. "We really need to live our faith in the world."

The intensity and depth of the commitment was more than some collegians had time for or liked. Some people came to meetings a few times and didn't return. Others came and stayed.

The Tuesday night meetings were switched to Friday nights so those with classes and jobs wouldn't feel a time constraint. Part of our meeting time focused on identifying with one another, being sensitive to each other's needs. That was my theme at our first meeting of the new year, January 1950.

"If we are to have a heart of compassion for people in Europe, we must start by having a heart of compassion for each other," I said as we started our prayer and sharing time.

Coke was feeling discouraged, perhaps due to a letdown after the high of the holiday season, or perhaps because of a reaction to being pursued by the media for stories about her change of careers. The media and many others, particularly the people with whom she had worked, found it hard to believe that she was going back to college that semester rather than taking the new contract offered by Twentieth Century Fox. Coke felt strongly that God had something else for her to do and she was excited to get back to school and train for whatever that would be.

"You're so warm, so Christ-centered, Papa Walt," she sighed. "With all your energy and enthusiasm, you make it sound and look so easy to have a heart of compassion. I think it's hard work!"

"I think it's hard work too, Cokie! That's why we have to practice. Having a heart of compassion means being able to reach beyond our preconceived ideas and empathize with another human being. Here we have the freedom to share all our feelings, not just the 'up' ones. That doesn't mean being abrasive or critical of others. It means being able to confront as well as support each other in love. It means trusting one another enough to be honest."

"You really demonstrate that, Walt," said Harriet, a bit shyly. "You are kind of like a daddy to the whole team. We're a diverse group, but you're binding us together. I know it's the Holy Spirit that does that, but you're his catalyst."

"That's true, Walt," said Ralph. "And you're teaching me not only how to trust other people, but how to trust the Lord's leading. You and I are both detailed planners. We like to have every detail tied down. But now I'm learning how to look for the confirmation of the Holy Spirit."

"If I really am doing those things, it's by God's grace," I said. "We have two decisions coming up where we once again need God's confirmation. The first is numbers. It looks like there will only be nine or ten spaces available on the European team. We've always known we'd have a home team and a European team, but now we're seeing the actual size. Out of the twenty-six of you, only nine or ten will be going to the work camps. The second decision is finances. The church will pay for two people, but the balance has to come from outside the church budget."

"Why can so few go, Walt?" said John Grund.

"Those in charge of the work camps feel that Americans shouldn't predominate," I answered. "And the cost of travel and not working for a summer is more than most Europeans can afford, so their participation is limited."

"What's our budget?" asked Duke.

Ralph answered. "Walt, Louie and I worked out an austere, no frills budget totaling $10,000. That's $850 per person plus a minimum for overhead. Since this mission is our commitment, I think the budget needs to start with us." He began passing around three-by-five cards. "Write down what you feel God wants you to contribute. You don't need to sign your names. We just need to begin by getting an idea of where we are financially."

There was silence, heads bowed in prayer and concentration. As the cards were returned, Ralph and Louie did some quick arithmetic, looked at each other...and rechecked their figures.

"You guys are amazing," said Ralph, his eyes shining. "You've promised $3,000."

I was really impressed. Most of these kids were in college and hardly had two dimes to rub together.

One young woman spoke up hesitantly. "Can my money be used even if I don't go?"

"What do you mean," I asked.

She blushed a little. "Well, I have $900 saved for vacation and I want that used whether I go or not."

"I've got an old car I'm selling," chimed in a young man. "I'll donate that money." Other offers started flowing until I held up my hand. "You people are incredible! But I'm hearing a few offers that concern me. Remember that you are students and your education has priority. Don't do anything that jeopardizes that!"

"Don't forget," Ralph said, "if God wants this, the money will come."

And the money did come, in amazing ways. I was telling my car dealer, who wasn't a member of the church, about this "wonderful group of kids and their project." He said, "Can anybody get into the act?" and wrote out a substantial check payable to the church and earmarked for our mission!

Carol Abrams came bursting into the meeting one evening in March. "Papa Walt! Guess what! I was telling my uncle about our mission. He asked how much it cost and then wrote out a check for $850. He said if I don't use it, another team member may."

The team had been accepted to participate in three different work camps, one in France and two in Germany. Dr. Evans (now a strong supporter of the group), Ralph and I all felt that the team members would be more effective in their six weeks in the work camps if they had some time beforehand to see the needs of Europe and get a perspective on the problems they would face there. Ralph put together a two-week orientation tour. In Geneva, center of many of the world's mightiest movements for world reconciliation, he arranged appointments with leaders from the World Council of Churches, The World Alliance of the YMCA and the Presbyterian Church. In London the team would meet with British collegians and with J.B. Phillips whose translation of Paul's New Testament letters had so inspired us.

Ralph was everywhere, doing everything from securing charter air flights to making packing lists. Weekly he published and distributed bulletins in which he encouraged, admonished, cajoled and corrected the group, expressing a tremendous sense of humor and keen insight. Watching him, Harriet summed up my own feelings.

"All that planning! All those contacts! He's a genius!"

Our genius had a new name. His last name had quickly become Cheese Burger, then was shortened to Cheesy, or when he was leading, the Big Cheese. He often looked flustered when the yell "Hey, Cheesy!" sounded across a room or work site, but he liked it.

I occasionally felt restless as the June departure date drew near. It had never been part of the plan for me to go with the team and I was regreting that a bit. But funds were limited and there was no way I would replace one of the collegians. Nor did I want to leave my family for eight weeks.

The group developed an esprit de corps I've seldom seen. Personal commitment to the disciplines of study, prayer and work had molded them into a unit that supported each other. I was no longer concerned that when the European team was chosen, it might create hard feelings or the others would drift away. The home team had a vital role to play in supporting the travelers in prayer, in keeping in touch and encouraging them through letters, in keeping the church abreast of the mission and in keeping the work projects going in our own communities.

A guiding principle of the group was "Pray about every detail until there is a consensus." We applied it to the team selection.

Ralph walked into my office early on the night we were choosing European team members.

"I have a conviction," he said, laying a three-by-five card with nine names on it on my desk. I laid my card beside his. The nine names were identical.

Knowing that no one could concentrate on anything else until the team selections were done, Ralph distributed cards as people entered. He and I looked at them as they were returned, then laid them out on the table with our own.

"Come look at this," he invited people, his voice barely more than a whisper.

Each card contained the same nine names.

"Ours is not the final selection," I cautioned the awed group. "The church screening committee makes that." But as I studied the cards once more, I really didn't have any doubts.

A week later Ralph walked into my office again saying, "I have a conviction."

"I know," I answered. "Kenny Grant's name should be added." He nodded, smiling broadly. The group consensus that night was unanimous. The list now numbered ten.

The miracle didn't stop. The Session, or governing body of the church, stayed closely in touch with our mission. Harriet's father, Sam Prichard, was the Deputation chairman on Session. That group, knowing how close Ralph and I were to the collegians, had established a screening committee to give a detached viewpoint on the applications. After going through all twenty-six applications and without knowing our selections, the committee chose the same ten: Ralph Hamburger, Louie Evans, Colleen Townsend, Harriet Prichard, Duke Benson, John Grund, Carol Abrams, Fran Kent, Lardner Moore and Kenny Grant.

The pace accelerated. Passports were secured and physical exams taken. Just a month before the team was to leave, Dr. Evans asked me to his office.

"Walt, do you have a passport?"

"Yes," I answered with my pulse quickening slightly. "Why do you ask?"

"I've been consulting with Session members and with team members and we all feel that a pastor/counselor should go with the group. Haven't you been feeling led that way yourself?"

"Where's the money going to come from?" I countered.

"I have a fund that could be used for a pastor's travels," he raised his hand forestalling my comment, "but not for a student's." My excitement was building, but I tried to suppress it.

"I really don't want to leave my family and work for eight weeks." He nodded. "We feel you should take the orientation tour and then spend some time in each work camp, see how the kids are doing, get a feel for the experience. Perhaps take a month. We'll need your perspective if World Deputation is going to become a regular part of the church's program rather than a one-time event."

I was convinced. Any more confirmation I needed was supplied by my wife Marguerite's whole-hearted support and the pleasure of the team when they heard I was coming.

"I wondered how we'd do this trip without our Papa!" exclaimed Coke as she gave me a hug.

Finally it was a week before departure date. With much clowning around, team pictures were taken on the front steps of the sanctuary. Ralph reconfirmed reservations, finished last minute details and stayed firm about the two suitcase limit per person.

"And no steamer trunks, please! You will be carrying your suitcases yourselves!" he reminded them.

The church's Sunday evening service was broadcast on radio. It was at that service, the Sunday before our departure, that Dr. Evans dedicated and commissioned the team. He asked many of us to take part.

Sitting in the chancel I could see my family, Marguerite, Beth and Ron in the front pew. As I heard Duke give the invocation and Colleen read the scripture, I was overcome with gratitude. My thoughts slipped back to that evening almost three years before on the mountain top with Louie when I joined in his prayer to be an expendable in God's service. Many in this group had made that same commitment. Looking down at the twenty-six dedicated young members of the home and European teams, I knew beyond doubt that God was honoring our commitment. The full-time demands of school or work, the soul-searching times of prayer, the hard labor of the work projects and the self-revealing moments experienced in a covenant group had produced deep spiritual growth in this wonderful group of kids. And in me, too.

After the service, people swarmed around the team members, congratulating them and wishing them a safe journey.

One small problem remained—money. We were $400 short. The next morning we met at the Evans' home for our pre-departure devotional.

"Did any of you receive love gifts at last night's service?" I asked. Heads nodded eagerly. "Empty your pockets! Let's see what we've got!"

Money began piling up on the coffee table. I did a quick tally. The total was $402.

CHAPTER FOUR

JOURNEY OF DISCOVERY

The Burbank Airport was in complete chaos when the team arrived on departure eve, June 17, 1950. In the midst of this wild scramble of bodies and baggage, we discovered that our charter flight was badly over-booked. If we didn't make this flight to New York, we would very likely miss our overseas charter to Rome. Warren Baird, a Beachcraft Aircraft distributor and one of the home team members, disappeared into the airline office.

I looked at Carol, one of the more sensitive and cautious team members. "What do you think?" I asked.

"We'll get on!" she replied confidently.

Warren emerged from the airline office.

"The flight's three-times over booked," he told us, his raised eyebrows indicating his opinion of such proceedings. "But I told them about your mission abroad and they'll get you all on."

Sixteen hours and not much sleep later we were in New York and due immediately at Presbyterian headquarters for an orientation meeting arranged by Jane Williams, director of the Youth Department's foreign missions. What Miss Seese, the Brethren work camp representative, had to say particularly stuck with me.

"People experienced in work camps recommend that Americans be kept in a minority for the enrichment of their experience. We feel that there is an opportunity for Americans to get to Europe, but little opportunity for the Europeans to get to America. We hope that through the selection of sincere and well-chosen participants, the total experience will not be handicapped by superfluous Americans, but that their numbers will show the Europeans that the interest of Americans in the problem of international understanding is considerable."

The orientation was lengthy. When completed, it was time for a late dinner and a brief prayer session at our hotel. "Please, Lord, let us not be superfluous Americans!" was at the heart of our prayers.

By 6:00 the next morning we were at Idylwild International Airport for our flight to Rome. Charter flights were mighty primitive in those early days of transatlantic flight. Flying Tiger Lines was just getting started and Bob Prescott, company president, apologetically announced that there would be a few hours delay due to "mechanical difficulties." The group groaned, but rallied when I suggested we use the time for corporate prayer, which had been squeezed out of our schedule for the last two days.

"Where can we find some privacy?" I wondered, looking around the busy terminal.

"I saw just the place," said Duke with a grin.

A few minutes later we settled down in a bar not yet opened for business. The bartender must have been more than a little surprised to find himself hosting a prayer meeting when he arrived to set up, but in typical New Yorker style, he didn't show it. We were still praying as opening time drew near, so he stationed himself in front of the door and shooed away early arrivers.

Finally it was time to board our Flying Tiger, a DC-4.

Louie bounded up the ramp and stopped in shock at the top. I saw why. We were flying in a cargo plane with temporary seats bolted to the floor and huge life rafts stacked aft along with the food. Louie glanced sideways at Ralph and murmured, "No wonder the ticket prices were so good, Cheesy!" Ralph smiled weakly.

The eight crew members were already on board and Louie started talking with one. He learned that the flight was twenty-six hours with two fuel stops; that two full crews came along to work in shifts. The pilots were Air Force veterans, members of the famed Flying Tigers unit, who just years before had been "flying the Hump" into China, on that perilous, 500-mile route over the Himalayas that the Air Force had used during the war to keep China supplied when land access was cut off.

The plane was heavily loaded with passengers and freight. But it roared into the air with power to spare and didn't quiet down much once it was airborne. Gander, Newfoundland was our first fuel stop. En route, the plane's heaters failed. Bob Prescott passed out blankets and started tearing others into strips stuffing them into air vents to block the cold. But many passengers were shivering, scared and complaining.

"Hey, Louie!" Kenny Grant, a red-headed theology student with a lively sense of humor, called across the aisle loudly. "Who's on first?"

Louie picked up his cue with a grin.

"Yea, who's on first?"

"That's right."

"So, go ahead and tell me."

"Who."

"The guy playing first base."

"Who."

"All I'm trying to find out is, what's the guy's name on first base?"

"Oh no, What's on second."

They went through the whole Abbott and Costello routine adding their own variations. I watched the passengers relaxing and even starting to laugh, particularly the eleven nuns with their Mother Superior traveling to Rome for Holy Year. As soon as Louie and Kenny finished, Lardner and Duke started with the Happy Hour Mortuary skit pantomimed by Coke. "We're the last ones to let you down!" Camp songs got started next and the whole team was "cutting up," pulling pranks and practical jokes. It reduced tension and helped us keep warm, so soon the other passengers, including the nuns, joined in. Even Bob Prescott, greatly relieved to have his passengers laughing, got in the act.

After several hours of noisy, grinding flight, we began descending in preparation for landing at Gander.

"Buckle up," came the order and minutes later we touched down. A beautiful landing...except our speed didn't decrease. The runway kept whizzing by.

"The left brakes are gone!" the co-pilot yelled back to Bob Prescott.

The pilot worked the remaining brakes and our speed slowly lessened. Praying for a long runway, I pushed my head against the window. Ahead of us was the cold, grey Atlantic Ocean. At the last possible moment the pilot grabbed the small wheel that controlled the nose and turned it hard left. At the same time the co-pilot idled the left engine and revved the right putting that huge plane into a perfect ground-loop that sent loose gear crashing and throwing passengers against their safety belts. Suddenly we were looking at a long expanse of runway instead of the ocean. Silence rather than the sound of screaming tires echoed in the aircraft.

Coke's voice came shakily into it.

"I don't think I brought a swimming suit."

Laughter filled the plane, then cheers for the pilot.

We had five hours to explore while the brakes and heating systems were repaired, so we set off on a quick tour of this "new found land." As we trooped back on the plane, greeting the other passengers like long, lost friends, I mused over how adversity could so quickly bind strangers together. Next stop, Shannon, Ireland.

The Emerald Isle was our breakfast and refueling stop. While we were eating, Coke let it slip that today was Louie's twenty-third birthday. I saw Ralph leave quietly. Not very long after, the kitchen doors swung slowly open and Ralph came through carrying a beautiful birthday cake with twenty-three candles on it. It made my eyes fill with tears to think how Ralph would take care of the small details that made life beautiful for every single member of the team.

We cleared customs in Rome on Tuesday night after twenty-six hours of flying time. Because it was Holy Year, Rome was packed with pilgrims and we had no hotel reservations. Bob Prescott, our now fine friend, had anticipated our dilemma, radioed ahead and found a hotel for us.

The sights, sounds and smells of this ancient city were overpowering to our tired minds. And I was not doing well at computing dollars to Italian lire. I watched in alarm as Ralph counted out hundreds of lire and handed it to the bus driver.

"How much was that?"

"Two dollars."

"Per person?"

"No, for the entire group."

The Albergo Termini, the family-style hotel that Bob had found for us, was small, clean and run by a warm, welcoming family. The cost was 700 lire or $1.25 a day. Bob certainly knew how to return a favor.

We started the next morning with a tour of the Vatican arranged by one of our flight companions, the Mother Superior. Coming into St. Peter's Basilica through the door only opened for Holy Year, one of the first things we saw was a bronze sculpture of St. Peter. It was on a pedestal and its toes, at eye level, had been kissed absolutely smooth by the thousands of pilgrims through the years. Our Protestant beliefs kept us from kissing it as the sisters did, but our fingers were irresistibly drawn to touch with reverence and wonder that cool, hard bronze. In the Sistine Chapel the group ended up almost lying on the floor to admire Michelangelo's ceiling frescos.

"I think Mother Superior would have arranged an interview with the Pope if we'd had more time," said Ralph in admiration as we were leaving.

"That's what she told me," I said. His eyes rounded in amazement.

The high points of the tour were the art and the catacombs in this ancient city that contains so many historic roots of our faith.

After breakfast Wednesday morning with Bob Prescott, it was time to catch the train. We were due in Geneva for orientation on Sunday and wanted to sightsee northwards through Italy on our way to those appointments.

It was almost more than our minds could absorb—the antiquity of Florence; our first close-up look at bomb damage in Padua where the railroad station was still in shambles, the narrow sidewalks, bridges and waterways of Venice, where we spent the night. In Milan we had an hour between trains. I stayed with the luggage while the team tore into town to see the Milan Cathedral, the third largest in Europe. They made it back with minutes to spare. The train started to move just as Louie and I jumped on. Louie grinned at me.

"Little close for comfort, Papa Walt?" I grinned back, shaking my head.

"I don't know if you all are keeping me young or making me old before my time!" I automatically patted my hip pocket for my passport and return tickets. It was empty! I whirled around with some wild idea of jumping back out on the platform. Duke stood there grinning, the passport and tickets he'd picked from my pocket held out in front of him.

It was evening with a full moon shining as the train started up into the Alps. Just before leaving Italy, we passed Lake Maggiore, with the moon coming from behind snowcapped peaks across that magnificent mirror of water. The setting was breath-taking; the air fresh and cool. It was too awesome to watch as individuals. So all eleven of us crowded into a compartment intended for eight. Lardner, the son of missionaries and a bit unsophisticated but strong and solid, was our unofficial song leader. He started singing softly and we all joined him:

"I'd rather have Jesus than silver or gold,
I'd rather be His than have riches untold;
I'd rather have Jesus than houses or lands,
I'd rather be led by His nail-pierced hand
Than to be the king of a vast domain,
Or be held in sin's dread sway;
I'd rather have Jesus than anything this world affords today."

Other hymns followed, particularly gospel and spirituals, one person after another starting their favorites. The minor tensions and fatigue of travel melted away in the fellowship of the group and the splendor of the setting. The conductor stopped to look in.

"Do you mind if we sing?" asked Carol.

"We're singing because we're happy," said Coke.

"C'est tres beau! C'est tres beau!" he answered.

Carol, or "Ma," as the group was beginning to call her because of her sensitivity to others, got up and closed the door, fearing we were bothering the other passengers. Within minutes a woman was at the door, opening it.

"Will you please leave your door open? Your singing is so beautiful, everyone in the train wants to hear it."

We arrived in Geneva at 1:00 in the morning. As we collected luggage and got off the train, a fellow passenger came up and thanked us for our singing. He asked me who we were and where we were going, so I gave him a quick rundown. He looked thoughtful when I finished, then asked a very practical question.

"Do you have reservations here?"

"No. Can you recommend a good, inexpensive place?"

"I think so. Wait here a moment, please."

He went to a telephone while I joined the other team members at the drinking fountain, drinking all the water I could hold. Never have I tasted anything so wonderful as that fresh, cold water! Our friend returned.

"The Hotel Balmoral has room for you all," he said. "It's small, but nice."

We thanked him profusely, but he waved it aside with a smile and went to round up taxis for our transportation.

"Walt," Ralph said reflectively as we settled back into the taxi, "does it seem to you that this trip is going smoothly?"

"Yes it does. Almost miraculously so."

"Perhaps we could say, providentially so?"

"Yes," I answered, "I think we should say that."

Each day began with a team gathering where Ralph outlined the day's schedule, we reviewed our biblical guidelines and had a time of prayer.

The next morning, rested and eager to see Geneva, we had our usual meeting.

"We've been traveling together a week now," I said. "How's it going? Any problems or concerns? Any gripes that need airing?"

"I credit Ralph's planning with how well we've done," said Louie. "Having a disciplined plan of travel, so we always know when we need to be up, when our group time will be and when we need to be somewhere, has done a lot toward building our group cohesiveness." Voices chimed in around the room affirming Ralph for his loving leadership.

"Given our growing sophistication," said Duke, his face quite serious, "I think it's time we stopped calling Ralph, 'Cheesy.'"

We looked at him in surprise.

"From now on we should call him 'Le Grand Fromage'!" Laughter broke out at his translation of "the Big Cheese" into French.

After a rich time of prayer, the gang took off in every direction having agreed to meet back at the hotel for dinner.

Dinner was a grand, noisy event as everyone related their experiences. We ended the day with a magnificent moonlight boat trip on Lake Geneva.

The next morning, Sunday, we attended church at St. Peter's Cathedral. Intriguing to us as Protestants was the modest church next to the cathedral, at the time not even in use as a place of worship. It was the church of John Knox, the author of the Presbyterian expression of the Protestant Reformation. It did something to me deep down just to be on the spot where both John Calvin and John Knox had regularly preached and met with their people.

I saw Duke across the street from both churches gazing up at them, his blond hair catching the sunlight, his hands deep in his pockets, his face thoughtful. I walked over.

"It is really awesome to be where so much history has occurred, Walt. The Navy taught me how to travel—just take one step at a time—so I haven't been much affected by the cultural differences, but I wasn't prepared for how moved I would be by all this history."

Our purpose in Geneva was to continue our training. Our first appointment was that afternoon with Professor Kraemer, a noted Dutch theologian and head of the Bossey International Institute under the World Council of Churches and financed by the Rockefeller Foundation. Its objective was to help establish a vital relationship between the Church and the world, and to that end groups of students, ministers and professional people from all over the world came to attend the Institute.

As Colleen said, Professor Kraemer could have been type-cast as the typical college professor—slightly stooped, balding and grey, with spectacles and a slightly distracted manner. But as soon as he focused on the group, the distraction disappeared. He was sharp, vibrant and shrewd.

"We are searching for a ministry of reconciliation," Ralph said, "by uniting with Christian students and others from the recently contending forces here in Europe. We would appreciate your counsel and guidance."

Professor Kraemer's face lighted up.

"We exist here at Bossey for the purpose of reconciliation," he said. "We work for reconciliation not only among individuals, but also among nations and among different segments of society. We ask the question, 'What does the Christian faith have to say to the problems of the world?' We provide an arena of contact for leaders of Christian movements from various countries to come together for mutual support and growth. It allows a cross-fertilization of ideas to take place."

The questions started coming as the group explored this concept of ecumenism, of reconciliation coming from the Church united rather than from one congregation. Professor Kraemer was questioned in depth for over an hour.

"We come from a dynamic church that is seeking to serve the needs of the community," Harriet spoke hesitantly. "But right now, I feel rather young and raw in the face of this world-wide, ecumenical movement with all of its maturity and compassion for the world." Team members murmured agreement.

"What we're doing is such a drop in the bucket," said Duke.

Professor Kraemer gently reprimanded them. "The Apostle Paul says that each part of the body must be content to serve its function well. And that is what you must do. Serve in the work camps so that people know who it is you truly serve. And when that part of your service is done, continue serving in that manner wherever our Lord calls you."

"That goes back to our first commitment," said Louie, "to be expendables in Christ's service."

"Thank you, Professor," I said, standing and extending my hand to him. "You have expanded the horizons of our understanding to include the whole world."

The next morning, Monday, we rented bicycles to get to our three interviews. What an adventure! We made it with a minimum of wrong turns, discovering that Geneva has more hills on a bike than it does in a bus.

Our first interview that day was with Miss Eleanor French of the World Council of the YWCA.

"What can we do here in Europe to accomplish our mission?" Louie asked. "What should we be sensitive to?"

An American in her mid-thirties, Miss French reflected a moment, then answered Louie's questions in reverse order.

"As to what you should be sensitive to… well, try this perspective. Look at yourselves, as Americans from a European point of view. I'm afraid you'll see it's a point of view in which we come off rather badly. Europeans see America as having great power, but being young, awkward and not politically astute. We seem terribly adolescent to them. As Europeans have seen their countries' power waning, they have fallen back on their culture as a source of pride. Consequently, it's very important to them. Remember, the collections in their museums predate Christ and in the United States we haven't even celebrated our bicentennial yet.

"If I understand you correctly, you see your mission in the work camps as reconciliation?" I nodded assent. "My advice would be to listen first and then speak carefully, but frankly. The Christians you will meet are up against the currents of the world and have to rethink their Christianity. Theirs is often a deep faith but they need your enthusiasm. You may find yourselves in the position of having more to receive than to give. Be open to that. What you have to gain is a sense of identity with Christians around the world."

What she was saying struck a strong cord within me.

The next interview was with a man it seemed I had always known about and had always admired—Tracy Strong, general secretary of the YMCA. In his early fifties, with rugged good looks and a sharp mind, Mr. Strong seemed quite at ease with these young Americans. I felt privileged to interview him and a bit proud to include in my introductions the fact that I'd been with the YMCA for years. He didn't seem at all impressed. In fact, he was abrupt, almost abrasive, barely waiting for our questions.

"Be yourselves in the work camps. Be serious. Europeans are very politically conscious and they will ask you serious political as well as theological questions. But don't end up taking yourselves too seriously."

He had been scrutinizing the group intently. Now he changed tacks. Pointing his finger accusingly at Carol, he asked belligerently, "Do you smoke?" I felt the group draw protectively around her.

"No."

"Why not?" he barked.

"I just don't."

"Is it because of your religion?"

Carol had been sinking into her chair, but she straightened, squared her shoulders and answered clearly and quietly.

"It just doesn't appeal to me."

He switched to Colleen.

"You believe that being a movie star gives you special privileges, don't you?"

He worked his way through the group, challenging our concepts, testing our dispositions, having an uncanny ability as to how to needle each person. As the tension in the room rose, he became even more obnoxious. Several times I started to intervene only to feel Ralph's restraining hand on my arm. Suddenly, Mr. Strong leaned back in his chair, a warm smile spreading over his face.

"That's only a small sample of the kind of questions you will be asked in the work camps," he said. "I thought you needed a taste of what you may experience. People will want to see how serious or superficial your faith is in relationship to real life."

He looked around at us thoughtfully.

"You'll do."

From him, that was high praise.

Rather shakily, we went to our last interview. It was with George Booth, a young man in charge of work camps for the World Council of Churches. He gave us advice on how to avoid the "ugly American" syndrome.

"Don't display money or possessions. The European campers have very little of either, often owning no more than the clothes on their backs. They are much more limited than you in what they can do.

"Be modest; be unsolicitous. Americans' instant openness is often alarming to Europeans. But be yourselves. Make your contribution."

We biked back to the Hotel Balmoral. After dinner we gathered for our last group time in Geneva.

"Carol," I said, "you handled yourself well with Mr. Strong today. All of you did. Our thinking and understanding have been challenged in subtle and direct ways ever since we left Hollywood and I'm impressed by the growth I've seen in each of you."

"I want to thank you and Ralph for this orientation time," said Carol. "I can't imagine going to the work camps without it."

"There's only so much understanding of life here," said Ralph, "that you can gain in the States. The exposure to the life and history of the Church and to the suffering the war produced is something that must be personally experienced. We've still just touched on it.

"When Miss French said Europeans view Americans as politically naive, she was right," Ralph continued. "Most Americans are, at least on an international level, because our nation hasn't had hundreds of years of political intrigue right on its borders. And, fortunately, you haven't experienced two world wars on your own soil.

"Think of the French, many of whom you'll meet in the CIMADE work camp. Their armies were defeated in their homeland, millions of their countrymen were killed, they were occupied by German armies, a quisling government was set up and it was impossible to know who could be trusted.

"Or consider the Germans, since we'll be in two of their work camps. They were impacted by the tyrannical leadership of Adolph Hitler, by the devastation of all-out war, and finally by the horrible bombing and the ravaging, raping and pillaging by the Russian forces in retaliation for the horror the Germans had visited on them. Only through Christ can reconciliation begin to overcome the hatred bred by such experiences, the hatred we will see and encounter," Ralph concluded.

"In these last few days I've been shaken," said Louie. "I realize that I've needed shaking. I've needed to be challenged to be refined and strengthened for our mission." Murmured assent came from the others.

The next morning, Tuesday, June 27, we travelled by train to Paris for a night and en route were once again adopted by a fellow passenger, Gilbert, who found a hotel for us when we reached Paris at 10:15 p.m. He even paid our taxi fare since we had no French money.

Wednesday we took the train to Dunkerque and boarded the HMS Brighton for New Haven, England. As the boat pulled away, I looked back, trying to imagine what it must have been like in late May 1940, almost ten years before, when the German armies had the Allied forces trapped on the beaches. British rescue ships, including fishing boats and motorboats, had crossed the channel and the more than 336,000 British, French and Belgian troops had waded out to them and been evacuated as the tiny Royal Air Force fought off German bombers overhead. My reverie was interrupted as we hit heavy seas.

By 5:00 p.m. we had docked and were on the express train to Victoria Station, London. It felt good to hear English spoken again, particularly with the British accent. I had the strange sensation of homecoming in a land I'd never seen.

Sitting with Ralph behind the others, I studied the team: Carol and Fran, growing daily in how to apply their already strong faith; Kenny and Duke, great impetuous boys, missing their fiancées deeply; John and Lardner, both deeply committed Christians, the first so intense, the second solid and serene; Harriet, warm-hearted and enthusiastic, yet not quite trusting the depth of her gifts; Ralph, bit by bit letting us see the warm, loving, humorous person he was; and Coke and Lou, beginning to feel the pain of their pending separation, but having no reluctance concerning the mission. (I was the only one who knew the depth of their relationship, since we'd agreed that romance wasn't to interfere with group cohesiveness.)

Thursday morning, just as we finished our group time, Allan Strong, a young man from the Student Christian Movement with whom team members were meeting on Saturday, showed up and asked if we would like him to show us around.

"We've been waiting for you!" Duke said. Allan looked completely mystified as no plans had been made for him to come.

"At every turn in our trip," Colleen quickly explained, "someone has come along to help us. God has really been caring for us."

Allan was an excellent guide. We toured the city by bus, had a late lunch at one of his favorite places, the Lyon's Corner House, then went to Evensong at St. Paul's Cathedral, untouched in the midst of great bomb damage. Everywhere—Parliament, Westminster Abbey, the Tower of London—there was scaffolding where reconstruction was underway from damage.

We made dinner a special event, a party celebrating our last night together since the CIMADE team would be leaving for Paris the next afternoon.

The next day, Friday, we met with J. B. Phillips, our reason for being in London. In this one man we found the incarnation of a life and spirit which was to mold, shape and inspire us throughout the years.

Arriving at his parish in Redhill, Surrey, about twenty miles out of London, we were a bit intimidated, not sure what to expect from this man who had translated the New Testament into colloquial English from the original Greek. We found him to be a proper, British vicar wearing his clerical collar, looking rather frail but bright-eyed and vibrant. At first he seemed slightly stiff with our American informality and slightly challenging to our lightness and enthusiasm.

But he warmed quickly, particularly when Louie told him about the disgruntled clerks at the Hollywood Bookstore.

"They would just get a display of your books set up and we'd come through like a swarm of locusts and wipe out the whole thing. After about the fourth time this happened, they wouldn't even put *Letters To Young Churches* on the shelves anymore. They'd just stack them on the floor and wave us in the general direction when we came in."

After some persuasion, he told us how he'd decided to do his translation.

"I was vicar of The Church of the Good Shepherd in London during the bombing. The Germans would send over those horrible flying bombs. You could hear and see them sputtering and skimming over the housetops and wherever they up-ended, an entire city block would go up in dust, smoke and flames. One never knew at what hour or moment they might appear. More than a mile-and-a-half of my parish was devastated by them, including my church." He looked mildly surprised by the shocked gasps his words caused. "You do know, don't you young people, that more than 30,000 Londoners were killed in the bombing, about eighty percent of our houses were destroyed and most of the city lay in ruins by the time Germany was defeated?

"Only the parish hall, a corrugated iron structure less than six feet from the church itself, remained of my beautiful church. But we had to go on and I could see the anxiety and apprehension of people as they traveled to and from their places of employment. So in the parish hall, I started a Bible study and prayer time. St. Paul's letters seemed appropriate since they were written to people under persecution. One day I was reading to them from his letter to the Colossian church. At the conclusion I said triumphantly, 'Now you understand!' Blank stares answered me. 'But surely you see how this applies to our times?' I asked. Finally, one woman spoke up.

'It's all those thee's and thou's, Vicar.'

'You didn't understand it?'

'Not one word.'

'Not at all.'

"I was dumfounded. How could the Word of God uplift and comfort these people if they couldn't understand it? So I dusted off my Greek testament and translated Colossians into modern English. That seemed to do the trick. The Bible studies really came alive. With C. S. Lewis' encouragement, I went ahead and translated the rest of Paul's letters. Now I'm working on the Gospels."

Team members were eager to ask his opinion on all their ideas germinated through our travels: ecumenism, the Church universal, the morality of war, pacifism and personal witness. Mrs. Phillips came to invite us to tea. Much too soon it was time to go. The kids and I felt a real warmth for J. B., just a year older than I. I knew it was the beginning of a priceless relationship for us. It was a meeting of kindred spirits that sparked and encouraged all of us to new insights, deeper growth and excitement to be about our mission. It was time to get to work.

But the separation of the team was painful. For the past ten months we had prayed together, studied together, labored together, encouraged and confronted one another, creating a closeness I had never before or have ever since encountered within a group. I was both mentor and participant, both father and brother. And the beginning of the work camps was also an ending. Our individual friendships would remain and with some even grow, but once we went our different ways, the particular entity we had become would end. I knew these kids would become the yeast creating growth in new groups, but as Fran, Colleen, Kenny and I boarded the train that Saturday afternoon, the sight of all those dear people—Ralph, Duke, Harriet, Louie, John, Lardner, and Carol—on the platform waving good-bye brought a giant-sized lump to my throat.

They had appointments in London with members of the Student Christian Movement and would leave Monday for their camps. We were to be at our camp by Monday morning.

As we left England, I couldn't forget the scenes of that indiscriminate bombing, long rows of buildings laid low like swaths in a wheat field partially cut: the great cathedral, St. Paul's, with five such swaths around it, but the cathedral itself untouched; Westminster Abbey with minimal damage because the defense people were up on the roof, disposing of the incendiary bombs as they landed, protecting their cherished cathedral at the risk of their own lives. There had been horrible destruction, great loss of life and property, but the spirit of the people, the integrity of their lives, was intact. We were prepared for the physical devastation the war had caused.

In spite of all our training, nothing had prepared us for the devastation of the human spirit, the broken, often hostile people we would encounter in the work camps.

Colleen, Fran, Kenny and I went to France two days before our work camp started, to attend an orientation for all American students going to work camps that summer. We met at Roche de Dieu, Louis XV's hunting lodge, for orientation by Brink Hoffman, a Swedish representative of the World Council of Churches who worked in the Russian Zone of East Germany.

Some of the things he said made our blood run cold: The Soviets aggressively claimed they were the real conquerors of the Hitler regime with little help from their Allies; the Russian Zone of East Germany was already firmly under their totalitarian control and the youth were being politicized for Marxism as they had been for Nazism; the Church had lost its former state support and its members were being persecuted. Still, the Church continued in East Germany, smaller in numbers, but very strong.

What impressed me most about the orientation was the man himself, Brink Hoffman. He was doing what we wanted to do—linking his life with his Christian brothers and sisters right where they lived, in the East, behind the Iron Curtain.

The four of us arrived early Monday morning at the CIMADE work camp, set on the grounds of a lovely old chateau in the Paris suburb of Sevres. Kenny was immediately off and away with collegians of other backgrounds and languages, none of whom he had ever met. Our project at CIMADE was to prepare an area of ground within the work camp for army barracks that would be brought in and reassembled to house refugees from Eastern Europe. Kenny was part of a crew going to the Alsace region of France to dismantle the barracks and bring them back.

I was assigned to a crew whose job was to clear the ground, level the area and prepare the foundation for the barracks. Fran and Coke worked with a group chipping mortar off old bricks so they could be reused for foundations and sidewalks.

In spite of the team's desire to avoid publicity for fear it would impeach our mission, word always seemed to leak out about the team from Hollywood with the lovely young starlet. It was difficult for the media to believe anyone would leave Hollywood for a religious vocation, and foreign reporters were as persistent as American reporters in trying to find out if Colleen intended to "go back" to films.

The first morning we were at CIMADE, she was summoned to the chateau for a telephone call, a very unusual event for a work camper. Raised eyebrows followed her and quizzical expressions greeted her return. She set cheerfully to work again chipping mortar, but Fran and I could see a tightness to her smile. The comradeship she and Fran had had with the other workers took a while to re-surface.

When we stopped for lunch, Fran and I held back as the others left.

"It was the International News Service, Papa Walt!" Coke said with exasperation. "They say a film actress in a refugee camp is headline stuff and they want to come out and interview me. I told them as lovingly as I could," her expression showed that she doubted it sounded very loving, "that we're not here for the publicity. We're here because there's a job to be done. We want to do that job in the name of Christ, so please, no publicity."

"It sounds like you handled it very well."

"I'm not sure they believed me."

"Well!" said a voice, "is the beautiful actress giving interviews while the rest of us work?"

It was George, a German pastor. In talking to him haltingly during the morning, I'd found him a proud, sophisticated theologian of the "old school." He walked away before any of us could reply. Coke looked stricken and Fran quickly put her arm around her.

"Cokie, look at your hands." Fran held out her own. Both girls' hands and my own as well were smudged with grime and a bit sunburned. "Your face looks the same, you beautiful actress you," she said. Coke and Fran burst into suppressed giggles.

"You'll do," I thought, remembering the high praise of those words from Tracy Strong in Geneva after he'd harassed the team. Arms linked, the girls walked to lunch. I followed more slowly, admiring my surroundings.

The old French chateau, graceful and elegant, was set on a beautiful plot of land and surrounded by high, ancient trees, broad, grassy lawns and flower beds. But now those magnificent grounds had been turned into a camp with tents in orderly rows, outdoor lavatories and a rude trough with cold running water for washing up. The only showers were a few primitive ones inside the chateau and those were only for occasional use.

That afternoon, before my muscles got stiff and tight, I chopped down and trimmed four apple trees. The German pastor, George, not accustomed to such manual labor or to seeing clergy in such a role, grimaced and said loudly, "Humph, the fat one works for two!"

As I chopped, I reviewed what I knew of the organizers of this work camp known as CIMADE (Comité Inter-Mouvements Auprés Des Evacués. Protestant in orientation and a combination of six youth movements, it was under the leadership of Madeleine Barot. Its mission was to go to those who were suffering, helping people come to know Jesus Christ by identifying with them in their suffering. It struck me how similar this sounded to what Corrie ten Boom had told us to do. During the war, CIMADE members had carried this identification to the extent of voluntarily becoming prisoners in the concentration camps. After the war they ministered to the German soldiers who were now the prisoners.

The CIMADE program in which we were involved was a refugee center founded in 1948 as an evangelistic outreach to the great flood of young political refugees streaming in by the thousands, first from Spain and then from Eastern Europe. This center was close to a seminary and provided housing for refugees interested in ministry. Paul Evdokimoff, the CIMADE director, was himself a refugee from the 1919 Russian Revolution. A trim, wiry man, keen and alert, he was an intellectual with great vision, compassion and a deep faith.

Helped by campers, our Polish cook fed us well that night. It was strong on grease and starch, but still a tasty stew. Bible study followed the meal. There were a multitude of languages spoken at the camp—English, French, Polish, Dutch, German, Belgian, even Latvian and Russian. Whenever any kind of presentation was made, the buzz of translators could be heard throughout the group.

I began to get a feel for this group of which Fran, Coke and I were a part. The CIMADE movement was a living example of all that we had dreamed of and were striving to achieve. These work campers seemed for the most part to be mature, young Christians, more traditional and liturgical than we, and also more theologically sophisticated. They were a remarkable group of people from different nations who had come together in a common cause: to find in Christian community an alternative to war as a way of settling differences.

Following the Bible study, the three of us met briefly.

"Do we really have anything to offer them?" asked Fran.

"I'm not sure," I admitted. "But we're exhausted and sore right now. Let's get some sleep and remember what Miss French in Geneva said, we may have more to gain than to give."

I got to sleep in until 5:30 the next morning, but the girls were up at 5:00 to help make the oatmeal and coffee for breakfast. Their good spirits restored, their cheeks rosy from the hot stove, they joined me as I was having my second cup of coffee.

"Happy Fourth of July!" I said.

"That's right! It is the Fourth," said Coke.

"Did you see the schedule?" asked Fran. "We only work until 12:30 today. I guess it's to give our aching muscles a chance to recover."

"Then let's go see gay Parie!" I suggested.

"Wonderful idea!" responded Coke. "Let's ask Marie, our tent-mate, to come, Fran."

"And Nina too," added Fran. Nina was CIMADE director Paul Evdokimoff's daughter, a robust, vigorous, energetic girl whose sense of humor and enthusiasm had immediately captured our hearts.

Fran and I had risen to leave, and Coke was about to, as George came by.

"Isn't the actress working today?" he asked, again not waiting for a reply.

"Have I offended him in some way?"

"You mean other than by being young, beautiful and looking like a model in jeans?" asked Fran. "Come on, actress," she said. "Let's beat him to work."

George's opinion of Colleen wasn't helped when she was again called off the job site by a call from the International News Service.

"This time I just told them no," she said abruptly.

During the morning, I chopped down three more trees. The girls helped with the mid-morning brunch and with dinner at noon. With Marie, Nina and a couple of other campers, we were leaving to catch the metro into the city. Coke stopped suddenly. A reporter and cameraman were headed toward us.

"Miss Townsend?" said a good-looking young man whose English had a thick, French accent. "How fortunate I am to run into you! My newspaper, "France-Soir," has sent me to get the story on you or else I lose my job!"

She turned to us in appeal.

"What do I do now, Papa Walt? Fran?"

"Please, Mademoiselle. This is my first assignment," said the young man pleadingly.

Fran answered slowly, "What's the most gracious, the most loving thing to be done? Stick to our guns, or give them the story?"

"Walt?"

"I trust your judgment, Cokie. You've always handled this kind of situation well."

Colleen turned back to the young man slowly. "All right. I'll answer some questions, but only on the condition that you write a story about the team and the work here at the camp, not just about me."

"Gladly, Mademoiselle!"

The campers with us had seen Colleen's real distress and had gathered around her protectively. As she answered the reporter's questions firmly turning the interview to the team and the work camps, I could see their respect for her growing. I was thrilled with the integrity this twenty-year-old brought to tough situations. After about fifteen minutes, she ended it graciously, but firmly.

"We've got to catch the metro. Good-day, gentlemen."

I reflected how once again the Lord had taken a problem and turned it into a positive situation.

Thunderclouds were building on the horizon when we returned to camp for dinner. We were met by a grim-looking Paul Evdokimoff. George, looking equally grim, was with him.

"My dear Miss," said Paul to Colleen. "Will you please tell me why you turn down an interview with the respected International News Service and then grant one to "France-Soir?" I have received a very angry call from the News Service."

"She didn't have much choice with the Francois, Papa," Nina told her father.

"I didn't want to give any interviews, Paul," Colleen explained. "But when the reporters were on our doorstep, it didn't seem gracious to slam the door in their faces."

He studied her for a few moments.

"I see that this is difficult for you. But what do we do about the News Service?"

"I really don't want reporters out here again. Would it be all right with you if I called the News Service and just answered questions over the telephone?"

"Yes, I think that should take care of it."

George spoke up. "If you would stop wearing that lipstick and stop looking so... so..."

"Attractive?" supplied Nina.

"The way you look causes the problems!" he exploded, stalking away angrily. Nina and Paul looked surprised.

"I have not seen him this way before," Nina said linking arms with the girls as they walked toward their tent.

That evening George led the camp in a worship service. Echoing the rumbling thunder of the coming storm, a ripple of unrest ran through the campers as they realized that a German, a man whose country had been the aggressor in both world wars, was going to speak to them. I hadn't sensed this tension at the Bible study the night before. Whether I had been too tired to notice it, or whether having a German in charge provoked it, I'm not sure. George talked clearly and concisely about Christian community, saying that Christ calls us to put aside national loyalties and animosities in our service to him.

Last night's Bible study had been an intellectual exercise without emotional involvement. Tonight, I sensed in the campers the same rancor and estrangement I had seen in Ralph before Christ had replaced inner chaos with his own Presence. The sense of community from the night before was fragmented. The visceral bitterness of the French, the Dutch, the Poles and the Russians toward the Germans and of the Germans toward them was a wall to fellowship. That service showed me that the goal of Christian reconciliation, accepted in the minds, had yet to reach the hearts. By putting a German in charge of the service, Paul was challenging us to break through these walls of separation and work toward real fellowship and community.

Colleen approached George after the service.

"Thank you for that message," she said. "Christian community is the goal of our group."

"Will you leave the security of your group to find it?" he asked.

"What do you mean?"

"While you are secure with your American friends, you won't really get to know other people."

Colleen studied his face. "I'll think about that," she answered.

George had hit upon something already bothering me. We were the only ones in the camp who had come as a team. After only two days I could see that the wonderful closeness we had between us actually separated us from our fellow campers. We met outside for prayer after the service. Lightning flashed above us.

"Did you hear what George said?" Colleen asked. Fran and I both nodded.

"I think he hit a nerve," I said. They agreed. We stood silently for a few minutes, feeling miserable.

"Let's pray," I said and grabbed their hands.

"Father, you've brought us together and given us this mission," I prayed. "If we have to let go of our relationships with one another to really identify individually with our fellow campers, to not be a clique, then guide us in this, Father. Give us the ability to do it cheerfully."

"Amen," we all said. Feeling comforted, we ran to our tents just as the storm broke.

As I finished chopping and stacking logs the next morning, I thought about what it would take to break down these walls of separation and make fellowship a reality. Having Christ in common was the starting point. That point made the integral difference between the attitudes here and what I would find in Kassel.

Watching Rolf, an aloof, stoic German boy, begin to loosen up as he worked side by side with a Dutch boy close to his own age, I witnessed what I later saw so vividly in Kassel, that the work itself was one of the most redemptive and immediate ways of bringing us together. Everybody was committed to the task and convinced of its vital importance. It was hard labor. Some of the girls cried themselves to sleep at night because their muscles were so sore, yet all worked in a spirit of unity. With the commitment to Christ and to the work and with the common Bible study and prayer time, we had all the right elements for fellowship. Only time would tell how they combined.

By midday the chopping was finished. After our noon dinner Paul asked me to be in charge of the leveling needed on the hillside to create a pad for the barracks. This was done with pickaxes, shovels and wheelbarrows. What I wouldn't have given for a bulldozer!

Nina's job was keeping us well supplied with water, so she was continually up and down the hill filling the water buckets.

"Nina! J'ai beaucoup de soif!" (I have a great thirst!) I would call out in my inimitable French. It got to be a game between us.

Aching muscles and all, our Bible study and prayer time were warmer that night than they had been. I could see tentative friendships forming, and individual love, compassion and respect growing. Fran, Colleen and I exchanged hugs, but sat with new friends. I happened to catch George's raised eyebrows as he watched Colleen seek out and sit with two German girls.

Thursday and Friday we continued working as rapidly as possible, hoping to have the pads prepared before the barracks arrived on Saturday. The same esprit de corps I had seen develop within our Hollywood group through hard work on a project, prayer and Bible study was developing here. I don't think a finer, more representative group of young Christians could have been found anywhere. They were willing to work through their prejudices, even toward us callow Americans, and to see people as individuals.

Still George continued to bait Colleen, finding it impossible to believe she could be an authentic Christian. I would see her slip away to find a quiet spot to immerse herself in prayer for love, understanding and even appreciation of this man. Again and again Fran and I were amazed at the honest and spontaneous love, a natural for Colleen, that kept flowing from her. Nina tried to intervene with George but to no avail.

On Thursday, three young men who had escaped from an East German prison camp came into camp. Talking to them after our evening Bible study turned out to be a life-changing experience. In the past three weeks they had walked at least 450 miles, always by night and never by public road for fear of being recaptured. It was a revelation for them to see Americans, Germans, Dutch, French and even Russians working and living together in a spirit of reconciliation.

"Why are these people here?" they asked me. "Why these young Americans, this young actress? What are they doing here?" I considered my response carefully.

"They are convinced Christians," I answered slowly. "And when people are committed to Christ, his love grows in their hearts, compelling and constraining them to care about, to love and to work for people less fortunate than themselves."

I watched as they thought this over and was thrilled to see a beautiful light of belief and acceptance flood their faces. But it only lasted a moment, then ebbed into doubt. A look passed between them.

"Let's be cautious," it seemed to signal. "This could be a clever political move, a clever stratagem for political purposes."

One said to me, "You say these people are here because they care about people less fortunate than themselves. Let me ask you a question. What is your church in Hollywood doing to help the Mexican population in East Los

Angeles? What is your church doing to help the Negroes in Watts?"

I was dumfounded. As the conversation continued into the night, I found that these young men, three weeks away from a prison camp in Eastern Europe, knew more about the Los Angeles ghettos and barrios than I knew, and I worked there. My answers sounded inadequate to me.

When the discussion finally wound down in the early hours of the morning, I was still pondering their question. I knew what we were doing in the ghettos and barrios, but was it enough? Their challenge stayed with me for three years until I ultimately changed jobs to make the ghettos and barrios the focus of my ministry. As would happen so often in the future, Christians from the East, under oppression, gave me a clarity I hadn't gained in my freedom.

The three hours of sleep I got Thursday night left me groggy for work, but after the Bible study Friday night, I was still up for a bull session with Colleen, Fran and two other Americans in the camp, Dave Romig and Bill Perkins. We covered everything from American foreign policy to pacifism. It was a privilege to get to know both young men, each of whom were to become career leaders of the church in Europe. It was worth another night's limited sleep.

The foundations were ready when Kenny and the barracks arrived the next day from Alsace. Sunburned, but with humor intact, he seemed to have gained maturity from the week on his own. We worked through the morning unloading the barracks. The girls were just as involved in the labor as the guys. With the hot summer sun beating down, Nina was hard pressed to keep up with the water calls. As we broke for the noon dinner, I saw George once again go stomping up to Coke.

Something inside me snapped. I was tired from work and lack of sleep and suddenly my determination to let Coke work this out on her own vanished. George had no right to be a bully! I strode up to the two of them, stopping short in amazement as I looked at George.

His eyes brimming and tender, this proud man was saying to Colleen, "You've got something in your spirit; I want what you've got." Her own eyes full, Coke gently took his hand and for the first time the barriers were down between these two Christians. In their loving voices I heard the sound of tumbling walls.

The truth of Corrie ten Boom's challenge to identify with people and earn the right to be heard became crystal clear to me. Had we come as a gospel team to George's church with the message of Christ's reconciling love, he wouldn't have heard us. But Colleen's loving presence in the midst of hard labor finally touched his heart.

We ended the day with a picnic. Kenny introduced us to his buddies and he met ours. It was a lovely evening of sharing and fellowship, translations occurring so naturally I sometimes forgot that this wasn't always our pattern of conversation. We'd become a real family.

Monday was my last day at CIMADE, the day I must move on to the other camps in Germany at Kassel and Ellierode. After breakfast I spoke to the campers about Christian youth movements in America. Then people came crowding around me to say good-bye. It was hard to leave. I would see my own crew at home, but for these new friends, who could say if our paths would ever cross again?

Kenny, Colleen and Fran escorted me to the train station. En route we decided on a real "binge!" We would treat ourselves to a steak dinner at a nice restaurant. We found one with linen table cloths and napkins. When we had ordered, I turned to Fran.

"After our first night, you asked the question, 'Do we have anything to offer these people?' How do you feel about that now?"

"Not nearly as tired, sore, discouraged and intimidated as I did then! But I'm still not sure of the answer," she replied.

"I think I was expecting more of a leadership role," said Kenny. "But they have plenty of leaders here."

"They surely do!" agreed Coke. "Perhaps it's because this camp has so many seminary students."

"They are a fine group of people," I agreed. "But I still think we've given them something mighty important. The same thing they've given us."

They looked at me puzzled.

"What are Germans like, Coke?"

"Well, that's hard to say. I know people say they are arrogant and rude, but the two girls I'm getting to know aren't. George started out that way, but that's just a small part of him and the three refugee boys…" Her voice trailed off as she looked at me. "I think I see where you're leading us, Papa Walt. We're seeing people as individuals, not as the Germans, or the French or the Poles."

"No more good guys and bad guys," affirmed Kenny. "Just people, some of whom I like and some I don't."

"And that's how they're seeing us," said Fran. "I don't think we're 'those

Americans' anymore."

"Our goal was to earn the right to be heard by eating what they eat, sleeping where they sleep, working as they work," I said. "It's working. Not quite as I'd anticipated, but it is working. And you three with your open, honest, loving outreach are the reason."

"And you too," laughed Coke. "After all, you do the work of two."

She was telling Kenny about George's remark, "The fat one works for two," when Fran suddenly grabbed her arm.

"Look!" she said with horror in her voice.

We followed her gaze to a neighboring table where a man had just gotten his order of escargot.

"That's snails!" whispered Fran.

Using a tiny fork, the man delicately fished the steaming inhabitant out of its shell, held it poised, then swallowed it whole. My three, sophisticated Californians gagged in unison. I started to explain how snails were farmed, hoping to relieve some of the strangeness, but Coke held up her hand weakly, her skin, like Fran's, slightly green.

"Please, Walt. Could we just talk about something else?"

"But girls, remember what Corrie ten Boom told us," began Kenny, his face serious, "we're supposed to eat what they eat..." At the looks on their faces, he burst into laughter.

Just then the waiter arrived with our steaks. Angling our chairs slightly away from the other table, we tore into them with gusto. I noticed the man with the escargot looking at us as we had looked at him.

"Do you enjoy horse meat?" he asked as he got up to leave.

"No way!" we answered.

"Didn't you just have steaks?"

"Yes. They where delicious."

His eyebrows rose. "If you had the steaks, you've had horse meat."

Now we really looked green.

Good-byes were tough and traveling by myself felt strange. As I boarded the train in Paris for Kassel, the atmosphere changed. The train would cross the border from France into Germany—still an occupied country and still ruled by the Allied Military Government—so it was patrolled by the U.S. Army Military Police. My instinctive reaction was that there was something ominous about the very fact that M.P.s were considered necessary. There seemed more restraint, less freedom of movement, less warmth and neighborliness. Was this true, or was it just that this was the first time I was traveling without the youthful exuberance of the kids?

I traveled all night, sleeping restlessly. Since I had no German marks, I couldn't buy breakfast. Tired and hungry, I was feeling low. At the French border it became clear that the Germans had lost the war and were a people living under control of a foreign, military government. All nine hundred passengers were ordered out, carrying their baggage. First came the French passport control. As we passed single file along a cordoned-off pathway, officials looked at each person's passport, staring first at the passport picture, then intently at the face of the bearer. After passports were stamped, the next stop was the customs official.

"Anything to declare?"

Luggage and parcels were subject to strict inspection, even my Swiss chocolate presents for my family. Next I had to fill out forms recording all the money in my possession, which country it was from, the denominations and the totals. Travelers checks and any other forms of currency had to be detailed in the appropriate place. What a relief when all 900 of us had finally completed the process! Then with an overwhelming feeling of fatigue I found out it must be repeated on the German side! Only then were we free to re-board the train.

Frustrated, tired, hungry, lonely, I sank into the seat in my compartment and shut my eyes. Dozing, I slowly became conscious of voices discussing California beaches. I poked my head out the door and saw two, young M.P.s leaning beside an open window having a cigarette.

"California? Are you from California?"

They looked up eagerly at the sound of my voice. One was from Glendale, California, and had come to know Christ through my friend at the Glendale YMCA, Homer Gould. The other was from Redwood City, just south of San Francisco. The M.P.s no longer looked so ominous.

I changed trains in Frankfurt where my M.P. friends pointed me in the right direction to get money changed. I had time to buy breakfast and walk around before catching the train to Kassel. Frankfurt had been badly destroyed and reconstruction was slow. It was shocking to see bomb craters and destroyed buildings with the rubble still uncleared. That sight became more common as I traveled into the German uplands. It still didn't prepare me for what I would encounter in Kassel.

When Harriet, Duke, John and Ralph had arrived the week before in Kassel they were deeply disturbed by the hostile reaction of the townspeople. The Brethren staff finally managed to pacify the crowd. But the work campers proved more difficult.

There were forty-one participants, including a militant Israeli, from fourteen different countries. The German campers, disconcerted by this concentration of former enemies, became aloof; some were even hostile. One of the Germans was a giant young man, a former Nazi youth leader, named Uwe Hollm. Uwe had attended a Brethren work camp the previous summer and had been deeply moved by the spirit of pacifism and the commitment to non-violence he experienced there. He had come seeking that experience again. The rancor in the camp and the staff's seeming inability to do anything about it made him tense and irritable.

Mary, the camp leader, was a warm, friendly, young Brethren woman who believed in non-directive leadership. With this diverse group, that method wasn't working. Asking people who still saw each other as enemies to make decisions by consensus led to arguments, quarrels and even out-right fights. The camp was supposedly Christian, but so volatile were the feelings between campers that as simple a thing as starting meals with prayer provoked controversy.

So intense was the discord that the Brethren staff began to consider disbanding the camp.

Ralph, Harriet, Duke and John decided it was time to do something.

At dinner on the night of their decision, Duke made an announcement. Standing up in the semi-sheltered part of the men's barracks, which doubled as the dining area, he finally managed above the babble of voices in a variety of languages to get people's attention.

"Harriet, John, Ralph and I are starting a prayer group tonight. We'll meet out on the hillside. This isn't a secret meeting" he said with his infectious grin. "We want to pray together for our project. Please feel free to come."

The announcement didn't get booed down, but neither did it generate any great enthusiasm. The four began meeting each evening and other campers slowly began to drift in.

One of the first to come was the one Ralph least expected—Uwe. At dinner on the day Ralph and the others arrived in camp, Uwe had challenged them with his declaration: "When you destroyed Hitler, you destroyed God for me!"

Uwe learned that Ralph had been born, as he had, in Hamburg, Germany. He also found out that Ralph's father was Jewish and that the family had fled to Holland where Ralph worked in the Dutch underground. Uwe's anger and rancor over his lost ideals, his irritation at the discord in this camp, his uncertainty about his own beliefs—all these feelings seemed to focus on Ralph. He began to perceive him as the enemy and found almost diabolical ways to take out his hostility on him.

And Ralph was fighting his own demons. Uwe appeared the prototype German, big, brash and arrogant with no apologies for the war. In Hollywood, Ralph's visceral hatred of Nazis, particularly German Nazis, had been conquered intellectually by Christ's love.

But now the distance was gone and he was face to face with the people who had beaten his father, killed his friends, wreaked havoc on his country, terrorized and disenfranchised him. The emotions came surging back. His faith was being severely tested by this abrasive arrogance. He would slip away for quiet times of prayer, asking God to show him how to love Uwe.

Only in the prayer meetings would Uwe's rancor abate. Those meetings and the kids themselves, particularly Duke and Harriet, were beginning to challenge Uwe, not with words, but with a way of life. Uwe's cot was beside Duke's in their roofless barracks where morning and evening he watched Duke read his Bible.

"Why do you do this?" Uwe asked.

"It's the best way I know to keep myself open to Christ and his guidance," Duke answered. He never pressed Uwe about his beliefs.

Uwe questioned both Duke and Harriet. "Here the camp is in deep crisis and you start a prayer meeting! What possible good do you think that will do?" He couldn't quite disguise the contempt in his voice.

"Our group has been asking God for guidance in everything we do," answered Harriet. "It's natural that we keep asking him here, where the need is so great."

"This camp needs a lot more than people sitting on a hill praying!"

"What do you think should be done?" Duke asked with genuine curiosity.

"We need some order, some organization, some respect for the rules to make people settle down and get to work!"

Duke chuckled. "This group doesn't seem to be responding too well to the staff's attempts at that, does it?"

"Christ's love is the only thing that can create that order and respect, Uwe," said Harriet quietly.

He wasn't convinced.

On a cold, blustery day, ten days after the work camp started, I arrived in Kassel. The railroad station, complete rubble and destruction, offered no shelter from the rain and wind. The other passengers left quickly and I was soon alone, hoping that Ralph had gotten the letter I'd mailed a week earlier with my arrival time. I had no idea where the camp was and it dawned on me that I had no contact person to call for information. After walking up and down the platform a few times to keep warm, I spotted a phone and tried to place a call to the Brethren Office. But I had no change or even any idea what the right change was. And I didn't speak German. In the middle of my attempted call, Ralph appeared at my side, glasses misted with rain and his smile as warming as a burst of sunshine. He'd received my letter ten minutes before.

With Ralph was Ed Sauer, the director of the Ellierode Camp where Louie, Lardner and Carol were. Their project was to build a home for forty boys orphaned by the war. Ed and Ralph were on their way to Ellierode, so I went along, delighted with a chance to see the other three so soon. Under the joy of the reunion, I sensed an edge, a tension. I had a sudden, uncomfortable feeling that the differences between the CIMADE camp and these two in Germany would be profound.

"What was the reaction in France to North Korea invading South Korea?" asked Lardner.

"The Embassy warned us to be ready to leave at a moment's notice, but no one in camp took it too seriously. What about here?" I responded.

"We're only thirteen kilometers from the border of East Germany," he answered. "There was real fear that it could be the start of World War III."

Louie spoke. "I said to one of the Germans, 'We're here as your friends. What would happen if war started again?' He answered, 'Then we would be enemies.'"

Carol gave an involuntary shiver.

I gave them a quick briefing on the CIMADE camp, going into detail about Coke's reconciling experience with George. Louie's face darkened, cleared and ended up all smiles.

"So within the first week national differences were starting to disappear?" asked Ralph pensively.

"Not so much to disappear as to become unimportant," I answered. "Isn't that happening here?"

"Not at Kassel," said Ralph emphatically.

"We've experienced some coldness, but Ellierode is a rural area and didn't get the destruction that Kassel did, so we've had nothing like the hostility the Kassel team's experiencing," explained Louie. "What's driving us crazy is how slowly the project's moving. We'll never get the home for the boys built at this rate!"

Lardner gave his deep chuckle, the one I swore would charm a baboon out of a tree. "My friend here's getting impatient."

"Remember, Lou," cautioned Ralph, "don't rush in. We're supposed to keep a low profile."

Carol was in charge of the kitchen, and according to Lardner and Louie, doing a great job of preparing meals with whatever supplies she had to work with.

I took her hands in mine, looking at the blisters as well as a burn.

"The burn looks like it came from a hot stove, but what about the blisters?" I asked.

"I'm helping with the foundation too."

"You have to see Carol swing her pickaxe," Louie said admiringly.

Ralph suddenly looked at his watch.

"We've got to get back to Kassel by dinner time, Walt. Do remember, Louie, easy does it."

"Our object is to get the house built, isn't it?" Louie was mumbling as Ralph and I left Ellierode.

Ralph filled me in on Kassel as we drove back.

As soon as I arrived in camp, Uwe wanted to talk to me. Considering what I'd heard from Ralph, I was surprised at what he had to say.

"You are a great man! The spiritual father of my spiritual friends," was his introductory statement.

"With the camp in deep crisis, Duke and the others from your church started this prayer meeting!" The surprise still echoed in his voice. "But there was this crisis and it was growing, so once I went along," he paused, looking reflective, almost subdued.

"What did you think?"

"This was a new and a strange experience! People were praying to Christ as if they knew who he was, as if they expected Him to intervene. They were doing it aloud and yet it was disciplined."

The tone in Uwe's voice told me that the disciplined part was very important to this former Nazi, this young giant who was barging into my life. He became very still, staring over my head, his dark eyes slightly unfocused, as he told me what happened next.

"So last night, I prayed," he said, his voice a whisper, "and for the first time in my life, I had the feeling that I was praying and receiving an answer, that I was not praying to the open air. As a child I went to confirmation classes—I'm studying theology now—but it was at these prayer meetings out in the bushes that I met Christ personally, not just as a concept." The wonder of this experience stayed on Uwe's face as his buoyancy resurfaced.

"And I'm not the only one affected. The camp is reforming itself through the spiritual leadership of your people."

What a thrill it was for me to hear those words! I had seen the beginning of understanding and dramatic reconciliation in the CIMADE work camp. The evidence of God's healing work here, too, validated those many months we had schooled ourselves in our three team disciplines: find biblical guidelines for reconciliation; pray about every detail and action; get practical experience in reconciliation by working in the ghettos, barrios and on the college campuses of Los Angeles.

At dinner that same evening I began to get a feel for this camp. Those at our table bowed for silent prayer before eating as did about half the people at other tables. The rest quieted momentarily, but didn't stop talking. Duke grinned at the expression on my face.

"This is a real improvement, Papa Walt. Last week I got my stew in my lap as the Israeli and a German tackled each other right across the table."

John spoke up. "And the silent prayer is our compromise with those who didn't want prayer at all."

"A good one. You're telling me I've got to know where you started to appreciate how far you've come?"

"For sure!" they chorused.

Harriet was sitting next to a tiny German woman, probably about forty, who didn't fit the work camper prototype at all.

"Walt," she said to me, "I'd like to introduce you to a new friend of mine. Anneliese, this is my pastor, Walt James." The introductions were a mixture of English and German.

Anneliese smiled shyly, then ducked her head. There was a serenity and a simplicity about her expression that caught my attention.

"Anneliese lives in the community and is working with us on our project." Admiration and protection were mixed in Harriet's voice.

"Walt," said Duke, seated between Uwe and another young man, "let me introduce Ricki." Duke had studied German and introduced the young German slowly in that language. Ricki was aloof, acknowledging the introduction with a brief handshake.

"So! We pray again tonight?" Uwe asked, smiling broadly at Duke's affirmative nod.

Uwe's excitement was contagious, even mixed as it was with the brashness and arrogance of his gestures, stance and tone. Then he saw Ralph.

"So! You are back. You have got Ellierode straightened out now?"

I was dumfounded at the antagonism in Uwe's voice, but Ralph's smile looked genuine as he responded.

"Nothing quite so grand as that. But the work has started."

Uwe shook his head in exasperation.

"The American men they had running the Brethren Camp I was in at Hamburg last year were very organized. They knew how to run a camp. Wonderful, spiritual men! What has happened to their camps this year?" Uwe's question seemed a challenge to Ralph.

"The Hamburg camp was their first, wasn't it?"

"Yes."

"I think this year their resources are spread out by trying to do so many more."

Uwe didn't seem pacified by this, but just then Duke unobtrusively intervened by standing up and making an announcement.

"We're praying again tonight. We'd like to have you join us."

The calmness, and authority with which Duke handled himself, humor still intact, were new. I was impressed. So was Uwe, beaming by my side, his attention now focused on Duke.

After dinner, Ricki walked away. Duke saw the direction of my gaze.

"Ricki's still a thoroughgoing Nazi. He won't have any part of our prayer times."

Anneliese was leaving too because, Harriet told me, she didn't like to walk home after dark. Ralph, Duke, John, Harriet, Uwe, Mary, the camp director, some other campers and I gathered on a gently sloping hillside for an hour of warm, loving prayer and sharing. For the first time since my arrival at Kassel I sensed a feeling of community and closeness. The only discordant note was Uwe's simmering attitude toward Ralph.

Like the other men, I slept on a straw mattress in the rubble of the bombed Luftwaffe barracks. It rained during the night, so we woke up damp and cold. The only indoor accommodation was the basement where the women slept and did the cooking. Many, many families were in the same situation. One of our goals was to identify with the people. We were.

Riding with the work campers in the back of an old truck through the city to the work site the next morning, I was overwhelmed by the magnitude of the destruction. Were we hopelessly naive to even consider reconciliation in such a place? The city was still in ruins. Vendors were doing business in holes they had excavated in the rubble of bombed buildings. Seeing my shock, the work campers began to fill me in on Kassel.

"There are still bodies buried in that rubble," Ricki told me in German with Uwe translating.

"It took about twenty minutes to accomplish this kind of destruction," said John, his face taut with pain.

"The Kassel residents are suffering from severe unemployment," said Ralph. "Survival is the one great task. Daily, a family member goes out to the farms and tries to barter for food, one or two eggs, some potatoes, usually in trade for a prized possession."

I sat silently trying to comprehend the destruction surrounding me, trying to conceive of not having enough food to feed my family.

At the work site, observing the friction between the different nationalities so recently on opposing sides of World War II, I realized that while the camp might be coming together through the team's spiritual leadership, the process was far from complete. This was particularly evident during the breaks and at the noon meal prepared and brought up to the work site by Harriet and some of the other young women.

Neither Ricki nor Uwe had any hesitancy about diving headlong into social and political discussions about Nazism, the Jews and even Germany's role in the war. In fact, these two started the discussions as if their clear consciences demanded that they exonerate at least some of Germany's guilt. Many of the other campers, particularly the Israeli, eagerly leaped into the fray.

Ralph and Uwe, the one slender and soft-spoken, the other big and brash, seemed to epitomize the depth of the divisions.

"Tell me," Uwe challenged Ralph at lunch time, "how you could be a Christian and also a member of the Resistance."

"I became a Christian during the war," said Ralph, "but why would that prevent me from being part of the Resistance?"

"Because Christians are pacifists. If you are a Christian, you must believe war is wrong!" I couldn't tell if Uwe was baiting Ralph or seeking answers.

"The use of force is wrong always," Ralph agreed. "Countries are destroyed, whole generations are uprooted and morality falls greatly. But not all Christians are pacifists. I believe sometimes war becomes necessary to stop a great evil."

"So if it is sometimes necessary to stop this 'great evil,' how can you say war is always wrong?"

"Because even if we must use it, destruction and despair will be our reaping."

"What then is the Christian response?"

"The Christian's fight is a spiritual one. We must tell people of God's love and grace, tell them that in Christ we have newness of life, power, a purpose for living. We must share what we ourselves have experienced, not a theory of life or religion, but the life and power of Christ himself," Ralph answered passionately.

"This life and power didn't do much for the Jews and Christians who opposed Hitler," said Uwe sarcastically.

"Where is Hitler now?" asked Ralph tiredly.

Uwe surged to his feet, glowering down at Ralph, then turned and stalked back to work.

The place I could see reconciliation beginning was in the project itself. The plan was to finish the demolition of a bombed out barracks and then on that site to use shovels in excavating basements for families whose homes had been destroyed in the bombing.

Here the different nationalities could come together in common cause. They all worked hard and through the shared effort, could begin to see each other as individuals rather than as Poles, Italians, Americans or even Germans.

The work was hard labor, physically demanding, and even dangerous, I discovered. That first morning I set to work to destroy a pillar of bricks. The easiest way seemed to be to fell it like a tree. What I hadn't realized was that bricks wouldn't fall in one direction the way a tree does. Using muscles hardened from labor at the first work camp, I was swinging my sledgehammer with gusto.

"Walt! Stop!" Ralph suddenly screamed.

Without warning, the pillar exploded around me! Instinctively, I went into a football roll and kept rolling as hundreds of bricks came crashing down where I'd just been working. Ralph and the others rushed to my side as the bricks were still falling and the dust swirling. Gingerly, they helped me up and we decided that I was still whole. Shared danger is another thing that breaks down barriers. From then on I was a part of the group.

Trying to live our faith in the midst of tension, fatigue, poor food and bad living conditions, the Kassel Camp was a real "baptism of fire" for the team and me. It was our first confrontation with what I had anticipated to be the postwar mentality, the arena in which reconciliation must be realized. It was a proving ground for our hopes and dreams of showing Christ as the basis for world brotherhood.

If young Uwe Hollm and I were going to share that brotherhood, I needed to get to know him, to understand what it was that drove him.

1950 Deputation Team—Front: (left to right) John Grund, Carol Abrams, Colleen Townsend and Duke Benson. Back: (left to right) Ralph Hamburger, Walt James, Harriett Prichard, Kenny Grant, Fran Kent, Louie Evans and Lardner Moore.

1950—Walt at CIMADE work camp in Paris. "The fat one works for two."

Ralph Hamburger at a work camp.

1950—In Paris Ralph Hamburger, Fran Kent and Colleen Townsend have an afternoon off from the CIMADE work camp.

1950—Louie Evans at Ellierode work camp.

From Uwe I learned what it was like to be a young German boy growing up in Nazi Germany.

Uwe's childhood had two major influences. The first was living in Holbe-Spaugen, a remote village by the North Sea where his father was the teacher in the one-room school house. An idealistic, politically naive man, he viewed this farming area as a rather romantic environment in which he and his wife, also a teacher, could raise their son and three daughters. The family did not even have a radio in the house.

The second major influence was Hitler. He was the center of Uwe's life. More than just a hero, he was a religious figure. In the big cities like Berlin the hard and harsh realities of Nazism were apparent, but to Uwe, Hitler was far away, a little bit like God.

Hitler's clarion call to restore Germany to her pre-World War I greatness struck an answering cord within young Uwe. And the Hitler Youth with its order, discipline and uniforms had strong appeal. Being the son of the teacher, an educated man in a rural community, made Uwe a candidate for leadership. So did his own natural ability. By age eleven, he had three boys under his command; by twelve, he had twelve boys.

His family's belief in education inadvertently deepened Uwe's exposure to Hitler and Nazism. To attend high school meant leaving the village and going to the regional school four miles away in Cuxhaven. Few villagers wanted their children to do that, so while Uwe daily biked back and forth to school, his friends' education stopped at age fourteen. Away from the insular village, Uwe was exposed to the influence of teachers who were either Nazis or who were forced to teach the party line:

"Germans are the highest species of humanity.

"They are superior to Jews and Slavs, images of the Lord, not monstrosities halfway between man and Ape.

"Jews are responsible for all the evils of the world.

"Democracy could only lead to Communism. A dictatorship is the only way to save Germany from the Communists and the Jews.

"Territories taken away at the end of World War I must be returned to the Fatherland. Because the German nation is growing, it is natural that it take growing space from the countries surrounding it."

Based on Hitler's *Mein Kampf*, this was what Uwe was taught at high school.

Germany had been devastated by World War I, dismembered and humiliated by the peace terms, and was failing economically. But Hitler said it could be great again, that it was destined to be great!

Any questions Uwe might have had regarding that doctrine were overridden by the magnetism of the Fuhrer, by his spell-binding oratory and his absolute conviction that he was leading Germany to her natural destiny as a world power. Any moderation Uwe's father might impose was limited because his father was seldom home. He had been drafted into the Navy in 1939 and was eventually sent to North Africa.

But men were supposed to be fighting for the Fatherland. And life at home was wonderful. High school and its ideas were exciting. Being there added to his prestige in the village. By 1944 he had risen to the top of the Hitler Youth in his area.

Not only was he the leader, but his group had been given real work, not just something to make kids feel good. He led a squad of young boys, drilling them on horseback; and had thirty horses in his charge. On Sunday mornings the squad would go cantering through the forest on patrol. It was exhilarating to be in command of such a formidable group, with the very real possibility that something dangerous might happen. For Uwe it was a great, great adventure.

But in the summer of 1944 the adventure started falling apart. Uwe returned home one afternoon to find his mother sitting at the kitchen table weeping.

"Mama! What's wrong?"

Wordlessly, she gestured to a telegram in front of her. Uwe reached out to grab it, then paused, suddenly hesitant and frightened. Slowly, he picked it up.

WE REGRET TO INFORM YOU THAT OFFICER HOLLM HAS BEEN CAPTURED AND IS A PRISONER-OF-WAR IN AFRICA.

"Father? A POW? How can he survive that?"

That his idealistic, scholarly father could even be a soldier had been hard enough for Uwe to believe. But a prisoner-of-war? The war suddenly seemed not so distant and glorious.

"Where is he? Is he wounded?"

"After the telegram came, I went to the post office and made some telephone calls. But there seems to be no way to find out." Months passed with no word from the military and no letters from Uwe's father.

In the fall of 1944, Uwe and his mother came into conflict.

"Uwe, it's time for you to take the church confirmation classes."

"Confirmation classes? That would be hypocritical since I don't believe in Christ."

"Don't say such things! Your father would want you to do this."

"Mother, it isn't fair to bring Father into this!"

"Why are you talking about fair? You know I'm right. Your father would insist if he were here."

Uwe sat silently, brooding.

"All right. I'll take the classes out of respect for you and Father. But please don't force me to go to Holy Communion. That would be hypocrisy and I really won't betray my sense of integrity."

She nodded. "Take the classes. Then if you still feel the same way, taking Holy Communion will be your own decision."

The war was coming even to Holbe-Spaugen. Uwe was biking home from school one afternoon when he heard the whine of a fighter plane. Shielding his eyes, he looked up and squinting against the glare, saw a fighter diving toward him. Stunned, Uwe realized he was the target and leaping off his bike, dived behind a stone fence as bullets strafed the road.

That terrifying experience became common. For no apparent reason, the fighters would suddenly scream out of the sky and strafe the village, the roads, the farms.

Then the bombers started. Day after day the villagers were deafened by the massive sweep of a thousand bombers flying in formation so close together that they literally blotted out the sun. They could take as long as six hours passing over, going and returning from bombing Berlin. One day on a return flight, one dumped its unused bombs on Holbe-Spaugen.

By 1945 it was impossible even in remote areas to believe the war was going well for Germany. Desperately, Uwe and his comrades wished for some way to join the army and defend their beloved country.

"If only I were six months older!" Uwe declared passionately to his mother. "Then I could fight against those U.S. Imperialists and Soviet Communists. If we don't defeat them, how can we maintain freedom and human dignity in Germany and the rest of Europe?"

"I thank God you are no older!" replied his mother. "How can our leaders be drafting sixteen-year-olds? That's criminal!"

"Please, Mother! Watch what you say!"

Finally, at the end of April, Uwe, his mother and sisters, gathering with the other villagers, heard the news over German radio. Hitler had fought his last battle at the front with his soldiers and then as a soldier, as a hero, he was killed by Russian guns.

Uwe was in mourning. His god was dead. What would happen now to all the high ideals, to the camaraderie of his patrol squad, to the greatness for which Germany was destined? Still, he was fifteen, his own idealism was intact and he tried to comfort the younger members of his squad.

"All right, so he is dead. But he died the death of a hero."

Then a few days later came the worst shock of his life. Uwe's mother heard it first and tried to cushion the blow for her son.

"Uwe, did you hear the latest reports from Berlin?"

"No. What?"

"It would seem the first report we heard about how the Fuhrer died was not accurate."

"What do you mean?"

"He did not die at the front. He...killed himself."

"No! He could not be so cowardly. You must be wrong!"

Silently she shook her head.

"He had not even the courage to stand up and take the responsibility for what he had done as a leader?" Uwe's voice trembled.

His mother nodded. "He was a coward and took his own life."

Uwe was badly shaken. If the Fuhrer, his god, was in truth a coward, if he could not stand up for his own actions, what remained of his values?

Shock followed shock. Uwe and his family were in Cuxhaven when the British troops occupied the area. Everyone was forced to see the films taken at the concentration camps. Uwe emerged from them stumbling, physically sick.

"Do you believe this?" he asked his mother.

She shook her head in horror. "I don't want to, but how can I doubt it?"

"Did you know about these camps the way the soldiers said we must have known?"

"I knew about camps, but not about this killing of the Jews and other people. My understanding was that the camps were work camps where people who didn't want to work were forced to go."

"I heard at school that everyone who wanted to overthrow Hitler or the government was shot. This is the normal thing one does with traitors to the country—but not this killing of the Jews."

"This is the deepest shame which could come to Germany," said his mother. "How can we believe that such a thing could happen in the name of Germany?"

The family returned to Holbe-Spaugen only to find that the world had streamed into their small village. Inundated with refugees, it had grown from 170 inhabitants to 600. They were crammed into all the houses. It was a complete change.

Uwe's home was changed; his god was dead; his country was defeated and dismembered. He was a disillusioned, disenchanted young man. The one bright spot was the safe return of his father, released by the Allies two years after the war was over. Amazingly, his idealistic, romantic nature was still intact, although badly shaken in spots by his time as a POW and by the stories of the concentration camps.

Uwe finished high school and decided to study at the University of Hamburg. He brought the subject up at dinner.

"Father, I would like to study theology at the University of Hamburg."

"Theology? That is odd considering your beliefs."

"I don't know if I'll end up taking the theological exam because I don't believe in Christ, but I have the feeling I must know more about this Christian belief."

"And you think a university is the place to learn that?"

"For me, yes. Please give me the opportunity to study for three semesters. After that, I will have to decide whether to go on or to stop."

"And will you study Greek and Hebrew, subjects that will be good for you even if you don't stay in theology?"

"Yes."

"All right, then. For three semesters."

What Uwe was looking for much more than an education, was a new purpose in life. He was open to all ideas. During his second year at the University he heard about an international work camp being held that summer of 1949 to rebuild a parish center that had been destroyed by bombs in Hamburg. Tracking down the information, Uwe found out the camp was being sponsored by a Christian denomination in America called the Church of the Brethren. The concept was to bring students from different countries together to help heal the wounds of war and to build foundations for peace. The theological students were being invited to come.

But no one was responding.

"Now this is a shame," Uwe said to one of his classmates. "These people are coming from the U.S., from Britain, Holland and Norway and no one cooperates with them."

The young man shrugged. "If they'd pay me, I might go. But I've got to work this summer to pay for school next fall. Why don't you go?"

Why not? Uwe decided.

The summer of 1949 was the first time Uwe had come into contact with Americans. Now he was in daily contact with three Brethren volunteers, deeply ethical men imbued with the Brethren spirit of pacifism. They worked hard to demonstrate the friendliness they felt toward the German people. A black man caught Uwe's attention.

"Tell me why you are here," Uwe asked forthrightly.

"Because I am a pacifist."

"I don't understand what that means."

"It means that I do not believe in war as a way to solve differences. I will not participate in a war or any military action."

"But if your country needs to fight, you are a traitor not to support it."

"No, not a traitor, but a voice calling my country to higher values."

"But what happens when you are drafted into the military?"

"Often our beliefs keep us from being drafted, or if we are, we work in non-military ways, such as in a hospital. That's what I did."

"But I still don't understand why you are here now."

"Because we want to heal the wounds of war and build foundations of trust and understanding that will prevent future wars."

Uwe was deeply impressed by this ideal of pacifism. It went counter to all he had absorbed in the Hitler Youth, but gave him fresh ideals to replace those that had failed so tragically. Still, he had been badly hurt and disillusioned by the call to high ideals that lacked the substance to create lasting change.

He returned to the University for the winter term, pondering pacifism, but not convinced he had found a new purpose in which to invest his life. Moved and intrigued however, he signed up the following summer, 1950, for another Brethren work camp. This one was in Kassel, Germany.

In the early morning dawn of my second day in Kassel, Duke gently shook my shoulder to wake me.

"Come on, Walt. We're going on a salvage operation before we start work!"

It was barely light, but Duke, Uwe, John and Ralph were already up. Feeling like I had just gotten to sleep, stiff from the straw mattress, I stumbled into my clothes and joined them.

"The Brethren staff discovered a huge, 350 pound cheese wheel in the old commissary, but it's so bug infested, no one thought it was edible," said John. "Then someone came up with the idea of putting it into a big vat of lye to see if it would kill the critters. We're going to help."

Much of the food was Army surplus, big barrels of dried milk, peanut butter, huge cans of marmalade jam gone to sugar and stale black bread.

I woke up in a hurry when I got a nose full of the combined odors of moldy cheese and lye. My stomach turned over at the thought of eating anything that smelled like that. With much hoisting, we got the cheese into the vat being careful not to splash the caustic liquid on ourselves. Sure enough, to the cheers of the group, the little residents came floating to the surface in large numbers. We skimmed them off, used fresh water to cleanse and purify the cheese, getting rid of most of the odor in the process, then lugged it to the kitchen. It was greeted with more cheers from the women who did the meal preparation, Harriet included.

I had thought the women well-housed, but as I looked around that dark basement filled with the odors of cooking and of bodies in close quarters, I wasn't so sure. Their roof was all that remained of the upper part of the building.

"What do you think of this?" I asked Harriet. She shivered.

"It gives me claustrophobia! And it's very difficult cooking down here and then transporting the food to the work site every day."

She looked tired, very tired, but a glimmer of humor surfaced. "But we do stay dry!"

"Your job is cooking?"

"I do a lot of cooking. Then after the food's delivered to the work site, I stay and work."

"What a trooper you are! By the way, who's your friend, Anneliese?"

"She lives in the community. I told you that. But I'm just finding out her story. During the Hitler times, she was sent to a concentration camp because she's slightly retarded. She bore her own suffering in that terrible camp and she saw most of her friends there die. Somehow, she miraculously escaped. The courage of that woman in the midst of terrible suffering is such a testimony to me. She has such a beautiful attitude, but needs lots of friendship and love."

That afternoon after work Ralph, Harriet, Duke, John and I got to see a wonderful example of reconciliation in action, another Brethren work camp, the Hessisch Lichtenau Project just outside Kassel. It was a children's orthopedic hospital set up in an abandoned Hitler youth camp. Work project campers in their six-week stretches were doing the additions and modifications needed to convert barracks into hospital wards.

Here nationalities had truly ceased to matter. Campers and staff were united in their goal of creating out of the debris of war one of the finest of children's orthopedic hospitals. The kids and I left refreshed and enthused.

On our way back to Kassel we detoured by Ellierode to see how the boys' home that Louie, Lardner and Carol were working on was progressing.

"Louie has reorganized the whole thing," Lardner laughed.

Since our guidelines were to be low key, not to jump in and take over, Louie tried to look contrite, but couldn't quite manage it.

"Okay, Lou." I said. "Let's hear it."

"Their system wasn't working," he responded emphatically. "The seven strongest guys were mixing mortar on the bare ground at the lower end of the area where we're building the house. Then it took all of them just to transport it up the hill to the work site. That left the girl campers and the boys living here to lay the brick.

"Yesterday I took Wolfgang, my fourteen-year-old buddy, and we went down to the village and bought some lumber— real cheap lumber, Walt—and built a mortar boat, about six-by-three feet and sloped on the ends. The day before I'd gone to the village blacksmith with a sketch for a mortar hoe—you know, it looks like a big hoe with two holes in it to let the mortar flow through and mix?"

I nodded.

"The blacksmith is this dear old guy. He wears heavy boots, black stockings, knickers and a leather cap. I love to watch him work. He doesn't speak a word of English, so I showed him my sketch and he scratched his head, spouted German that I couldn't comprehend, and finally nodded that he could do it. He had it ready this morning and followed Wolfgang and me up to the site to see what we were going to do with it.

"We set the mortar boat up at the top of the site and I taught Wolfgang how to mix mortar. With the boat and the hoe he was producing faster than the seven men and instead of having to carry it up, we could lower buckets of it to the people on the site.

"We didn't try to talk anybody into anything. Just did our thing. The blacksmith was impressed. He called down to the men mixing the mortar, they came up and watched awhile, closed up their own operation and went to work laying bricks. That's what they wanted to do anyway."

"Did you sense any resentment?" I asked. Carol spoke up. "They wouldn't resent someone who freed them up to do what they wanted to do. People are singing as they work now."

"Everyone is happy to have the work progressing," Lardner agreed.

We were sitting on the grass under a lovely old oak tree talking and praying as the twilight deepened around us. Our prayer time seemed particularly meaningful to Harriet who was really being drained by the dissension and by the harsh working and living conditions at Kassel. And I knew Uwe's anger was wearing Ralph down.

"In the middle of an experience it's hard to evaluate it, but what are your thoughts and feelings?" I asked.

"Our guidelines are crucial," said Harriet.

"Thank goodness—no, thank Walt and Ralph—that we were so well drilled to look for the biblical guidelines, to pray and then to act," said Duke. "If we hadn't been, I would be way out of my depth here."

"Me too," John chimed in. "Without our training and the orientation, I'd be paralyzed by the bitterness and hostility not only coming at me, but flaring up between the different nationalities."

"Looking for the leading of the Spirit during our training has carried over to camp," said Harriet. "I know the Spirit led John, Duke and me to start the evening prayer meeting." She continued. "The environment is so depressing and the work so tiring, if I didn't have the structure we established as a group, I think I'd just go to sleep at night instead of going to the prayer meeting."

"I agree," said Carol. "Some evenings it takes every ounce of my determination to go to the meeting instead of going to bed!"

"Our camp's not as international as the other two," Louie reflected. "The campers are mostly German, but very diverse. Among the Germans themselves, there's an incredible need for reconciliation."

Ralph was nodding agreement.

"Yes. Perhaps the greatest need for reconciliation is in Germany itself."

"How are you doing, Ralph?" asked Louie

"It's tougher being here than I anticipated. I need your prayers that I may see Uwe as Christ sees him."

We joined hands then and prayed for Ralph, for each other and for specific campers. Christ's refreshing love washed over and renewed us in the process.

"Anything else?" I asked, looking particularly at John, who had become very quiet.

"The massive, senseless destruction is really eating away at me," he said grimly. "I have a hard time believing that war is ever right or justified."

"I hear you, John." said Louie. "I've been sickened by the stupidity of humanity in wreaking such destruction on beauties that cultures have built up through the centuries."

"The sheer numbers of people killed in the war is beyond my comprehension," Carol said.

"And the mass suffering of the survivors..." Harriet's voice trailed off.

We sat in a subdued silence.

"There aren't any right answers about war," I responded heavily. "We can only keep our focus on Christ. Christ is the only real answer."

Once again we took our concerns to our Master, seeking his vision for issues so far beyond our solutions.

"Oh look!" said Carol. "There's Pastor Kropetschek. It's his church, you know, that's sponsoring the Ellierode project." She waved to a robust, rugged looking man striding up the hill. He came over with seeming delight to meet me and the other team members and invited us to his home. It was so big that it seemed more of a lodge than a family residence. The campers slept upstairs and used the kitchen to get their meals.

Pastor Kropetschek was quite a man. He was born in China, had traveled the world, and at one time had been quite successful in business.

"The Holy Spirit got hold of me and now I am a pastor!" he told me, the light of heaven shining in his face. He introduced me to his wife, then took me into the bedrooms, proudly showing me his six children, most of them already asleep.

"I thank God daily for your young people," he said while beaming paternally at Louie, Carol and Lardner as we rejoined the group. "The Brethren are running this camp as they are the Kassel project. They are wonderful people, but talk more of labor and pacifism than of Christ. At the evening meetings your young people share their faith simply and openly and it is bringing the boys here to know the Lord. And that one," he added, pointing an accusing finger at Louie, "has reorganized the project so the house will get finished."

The days passed quickly, a blur of hard labor, nightly prayer and impromptu counseling. It seemed no time until it was Ralph's and my last evening at Kassel. We were leaving for Amsterdam the next day to see his parents. From there I would return home. Ralph would join Coke, Fran and Kenny at the CIMADE work camp.

During evening prayers, Ralph surprised me by sharing with the other campers some of his war experiences. He then told how Christ had moved into his heart, taking away the rage and hatred that had festered there, bringing reconciliation in ways he'd never thought possible.

"It was Christ or chaos for me," Ralph was saying. "Then wonderfully and quietly, Christ made himself known to me. Nothing dramatic. I was just walking home from the Hollywood church one evening and all of a sudden the lights went on in my heart. The Lord had come in. I felt his physical presence next to me. He was for real, he really lived and he could be trusted with my future!

"A few weeks later I realized how much I needed to forgive the Germans, the Nazis, to rid myself of the hate and rancor I still harbored in my heart. Guided by a friend, I spent a night in prayer and during that vigil, Christ's healing love washed through me. I learned how to forgive. I learned the reality of unconditional love.

"That same unconditional love is available to all of you."

Uwe was studying him intently, but didn't react. His face seemed made of stone. After the meeting other campers came up to question Ralph and thank him for sharing. Uwe left.

Because we were leaving very early the next morning, I said my good-byes that night. The parting wasn't as painful as at CIMADE since I hadn't been in Kassel as long, but I still had a sense of loss at leaving the people and the project. I particularly regretted not seeing any reconciliation between Ralph and Uwe.

It rained that night and Ralph and I woke at dawn, wet and weary, dressing as quickly as we could to try to get warm. Mist was rising from the soaked earth. As we left the rubble of the barracks, Uwe came walking toward us. He stopped and stood tensely, eyeing Ralph, nervously shifting his weight from foot to foot. Suddenly with almost a sob, he threw his arms around Ralph, and his voice breaking, spoke.

"You've got something. I want what you've got!"

Shocked, Ralph stood transfixed. Then, his eyes filling, he gathered as much of Uwe as he could into his arms, and answered.

"Not something. SOMEONE!"

They stood locked in a healing embrace for long moments, then Uwe moved back slightly.

"You are quite a great man—to be a Jew who has gone through all that suffering and to then become a Christian. What you said last night made an impression on me."

"I am not a great man," said Ralph firmly. "I'm committed to Christ and to letting him use me for reconciliation. He can heal your anger as he has healed mine."

They had stepped apart and now I could see Uwe, his cheeks shiny with tears, but a glint of laughter suddenly lurking in his eyes. He drew himself up and said arrogantly, "No matter what you say, to me you will always be a great man."

Ralph sagged, then looking sharply at Uwe, saw the humor in his face and realized he was being teased. Both began to laugh.

"I can sound so damned German, can't I?" said Uwe ruefully.

Uwe rode with us to the train station. My last memories of the Kassel Camp are of his encompassing bear hug and his tall, solid body standing on the misty platform waving as our train pulled away.

I knew that Uwe's life had been profoundly changed. But I had no way of knowing that our three lives were now inextricably linked and moving toward ministries that would involve people on both sides of the Iron Curtain.

I was soon back at work, catching up with my family and the home team members. But at times I had a strange sensation of being caught between two worlds, and the words of the young German refugees at CIMADE would echo in my mind, "What is your church doing for the oppressed in your own country?"

Letters from the European team kept me up-to-date. A long, newsy one from Ralph about the CIMADE camp and how different it was from the two in Germany gave me the impression that he was glad to be out of Germany in spite of his last encounter with Uwe. Colleen wrote about her new assignment. "A team of seven fellows was being sent to Boulogne near Dunkerque and they needed a cook. They hesitated sending a girl, as they thought it would be too rough. Can you imagine that?!! Well, we piled into the open truck and here we are. The fellows have two barracks to tear down. I cook their three meals for them. It's a real experience. I cook on a little wood deal. We chop our own wood and get all of the water from a pump down the road. There's a town nearby where I buy food each day. It takes all day to cook things because the stove is so small. It's pretty rugged here.

"This is a part of France I wanted to see, but it just tears my heart out to see the little kids who are poverty-stricken because of the terrible bombings during the war. Right now there is a whole gang of them outside the barracks, banging on the door and calling my name. They ask for bread, chocolate, anything! When I go outside they swarm around and grab me. This is something we didn't see in Sevres. As I said, I'm glad I'm seeing it, even if it does about break my heart. I never want to forget this."

She never has.

Harriet brought me up to date on Kassel.

"Well, the Lord has really been working in Kassel, Walt. He sees more than we anticipate so many times. We have organized a Tuesday night Bible study and discussion on the Book of John. The first week was only a warm-up, but last night was a real humdinger! These campers are so mixed-up with all sorts of doubts. I know they are watching us every moment. We have found that few of them know the real power of Christ working in their lives in a vital and living way. They have never really discussed their faith, but have accepted it because it is a tradition to belong to the church."

A letter from Louie described how well the construction was going on the boys' home. Then he talked about the group interaction.

"You know, Walt, the people we're with are mostly German students who support a gospel of pacifism and labor. Our emphasis on the centrality of Jesus Christ makes for good discussions. A couple of young Communists were biking through the area and stopped and stayed with us. We have opportunities at our evening meetings to make a witness, to talk about our faith. Some of the people are coming to Christ that way. Who knows what will happen with those two? Wolfgang, my fourteen-year-old friend, has come beautifully to the Lord!"

In August, while the teams were still hard at work in Europe, I was asked to bring a progress report to our congregation. As I stood in the pulpit, I realized that it hadn't been quite two months since I had stood here for the commissioning service prior to the teams leaving. How much I had learned in that short span of time!

"The heart of Europe is desperately hungry for some sure voice of reality, something real, something around which lives can be built.

"Our young people have been witnessing in Europe by every possible means to that Reality, to that which they have seen and heard concerning Jesus Christ. The world still responds to his voice of authority.

"Our young people are working hard. I wish you could see Harriet Prichard swinging a pick in Kassel and little Carol Abrams lifting tremendous rocks to build a foundation at Ellierode.

"Yet, the work is a means to an end. Through it they are earning the right to witness to our Lord's redeeming love. They are learning and demonstrating that unconditional love can break down all barriers." I talked about Coke's experience with George, the German pastor, and Ralph's with Uwe, and the Bible studies and prayer groups the kids had started. I told them what Ralph's father Donald had said to me in Amsterdam when I asked him why people seemed so deeply touched by our kids.

"Your young people! They come here so full of optimism, enthusiasm, faith, joy. We don't have young people like that anymore. We had almost forgotten they exist."

I finished by expressing my own convictions.

"I am convinced that the summer deputation to Europe was ordained and ordered of God. These young people have something tremendously worth sharing with the people of Europe, something Europe very much needs to have. We here at home also have something to share, something the world needs very much to have—reality in the person of Jesus Christ. We had better be about sharing him in every place we can and in every way we can.

"The problems in this country—the ghettos, the slums, the race riots, the gangsters—were the first things the team was asked about in Europe. The single most compelling incident for me personally was when three young refugees who had just escaped from the East asked me about these problems here in the U.S. I was glad I could tell them about our programs, but I wonder, in all honesty, if I could tell them enough. We have been admonished in the Gospels to have 'the mind of Christ', to see things from God's perspective.

"I wonder if the greatest challenge that exists in the world today is not a challenge to the Christian Church? A challenge to develop and send out inspired, dynamic, well-trained, well-equipped persons into all areas of life, to all nations. To send them not only into mission fields, but into places of political, social and economic leadership. I wonder if, above all else, this ought not to be the burden of our prayers?"

The day before the team was due home, I got a cable from Ralph. The charter company transporting them home—not Flying Tigers—had gone bankrupt. They were all stuck in Luxembourg City looking for alternative flights.

"DUKE FIRST," was the last line of the cable, a reassurance I was to pass on to Cookie, his fiancée. (Their wedding, at which I was officiating, was just two weeks away.) So rather than one big joyous homecoming, the kids trailed in by twos and threes over the next week.

The day after the cable, Duke's smiling face appeared around the edge of my office door. It was from him that I learned his teammate, John, was not returning with the group, one of the stipulations all had agreed to.

"He's registered as a conscientious objector with the draft board and he's going to work with the Brethren in Europe for a year, probably in Berlin," said Duke. "The horror of war hit him not in a deeper, but somehow in a different way than it did the rest of us."

"What do you think about him staying there?" I asked. Duke looked troubled. "I think he was too affected to be able to function back home. But I'm not sure it's good for him to stay."

Duke filled me in on the people at Kassel, ending with Uwe and Ricki.

"Uwe's faith was growing by leaps and bounds. He took communion for the first time in his life and that seemed to cement his new faith. I don't think we got to Ricki at all, but at least by the time we left, he and I were friends.

"The airport was a disaster! We weren't the only work campers on the charter that got canceled, so there were lots of people frantically looking for flights home. Good ol' Cheesy! He made the rounds of those airlines almost hourly. He'll get everyone out before he leaves."

We talked on for awhile, then Duke glanced at his watch and rose.

"I'm off to rent my tux," he said with a big grin. Then he paused. "You know, what I'll pay for my tux would feed a work camper for a month."

Just as Duke had predicted, Ralph was with the last group home. But, in spite of the hassle, they came home with hearts aflame. Months before, these young men and young women had caught a vision: To discover what God would accomplish with a life made wholly available to the service of Jesus Christ. In pursuing that vision they had found life in new dimensions altogether. They had experienced the energizing, transforming power of Agape love, a love which transcends and transforms every obstacle, every barrier.

In pursuing that vision they had also found a formula for reconciliation, one that proved successful beyond our wildest dreams. Corrie ten Boom had given us the model when she said: "If you really want to bear witness to what you believe, live it out. Go to a city destroyed by American bombs; go at your own expense without compensation; eat what they eat; sleep where they sleep. If you do it well enough and long enough, maybe they will hear what you have to say."

The team had done that. They had identified with people across all the post-war barriers: military, political, ideological, and, perhaps the most insidious, psychological. They had found a system that worked. They had seen walls come tumbling down—walls of hatred, suspicion, fear, hostility and heartbreak. By living and working together, they found their hearts and spirits inseparably linked with those from other lands, cultures and backgrounds. These bonds of Agape would continue to unite and mold them for years to come.

We had a reunion and debriefing session at my home as soon as everyone returned. Over dinner, we discussed the impact of the summer. The overwhelming consensus was that Deputation should be expanded to a denominational level, if possible.

"I would like to work on that, Walt," said Ralph. "We have found an answer to Dr. Einstein's challenge to discover some spiritual basis for world brother-hood, but more than just our church needs to be giving that answer."

"That's true," agreed Duke. "This trip was just a drop in the bucket. A worthwhile drop, but a drop nonetheless."

"What a paradox this whole experience is," mused Harriet. "Hollywood and post-war Europe are just about as opposite as you can get. We learned and received 110 percent more than we gave. And yet, Ralph is right. We do have an answer for Dr. Einstein's challenge."

"That's got to be the leading of the Holy Spirit," said Fran.

Lardner spoke up. "The Brethren camps are good. But their answer is incomplete because they don't stress the centrality of Christ." He grinned at Louie as he used what had been their key concept in the evening meetings.

"What's crucial too," said Carol "is that it's not just our opinions that the camps were influential in people's lives. We're already getting letters from our work camp friends that say the same thing."

"It's nice to get that kind of affirmation," agreed Kenny, with a pile of letters we'd all been sharing on his lap. "I'm still amazed that it happened!"

"The whole experience is amazing," said Colleen. "It took Walt and Ralph to put it together."

"That's right," agreed Harriet. "They believed it could be done."

"You made it work," said Louie as I started to protest. "And I thank God for the two of you and this experience. As you predicted, Ralph, it's had a pro-found impact on me. You two have created for me so many standards—of behavior, of work, of how to keep Christ in the center, of waiting for the leading of the Holy Spirit.

"You know, Walt, in Romans 12:2 Paul says, 'Do not be conformed to this world but be transformed by the renewal of your minds' (RSV). That's what you did. You took our minds and transformed them."

"Christ did the transforming, Louie. What Ralph and I did was just what you all did. We made ourselves available to be used."

Colleen changed the subject for me.

"Louie, do you think it's time to make our announcement?" His face turned all smiles.

"Colleen and I hope you'll all be home for Christmas because we want you to come to our wedding."

The meeting exploded into an uproar of congratulations. The kids stayed

late that night and left reluctantly. John's absence had been felt and we all
sensed that while we would be together again, this was really the end of the
group. That special bonding, that chemistry of people, would be deeply
missed and hard to replace. We finally ended, as we had so many times before,
with prayer and singing. The words of the last song echoed in my mind as the
door closed softly behind Ralph, the last to leave:

> "In Christ there is no East or West;
> In Him no North or South;
> But one great fellowship of love;
> Throughout the whole wide earth."

Duke and Cookie were married the next week with a full contingent of team
members present; the European team reported to our congregation and to
their peers in the College Briefing Conference at Forest Home Christian
Conference Center. School, seminary and jobs again took priority and the
summer became history. Letters continued crisscrossing the Atlantic and the
cardinal cry from Europe was "When can you come back?" A letter from
Malolo Vingiano, an Italian who had been at Ellierode with Louie, Carol and
Lardner, seemed to sum up the summer.

"Tell me that Ellierode and the project are not just a dream; that the life we
have lived together was real; that it is possible to have harmony and agreement
with unknown people; that thinking, working and playing together is possible!
So now I know that I must live my life among my people and testifying that a
life of love, brotherhood, friendship and understanding is possible and can
exist in this world as it did in Ellierode. Do you think we can realize it in bigger
proportions?"

That was the question. Could such an experience be multiplied, or was it a
one-time event?

Impressed by the team's report and by the letters of commendation from CIMADE, the Brethren Service Commission and the World Council of Churches, our church gave World Deputation the nod for another year.

The goals remained compelling: to find how God would use individuals' lives made wholly available to him and to demonstrate Christ's love as the spiritual basis for world brotherhood. Many of the same young people were involved and a high level of commitment was wonderfully evident. They were as determined as Ralph and I that Deputation not become just another program done by rote.

We used the three disciplines that had just proved so successful: study, prayer and field work. This second year we could be even more specific in the training because we had a successful model and resources from which to draw. When Ralph or Duke talked about identifying with people in pain, they could draw on personal experiences.

Ralph plunged into finding out how to make World Deputation a denominational program. Barraging national headquarters in New York with letters and visits, instead of returning to college he became the unpaid secretary for Deputation.

"Don't worry, Walt," he reassured me. "I'll graduate eventually. But right now expanding Deputation and supporting myself are all I can manage."

Enthusiasm and commitment continued high with Uwe, our new friend in Germany. He was back at the University of Hamburg studying theology, growing in his faith and becoming even more deeply committed to international work camps. He wrote to Duke and Harriet regularly.

"Six weeks before I came to the camp, I did not know how to pray. I had my deepest experience in faith in the camp. I told some of my fellow students about you people in California and they are anxious to work in one of the camps where you will have team members."

Uwe was working within his Lutheran denomination to get support for a work camp in Hamburg.

"The pastor told me that such a camp would be a great help in his work because people could see that Christians are really working for one another and their neighbor and do not only preach. There are many Communists in the district. You know, bad conditions breed Communism.

"It is hard for a pastor to preach the gospel in these places without having any real help. People won't listen because they don't know what Jesus Christ could mean to them. But if they could experience such a work camp spirit living in their lives, then they could see that Christ wants to help and can save the total man—body and soul."

The Christmas holidays were highlighted by Colleen and Louie's wedding, performed by Louie's dad, Dr. Evans, Sr. with Ralph, uncomfortable but resplendent in a tux, representing the team. Now Coke, Louie and Harriet were all away attending seminary. I missed them.

Spring was upon us and it was time to choose Deputation projects and participants for the summer. Our mission was widening. We had one team going to Haines, Alaska, to build a cabin at a summer conference grounds, to teach Bible school and to conduct church services for the Native Americans. We had a home team working again at Cleland House, the East Los Angeles neighborhood house. Three teams were going to Europe. Jean Simpson, a college student, and Ralph were going to a camp in Condé-sur-Noireau, a small, industrial town in France that was ninety-five percent destroyed by Allied planes on D-Day. Their project was digging foundations for a new parish house and building a children's playground. Harriet, Taylor Potter and Hugh Harris, all seminarians, were going to Loccum, twenty miles west of Hanover, West Germany, to construct a barracks youth center for refugee boys from the eastern zone of Germany.

The third camp was Agape in the Italian Alps near Turin, where the project was to complete a Christian retreat center by building a road, putting in retaining walls, terracing around the buildings and doing the finishing work inside. That team in Italy included university student Newton Russell, and seminarians Lardner Moore, Colleen and Louie.

This summer I was the one sending the letters abroad and receiving the flood of news from team members.

From Agape, Newt Russell wrote: "For the first time, Walt, I'm out from under the protective wing of the church and its ministers. I'm having to rely completely on God for guidance and he never fails me. The work camp experience is forcefully bringing home to me the tremendous importance of making every moment count for Christ. I know I have to live a Christ-filled life. The campers have to see it. I realize, too, that not only should my life count for Christ at the work camp, but equally at home or wherever I am."

In spite of heavy rain nearly the whole summer, Ralph's letters sounded euphoric. "The work camps have utterly changed my whole life and outlook. I find myself thankful and feasting continually on this rich experience. I feel that it has given me a drive and passion as never before to make my life count for Christ in the service of the Church." Hugh Harris, working with refugee boys at Loccum, was having a gut-wrenching reaction. "We Christians in America have a great responsibility toward the rest of the world. To see a Church that is torn, floundering and debilitated, actually fighting for its life, with but little in its hands—and then to see the smug complacency of many in America is enough to tear the heart out of anyone who desires to see the Kingdom of God furthered in this world. It is a shame that we who are rich spiritually as well as materially cannot send out hundreds of young people every year to the far corners of the earth as ambassadors in the name of our Lord Jesus Christ."

Loccum was our group's first in-depth exposure to the growing stream of refugees flowing out of the Soviet Zone of East Germany. Harriet Prichard's letter showed me the reasons for Hugh's reaction.

"This is a place of tremendous challenge," she wrote. "Outside the little village of Loccum in a barracks camp live five hundred boys, boys with tragedy written all over their faces. These boys, each one, can relate a story of heartbreak, disillusionment and fear. Some have walked hundreds of miles to cross the border at night and escape to freedom. They are young, ranging in age from fifteen to twenty-six.

"Their reasons for leaving the East are usually political— to escape duty in the Ural mines or to seek employment so that someday they can bring their families to the Western World.

"They have nothing but the clothes on their backs. They no longer have families, since they are barred from them by the Iron Curtain. They have no jobs, and worst of all, they have no hope.

"What's equally discouraging is that while the work campers have great interest in constructing the youth center, they have very little interest in working with the boys."

As the summer progressed, Hugh's and Harriet's letters reflected the changing attitudes they were facilitating in the work camp. Through prayer groups and Bible study, the Holy Spirit moved to create a genuine concern for the boys and a real witness to them. As a result, one of the work campers, Rudi

Kraft, a YMCA secretary, became the new center's director.

"Rudi's real concern," said Harriet in her last letter from Loccum, "is that these boys might find and know Jesus Christ as Lord and Savior."

At Agape in Italy Louie and Coke were also having contact with people from the East, but not refugees.

Colleen wrote: "We've prayed and feel led to travel in Germany during our days after camp. Here we have met a wonderful Christian boy, a theological student from the Eastern Zone who wants to take us around Berlin for several days. We're anxious to share with you his experiences in the Church in Communist Germany. You'll be thrilled to hear what God is doing behind the Iron Curtain. As he says, 'A real faith in Jesus Christ is the one thing they can't take away. They can't arrest a man's soul.'"

Toward the end of the summer, I heard from Uwe, co-leader of a Brethren work camp in Salzgitter, Germany.

"I have learned more than I would ever have thought, especially that international understanding is not only possible but necessary. Now I judge American people differently and I'm still surprised about the spiritual liveliness among the American campers. I am longing to see that country where this spirit and powerful faith prevail, and to learn more about it from its people.

"A spiritual basis for brotherhood is a strange idea to Germans. Again and again people ask me about it, wherever I speak of my camp experiences. Most Germans can't understand that our enemies (officially, the Americans are our enemies) want to help us. I am so happy to tell my friends that I know American work campers who are so different from the Americans they are reading about in the newspapers. Work campers must be like shock troops bringing to the whole world the message 'Peace on earth for Christ.'

"But before I set to work, I have to have firm ground under my feet in order to debate clearly. Words and phrases do not serve people. That firm ground I can get only by attending another camp or by going to the States."

The 1951 teams came home as inspired as the first team. From Cleland House in Los Angeles to Alaska and to Europe, team members saw the results of identifying with people and earning the right to witness to Christ's reconciling love. Colleen and Louie had been challenged by the level of integrity, conviction, courage and faithfulness of the Christians in the East.

"Walt, they have a dynamic quality of life, a zest, enthusiasm, sparkle, and a courage that's unique," Colleen reported.

"And their faith is standing the test in a militant, atheistic system dedicated to its eradication," said Louie. "They need our support, not so much in the work camp way of reconstruction, but more in the way of spiritual and emotional support. They need to know they aren't forgotten."

"Spiritual and emotional support" to beleaguered Christians that had a prophetic and scriptural ring to it. I wish I could say bells went off or lights came on in my head as a sign of how significant that sentiment would become in my own ministry. But they didn't.

Now with two years of solid examples to back it up, Deputation was assured of a long-lasting commitment from our Hollywood church.

Following Ralph's aggressive leadership and contact with national leaders of our denomination, the World Council of Churches and the Brethren Church, this Deputation program in the following years took on world-wide proportions: Korea, Japan, the Netherlands, Greece, Africa. In the States: Alaska, Harlem, in California among migrant agricultural workers and in the ghettos of Los Angeles. With Ralph as secretary of the movement, its growth was disciplined and orderly and done on a carefully developed basis.

Thinking back to our beginnings with a small group of collegians committed to making their lives wholly available to Christ and to seeking a spiritual basis for world brotherhood, I was awed and humbled by how the Lord had honored that commitment. Our horizons had been broadened to worldwide proportions. We had seen walls of hate, opposing ideologies, prejudice and distrust come tumbling down. And in the Lord's beautiful way of multiplying effects, not only the recipients of the team visits, but also the team members were deeply touched. In the years that followed, many who had served on a Deputation team chose a Christian vocation. I knew we'd never know all the rippling effects of Deputation. But the developing ministries of the few whose lives we could follow were intriguing, particularly the one that walked into my office one fine day in February 1952.

CHAPTER ELEVEN

UWE'S JOURNEY

Arriving early at my office in the Hollywood church, I heard classical music being played across the hall. I poked my head in to see who was playing so beautifully, and to my complete surprise, discovered Uwe. He was realizing his dream, following his conviction that to deepen his faith he needed to come to the country that had produced his Christian mentors.

From the outset of his visit, it was obvious to me that the 1950 Kassel work camp had been more than a healthy summer experience, more than a good ecumenical experience, for young Uwe. It had directed him to new life.

It was quite a reunion when Uwe met with Duke, Harriet and Ralph, his Kassel teammates. Uwe talked enthusiastically about Kassel and Salzgitter, the camp he'd just co-directed, and about his dreams for the future. His spiritual awakening had imbued Uwe with a compelling sense of mission.

"We German work campers are like prophets in our own country if we talk about international understanding," he said. "People don't like that because they see foreigners as part of the occupation army. But every single work camper gets the idea that Americans and other campers don't come as a broad-mouthed occupation army, but as individual people. And the most effective camps are the ones that witness to Christ, not just to Christian ideals."

Uwe enjoyed wholehearted rapport with the World Deputation group. He passed on some impressions—both positive and negative—being expressed about "the Hollywood groups" known, he said, in work camp circles all over Europe.

"Be understanding of other forms of worship," Uwe reminded us. "Don't jump the gun and think that if others do not express their faith in Christ exactly as you do that they were not Christians.

"Keep sending as many young people as possible. They are needed!"

Uwe spent a week with us, involving himself in the life of the church. He had already spent time on the East Coast and in Indiana working with the Brethren. Now he was off to northern California. Uwe had come to America as we had gone to Germany, not for a "good experience," but with a real sense of mission.

But this California project proved to be a shocking disappointment and a severe challenge to his young faith. The church where he was working started as a recreation center and that's what the teens in the area wanted. The minister was Uwe's age, serious and conscientious, but with no theological training and no idea of how or what to preach. Uwe's letters expressed a deep frustration.

"Circumstances here are really confused. That's why the Lord wanted me to be in Hollywood first, so that I might hear it once more very clearly: Christ is the center of all being. Here I have to know it. The minister doesn't know the Bible. He preaches good will and the simple life, but not Christ. The Sunday school teachers don't know Christ or the Bible. And the young people just come to play basketball. They are completely ignorant of the fact that the church has something to do with Christ and with the Holy Spirit. I started right out preaching Christ clearly.

"The volunteers who worked here before me were very young. They stood together with the young people against the minister. When the young people found I wouldn't do that, they started trying everything to upset me. It is as if the Devil himself is behind it. In fact, he is. Three boys in particular are really trying to upset things. They laugh and make jokes about prayer. It is not a question of conduct, but rather whether they are willing to take Christ seriously or not. That's why I can't throw them out. Christ wants them. He wants them all.

"We conclude our discussion with scripture, a meditation and prayer, even prayer fellowship. They have never experienced anything like this before. I told the camp leaders right from the beginning that I'd come to serve in the name of Christ and that He was my goal for the community. Many are skeptical of my efforts. They are of the opinion that young people are not mature enough to understand Christ. You know that this is the excuse of unbelief.

"I am handicapped quite a bit by my difficulty in speaking English, especially when I pray. I need to ask you to help me by your prayers. The following weeks will be difficult."

The following weeks were difficult. Uwe had no support for a Christ-centered ministry, no one with whom to start a prayer group, no one to reinforce his young faith. He became so frustrated that he lost his fluency in English. Realizing he was close to losing his faith as well, Uwe decided there were two things he needed to do immediately.

First, he went to a Lutheran minister and told him that he had to make a personal confession and take communion. It looked like he had found another stumbling block. The minister was from a closed group not allowed to give communion even to other Lutherans.

After some deep thought, he said, "I think this time I need to bend the rules and give you the help you need and want."

He listened to Uwe pour out his doubts, his frustrations, his anger, his feelings of failure, and then served him communion with his congregation. I wonder if that man has any idea what a crucial part he played in shoring up the faltering faith of a man who consequently went on to do the same for countless others?

The second step brought Uwe once more to my doorstep.

"I knew I had to get out of there and back to Walt James and the Hollywood Church," he told me as he collapsed in the big easy chair in my office. "I have to get Christian fellowship again where we can pray and work and be honest."

"I'm sorry you've had such a tough time."

He smiled wryly, "I learned how much I have to learn." His gaze turned inward and he became reflective. "When the myth of my childhood was taken from me, when Hitler was dead, it left a tremendous vacuum, a void that could not be filled. Then at Kassel I discovered that the void could be filled—filled with the Living Presence of Jesus Christ.

"My past has created within me an urgency, a compelling necessity to share the person of Jesus Christ, particularly with young people. I become impatient with all the things people try to substitute for him. It was basketball for those kids I just left. It was moral values for their teachers. Without Christ these are empty forms of conduct and behavior. There is no substitute!" No longer slouched, he was sitting upright, his look intense, his fists clenched.

"I know," I said quietly. He fell back in the chair and grinned at me.

"There are some valuable lessons to be learned from that experience."

He stared at me, his brow furrowed in concentration.

"I learned the value of team ministry, so you can support each other. I learned my own limitations…" he trailed off, looking at me questioningly.

"Also, hard work and all the good will and fine intentions in the world won't mean much unless Christ is at the center." Uwe continued. "That young minister and those teachers were fine, high principled people, but without Christ at the center of their program it's not going to have lasting impact."

Uwe spent the next weeks immersing himself in every aspect of our congregation's life, which included some of Marguerite's fine meals and the close scrutiny of our children, Beth and Ron.

Observing his strong appeal to my kids, I asked Uwe to make his final stop in the U.S. at Forest Home Christian Conference Center to be one of the speakers at a junior high conference.

Driving up to Forest Home, he shared with me the impact being in our congregation had had on his life.

"Walt," he said quietly, "through your congregation, God has called me into the ministry."

"Tell me about it", I said with delight.

"In Hollywood, for the first time, I've seen a picture of what a Christian congregation can be. It's not just an exotic group in a work camp, but it's normal people with families; weak Christians and strong Christians. I now know this organism to be the body of Christ."

He paused, struggling to express his deep conviction in a foreign language.

"I know now that if ministering to this organism means being a minister, then I would like to be a minister."

"Thank you for telling me this," I responded, my throat tight with emotion. "It's been quite a year for you."

"That, as you Americans say, is an understatement!"

The impact that this powerful young life would have was clearly revealed to me that weekend as Uwe's magnetic Christian charisma captured the hearts of those junior high campers and their leaders. I watched his leadership bloom as at first hesitantly, and then with more and more assurance, he shared his life and convictions with individuals, small groups and with the entire assembly of over 250 kids and their leaders.

I shall never forget that final, sustained ovation given to Uwe by the campers as he bade them all good-bye. On their feet, they were stomping and yelling, "UUU-VEE, UUU-VEE, UUU-VEE."

Uwe's presence, large in every way, was sorely missed. So it was with delight that we heard another German was on his way to see us. His mission and his invitation were to take me abroad once again.

CHAPTER TWELVE

ALFRED SCHRÖDER

During World War II, the German armies swept into Russia burning towns and villages and slaughtering the inhabitants. Advance scout tanks, guns blazing, were the first into remote villages, eliminating opposition for the invading troops.

One tank leader had a different approach.

Alfred Schröder clattered into towns and villages with the tank hatch wide open, his body fully exposed, waving his arms and yelling, "I am not your enemy! I am a pastor! The war is coming! Run into the woods until the troops have passed! Run for your lives!"

There were thirty-seven men in his command. Had any one of them betrayed him at any time, he would have been executed immediately.

Why was a pastor a tank leader instead of a chaplain? And what induced him to risk his own life so blatantly? The answers come from the schism regarding Hitler that shook the German Protestants so violently.

In February 1933 after Hitler secured his power in Germany, he worked to consolidate his gains. He needed the support and allegiance of the German churches, particularly the German Evangelical Church, the structure under which the powerful Lutheran and Reformed Churches worked together.

Hitler established a cabinet member as liaison between the government and the churches. Through intense pressure, rigged church elections and appeals for national unity, he got the man he wanted—Ludwig Müller, elected as the first national bishop of the newly reorganized "German Church." At first, the Protestant churches did not object to being organizationally incorporated, recognizing Hitler as head of the Church as well as the State. This position by the Church was based upon Romans 13:1-2, "Every Christian ought to obey the civil authorities, for all legitimate authority is derived from God's Authority, and the existing authority is appointed under God. To oppose authority then is to oppose God, and such opposition is bound to be punished."

The national bishop, on Hitler's orders, convened a Church conference on November 13, 1933 in the Sports Palace in Berlin. At this conference a senior Nazi official declared that the State Church and all its bishops, superintendents, theologians, pastors and people must immediately implement the tenets of National Socialism, that is, Nazism. Church membership must be confined to those of Aryan descent. Masonic connections must be cut off and Communism denounced. The Church must parallel National Socialism. Above all, he called for "liberation from the Old Testament with its Jewish money morality and from these stories of cattle-dealers and pimps."[4]

Christian opposition arose immediately and those who resisted this mandate were expelled from office and the Church and subjected to persecution.

Alfred Schröder was studying at Humboldt University in Berlin at this time. He and his fellow students were divided as to whether Hitler was harming or helping the Church.

"I can't agree with this Nazi program!" Alfred declared vehemently.

"The Church will gain power through this unification!" argued Paul, another student.

"But this national bishop obeys Hitler absolutely."

"By uniting, the Church finally has a chance to gain the prominence in German life that it should have."

"At what cost? My understanding of the Bible makes me feel that I must become part of this new Confessing Church which is against the State Church."

"Alfred! You must think carefully about joining that group. You will become an enemy of the State."

The Confessing Church and the Barmen Declaration of 1934 were the response of many leaders in German Protestant churches who came to realize that tragedy had struck; that somehow Christians had misunderstood what the thirteenth Chapter of Romans meant. The Barmen Declaration stated the Confessing Church's intention to withstand the destruction and subversion of the faith by the State. It decried the false doctrine and the use of force by the German Church and insisted that the Church in Germany could come only from the Word of God, in faith through the Holy Spirit.

The brilliant theologians, Martin Niemoeller and Dietrich Bonhoeffer, along with their dedicated army of colleagues facing martyrdom and death, moved to restore the "Gemeinde"—the true Church—to her rightful place of authority and leadership.

Alfred became part of this underground church. His first theological exams were given by professors of the Confessing Church in church basements or in parish houses rather than at the University.

After his first examinations, he was sent out into the country near Stettin to

---

[4] Eberhard Bethge, *Dietrich Bonhoeffer* (London: William Collins Sons & Co. Ltd., 1970, p. 263).

the Finkenwalde seminary led by Dietrich Bonhoeffer. The seminarians lived together in a rambling old farm house and were supported by congregations and individual patrons within the Confessing Church. With Bonhoeffer, who was only a few years their senior, they studied meditation, preaching and theological literature. Through life style and discussions, he imbued them with his deep sense of service and discipline.

Of the eighteen members of Alfred's Class of 1937, only he and two others survived the war. Just weeks after he left, the seminary was closed by the police.

Alfred initially was assigned to Forst, 250 miles southeast of Berlin, where he worked as an assistant minister. The pastor was ill, so much of the work fell to Alfred. He was given a tiny used car and told to organize the youth work in the province. The political climate made that complicated, if not illegal, for the Nazis had ordered all church youth groups dissolved. Youth between the ages of ten and eighteen were compelled to join the Hitler Youth Movement. Schools were forced to teach Nazi doctrines. The motto of the Third Reich became: "To serve Hitler is to serve Germany, to serve Germany is to serve God."[5]

For the next two years, Alfred traveled through the province holding meetings and starting youth groups. Since they were not legal, there could be no formal membership in these groups. In spite of that, the groups were strong.

Alfred had to work carefully, because Hitler Youth officials followed him and tried to find illegalities in what he was doing. His reaction was to invite them into the meetings, or just to take time and talk with them about his faith. Like the Roman guards of the Apostle Paul, many were converted by association with him.

In 1939 Alfred was assigned to a church north of Berlin. It was in a poor area with small houses and apartments. Most of the men worked in the Berlin factories and had to travel hours to and from work. Alfred and his wife, Elizabeth, lived in two rooms on the first floor of a small house. Parish taxes collected by the German government, supported the State Church and pastors. But since the Confessing Church was in opposition to the State Church, there was no support for it. To build a congregation, Alfred went house to house, introducing himself and visiting with the people. Reactions varied.

"A pastor of that church! Then you are a traitor!"

---

[5] Dr. Kenneth Scott Latourette, *A History of Christianity* (New York: Harper, 1953).

"The Confessing Church is not loyal to Germany! Don't spread your lies here!"

"I don't understand how the State Church can say Jews can't become Christians."

"Why do the Nazis believe old people should be killed?"

"My teenage daughter came home from school saying that it is a service to the State for unmarried girls to have babies. How can that be?"

Alfred was out late most nights visiting the workers as they returned home. The visits worked. The 150-seat hall where the congregation met started filling for Sunday services and soon became overcrowded. His Bible studies for women and for men were also well-attended.

In 1939, just after Alfred moved to this parish in Berlin, World War II started with Germany's invasion of Poland. Protected by his superintendent, Alfred continued his work. But as the war intensified, the Nazis became more and more intolerant of opposition and strove to crush it all, including the Confessing Church.

"Church publications were curtailed and, many pastors and laymen were arrested; some for protesting the cruelties against the Jews; some for opposition to the euthanasia of the aged and infirm; and some for protesting the glorification of the unmarried mother; and some for other criticisms of the Government. Further difficulties were placed in the way of giving religious instruction to children and youth. It is said that eighty-five percent of the pastors of the Confessing Church were taken into the armies."[6]

In 1941 Alfred's identity as a Confessing pastor was uncovered. He was inducted into the army not as a chaplain, as were the State Church pastors, but as a soldier. He was trained in the use of all types of military vehicles. The colonel in charge knew him to be a Confessing Church pastor and did his best to make life difficult. After training, Alfred was sent to the front, first near Leningrad and then, at the beginning of the winter, to Moscow.

The Germans expected another *Blitzkrieg*, a lightning war, when they invaded Russia in June 1941. They made no preparation for a long fight, not even issuing winter uniforms to the soldiers. But the Russian counterattack and the bitter cold of winter stopped the German advance on the outskirts of Moscow. The mud and snow froze around the wheels of the cars, trucks and tanks, immobilizing them. Troops, with no protection other than summer uniforms, had to walk back to the German defensive positions. Alfred's

---

[6] op. cit.

company was among them.

"Pastor! I can't feel my toes anymore!"

"Run in place. You must get the circulation going again."

"I'm too tired to run."

"You must! We'll do it together."

"Pastor, I have no feeling in my fingers…"

It was agonizing for Alfred. He would pull soldiers' boots off and rub their feet, trying to restore circulation. He did the same with hands. But it was often useless.

"My toes are black! What does that mean?"

Hundreds from that retreat had to be evacuated back to Germany for the amputation of fingers, hands, toes, feet even whole legs.

The next August, Alfred's company was ordered into the attack on Stalingrad. For five months the Germans battled to take the city, until they once more became engulfed in a Russian winter. Over 260,000 German soldiers were killed and around 90,000 were taken prisoner, including twenty-four generals.

In November, a month before German Field Marshall von Paulus disobeyed Hitler's orders and surrendered his half-frozen, starving army to the Russians, Alfred and his company were ordered out of Stalingrad and into Czechoslovakia.

The slaughter Alfred had seen in Russia confirmed his original resolve. His purpose as a pastor was to save lives, not end them. Whenever and wherever the unit's targets were civilian rather than military, he did his best to protect both his men and the noncombatants. As did many other German leaders, he quietly disregarded Hitler's scorched earth policy, the policy of devastating any area Germany occupied.

In April of 1945, just weeks before Germany's surrender, Alfred's company was ordered to join the German units defending Prague. His company was at the outskirts of the city when Alfred saw Russian tanks already there. He called a halt. Climbing out of his tank, he stood musing. A sergeant joined him.

"What do we do, Pastor?"

"It is apparent that Germany must soon surrender. If we advance, we will either be killed or taken as prisoners by the Russians."

"But our orders are to advance," said the man tentatively.

"And be killed uselessly? I have higher orders and those are to bring you home safely. Your lives at home will be much more useful than your deaths here. We will retreat back toward the German border."

In doing so, the company met the American Army near Plauen, Germany and surrendered to them. The men were taken as "disarmed German forces" to a special camp near Hof. Within weeks after Germany surrendered on May 7, they were released to go home.

It was an emotional farewell between the troops and their leader. One of the last to say good-bye was Alfred's sergeant.

"You were right, Pastor. My family needs me much more at home now than the Fuhrer needed one more death. I will never forget you."

It was a long way back to Berlin. Having no alternative, Alfred began walking. Crossing into the Russian occupied zone, he saw a coal train refueling. "Where is this train going?" he asked the Russian officer in charge.

"Berlin."

He climbed into a coal car and two days later, grimy and covered with soot, arrived home.

Berlin was decimated. What the bombs hadn't destroyed, the house-to-house fighting between the invading Russians and the retreating Germans had accomplished. Anything left working, such as industrial equipment, telephone exchanges, buses, trains and generators, was packed up by the Russians and shipped back to Russia, part of what they considered reparations for the terrible damage the Germans had inflicted on them.

Close to half of the city's population had been killed. The Russian troops, mostly Mongols, considered rape and plunder their right. Few girls, women, and homes escaped them.

In the Potsdam Agreement, before the end of the war the Allies—the U.S., Great Britain, Russia and later France—had agreed to what areas of Germany each would occupy and govern. They were determined to rid the country of all traces of the Nazi regime before reuniting it. Berlin was deep inside the section of Germany assigned to Russia. Since it was the historic capital of Germany, the four powers divided the city into four sections and agreed to administer Berlin jointly.

The American and English troops were just arriving and the city was being partitioned when Alfred got back to Berlin. He walked the streets in shock. The once beautiful city, the center and heart of the nation, was broken and ravaged. It was a ruin full of hungry people.

The only joy and comfort he found was that his wife Elizabeth and young son Michael had survived the war.

Dazed, he sought out the Church leadership. It was then he found out that his seminary professor, the profound young theologian, Dietrich Bonhoeffer, had been taken from prison and executed on Hitler's orders just one month before Germany surrendered.

Many Confessing Church pastors had been killed in the war because, like Alfred, they had been put on the front lines and marked for death. The seminaries had been closed by the Nazis, so no pastors were being trained. A fresh start had to be made everywhere. But, thought Alfred, the start could at least be made in freedom without the tyranny of government oppression.

The bishop of Berlin-Brandenburg, Dr. Otto Dibelius, put him in charge of the youth work in the area of Berlin-Brandenburg. In the area's 250 parishes, he was to find what remained of the youth groups and begin rebuilding them. There was no used car available now and public transportation was destroyed. So Alfred began making his rounds on a bicycle. He worked with the ministers who were left or were returning from POW camps and helped them organize their youth work.

The first step was to recruit and train youth workers. He encountered opposition, hostility and lethargy.

"I'm hungry, Pastor. I don't have the energy for church work."

"Our church is destroyed. It's too depressing to meet in ruins."

"Hitler was my idol! You were against him."

"I'm starving, and you want me to come to church?"

"I'd never trust you. Your church disobeyed the Fuhrer. You worked against Germany!"

"My parents are dead! Hitler is dead! I've got to take care of myself."

"I'm hungry, Pastor. Does the church have food?"

Slowly, he began to find some young people with faith and others who were seeking answers. He became the teacher of these thirteen-to-twenty-year-olds, holding small Bible studies, counseling them, inspiring in them a real and living faith in a real and living Christ. His training was intensive, compelling and always practical.

"Pastor, I think my next door neighbor is still a Nazi. What should I do?"

"Do you still have one of those candy bars the GI gave you?"

"Yes."

"Take your neighbor a candy bar."

"What!"

ALFRED SCHRÖDER

"You can't make some big proclamation to him. Just be a living witness. Each day find some little thing you can do for him. That is how we must live our lives, as living witnesses to a living faith. And we do that through small tasks each day. What specific thing can you do today to be a witness?"

He grounded these young people in the Bible, in living each day as a witness, and then sent them out to do the same for their peers. They met in destroyed parish houses, each bringing one piece of wood or coal to heat the room.

As the numbers in the youth groups grew, so did the awful realization that the time of government opposition was not over. In their eastern sector of Berlin and in the zone of Germany they occupied, the Russians were imposing their own beliefs and system of government. In October 1946, Berlin held its first free election since 1933 and elected Ernst Reuther mayor. The Soviets had gambled on their ability to swing that free election. Stunned when their efforts failed and that their candidate had lost, the Russians declared Reuther anti-Soviet and vetoed the election. From that point on, in violation of the Potsdam Agreement, the Russians dropped the concept of German reunification and began to establish their section of Germany and Berlin as a separate Communist state.

Passage in and out of the Soviet Zone became more and more restricted. Even more threatening to the Berliners with memories of the Nazi indoctrination, the schools in the Soviet Zone were teaching Marxism.

On June 24, 1948, the Soviets cut off the Allies' land access to Berlin, isolating it within the Soviet Zone with no means of getting food, fuel or raw materials. The Soviet's intent was to force the Western Powers out. Instead, the West organized a gigantic airlift bringing in supplies for the more than two million West Berliners for almost a year. For the next eleven months, every pound of food, every piece of coal, everything needed to keep the West Berliners and the Allied forces in Berlin supplied was transported by air. In a total of 2,728 flights, American, British and French airmen brought in 2,343,301 tons of food and supplies. At the peak of the airlift, planes were landing in West Berlin at the rate of one every forty-five seconds.

The airlift is an indelible chapter in the history of the defense of freedom. So was the fortitude of the people of Berlin. They subsisted on a slim diet. During the winter, with fuel scarce, people were often miserably cold. For months, electric current was only available three hours in twenty-four. The Communists offered the West Berliners food and fuel if they would move to

East Berlin. All but a few thousand spurned the offer. Admiration for their courage and endurance helped greatly in rehabilitating the German people in the eyes of the world.

The blockade failed; land access was again guaranteed. But now Berlin was completely split with separate governments, currencies, police and public utilities. The Church was the only link between East and West Berlin.

Alfred continued going into East Berlin, even as the restrictions got tougher and tougher, because much of his work was there. He kept training and encouraging his youth leaders to live each day looking for the simple way to witness to their faith in the face of militant atheism.

Pastor Schröder, as Alfred's youth called him, always spoke and gave the Bible studies at each of the twenty district youth retreats. As the Landes-jugendpfarrer (youth pastor) of the Protestant Churches in Berlin he had approximately 45,000 youth in the churches of both East and West Berlin by 1952.

That year the German Evangelical Church leadership, seeing the rising stridency of Communism and their own, ever-more limited ability to go between parishes in East and West Berlin, decided to pursue contact with Christians from the Allied Powers who might be more able than Berliners to bypass Soviet restrictions.

That's when Pastor Schröder came to Hollywood.

1952—Pastor Alfred Schröder—"We are not shaken by this rubble. Christ is our foundation."

It was an instantaneous match between this Lutheran brother from Berlin and the California Christians. Vigorous, dynamic, spiritually alive and alert with an incorrigible zest for life, the disciplined and biblically-oriented Pastor Schröder captured our hearts.

He in turn was thrilled and charmed by our congregation and by the enthusiasm, maturity and commitment of the Deputation members. As he visited with us those few days in June 1952, one of his many stops in the States, he pressed for a team to come to Berlin. He wanted our participation in strengthening the bonds of Christian community between West Berlin and the Christians in East Berlin, and in all of East Germany where they were surrounded by Marxist-Leninist ideology.

Our congregation had heard Louie and Colleen Evans' report one year earlier that Berlin offered an opportunity to which we should respond. Now we had Pastor Schröder's urgent invitation to visit that Island City and see the work there. Dr. Evans, our senior pastor, Ralph and I were feeling that it was time to give Deputation an on-site review. Berlin could be investigated at the same time.

In November Warren Baird, leader of the international student work of our church's College Department, and I were commissioned by our church to go to Europe to "explore and evaluate the effectiveness of our World Deputation Ministry, also, to explore other possibilities, including Berlin and the East." One of the other possibilities was to link-up with students at European universities.

The first stop on our month-long journey of discovery was London. There we met students at the universities of London and Cambridge and worshipped with our good friend J. B. Phillips at his church in Redhill, Surrey, twenty miles south of London.

Then it was on to Paris and more student meetings. We went out to the CIMADE headquarters in Sevres, where we had the pleasure of seeing Paul Evdokimov, the CIMADE leader at the 1950 work camp. With pride he showed us the completed chapel and barracks, both projects that Colleen, Fran, Kenny, Ralph and I had worked on.

From Paris we took the train down to Geneva for more student meetings and for a reason we hadn't anticipated when we planned the trip. As we visited university after university, a deep, burning question was growing in our minds for which we had to have an answer. On every campus we found students and faculty—brilliant, thoughtful, responsible people; people with advanced degrees in a variety of subjects—who were, by their own confession, convinced Communists.

The tactics, the ruthless oppression, the brainwashing, the imprisonments, the annihilation of personal, human values and rights by the Marxist-Leninist regime were well known and acknowledged. In spite of all this, these people were, by conviction, Communists. How could this be?

The person to whom we turned was Dr. Philippe Maury, secretary-general of the World Student Christian Federation headquartered in Geneva. It was said of him that he knew students and the student mind better than any other youth leader in the world.

He listened carefully to our question and reflected before he answered:

"You men are Americans, so it will be hard for you to understand what I'm going to say. In America you're free. Your cities are unspoiled by war. Yours is a great democracy, probably the greatest in the world. Yours is a way of affluence and prosperity.

"But to the people you've been meeting, life looks much different. For these young people and faculty members, so-called twentieth century Christian civilization has utterly failed. The last 2,000 years of recorded history reveal world-wide warfare, hunger, poverty and discrimination. Nearly one-half of the world goes to bed hungry every night. Today our world is divided into two mighty, armed camps poised for yet another war, a war that could be the end of civilization.

"You in America have not experienced this...yet. But the people you've been meeting believe the time will come when America, too, will fall. It is simply a matter of time. You, too, have your poverty, your slums, your race riots and tensions, McCarthyism and your Gestapo in the form of the FBI and CIA.

"These students and professors are looking for a system that offers some ultimate hope for social justice. They do not like Communism either. They do not like its tactics. They do not like what it does. But they do not believe that twentieth century Christianity has the answer. And so, like it or not, they are convinced Communists."

We were badly shaken as we left Dr. Maury. Had twentieth century Christian civilization indeed failed? Had the Church of Jesus Christ failed? Did we, the

Christians of the world, not care enough to pay the price to find real answers? Did we really have the right answers to the challenge of Communism?

I thought of the miracles of reconciliation and conversion I had seen brought about through Deputation. I thought about the transformed lives I had seen when gang members met Christ personally.

"Yes," I thought, "we do have the Answer. But in the face of militant, aggressive, organized Communism, are we committed enough, do we care enough, do we have the courage to present that Answer? Will we pay the price? Am I personally serving Christ at the point of greatest need?" Going on to Basel, we met with Professor Karl Barth, the renowned theologian and teacher. He understood our concerns and agreed with Philippe Maury that intellectuals were turning to Communism in a desperate search for solutions.

"When we see the world-wide strategy of Communism, it is easy to become alarmed," he said. "But remember. Christ himself is the basis for world improvement. Not programs. Just Christ himself. It is not our job to build the kingdom. He himself does that. Our business is to present Christ."

Looking at Warren, knowing that he headed our church's work with international students, Professor Barth said, "Look for specific ways to present Christ. Strengthen the ties between your students and international students. Find them Christian homes in the states. Give them a Christian orientation. These students will come home to be leaders."

Warren nodded. The look in his eyes told me he was already designing ways to do that.

The next day we took the train to Frankfurt. As we boarded the Pan American flight from Frankfurt to Berlin, it never occurred to us that we were flying through a restricted air corridor patrolled by Soviets jets, the same corridor used just four years before during the Berlin Airlift. It was only when our plane broke through the low, overcast clouds and revealed the startling spectacle of row after row of ghostly, skeletal buildings destroyed by bombs that we suddenly realized we were entering a world different from any we had known.

Pastor Schröder came by our hotel to welcome us and to lay out our schedule. He had asked us to be in Berlin from November 16 to 19 so we could attend a church conference. The next day, Sunday, Dr. Arthur Siebens, pastor of the American Church in Berlin, would take us to his church for services, give us a city tour, then take us to the conference. On Monday we would move into the Dietrich Bonhoeffer House, a youth center, and continue attending the conference.

Nothing in Warren's or my experience prepared us for what we saw on the tour Dr. Siebens gave us. For openers, it was a hair-raising experience just to pass through the heavily armed check-point from the sectors controlled by the West into the Soviet Sector. It didn't look or feel like the war was over, and I wasn't sure the Soviet guards knew we were supposed to be allies.

We saw very few people even though it was the middle of the day. The body language of the ones we did see seemed to reflect the restrictive coerciveness of the Soviets. It was heartbreaking to see them walking listlessly and stoop-shouldered with lifeless faces.

The sector felt like a ghost town. The buses were old and decrepit. What had once been the very heart of Berlin's business and commercial center was now in utter ruins.

"Why isn't reconstruction happening here as it is in the other sectors?" I asked Dr. Siebens.

"Russia was devastated by Germany in the war, and retribution, not reconstruction, was uppermost in the Russian mind. Now, of course, its own reconstruction is its first priority," he answered.

Dr. Siebens showed us what had been the American Church, now a small mountain of rubble, piled high and useless. As he stood viewing it, his shoulders sagged and he looked despondent.

"When we worshipped here, many Germans worshipped with us. Now, all we have available are quarters on the U.S. military base and the Germans won't come there." He lifted his eyes, looking out at the city and spoke quietly, almost to himself. "There were more than 300 churches in Berlin, most of them in the Soviet Sector. Only one was left undamaged. Most are still unreconstructed, still in their damaged state."

Depressed as the grey sky above us, we continued our tour. In stark contrast to the rest of the sector stood the renamed Marx-Engels Square, totally rebuilt with tremendous flag displays and huge pictures of Stalin up and down the streets. The government stores had lavish window displays, but Dr. Siebens told us there was limited merchandise at unaffordable prices.

The only building not rebuilt in the square, perhaps as some sort of symbol, was the great Lutheran Cathedral Church, now an unsightly, abject ruin with weeds and debris its only occupants.

The devastation was even more total at our next stop, the Tiergarten, what had been the counterpart to our White House and Capital grounds. Divided by the East and West sectors, it was an absolute wasteland with great heaps of rubble piled high. Dr. Siebens pointed out two gigantic slabs of heavy concrete, sitting at weird angles. One was what remained of the entrance to Hitler's underground bunker where it is thought he and Eva Braun committed suicide. The other slab was said to have been where their bodies were burned. Nearby was the mountain of rubble which had been the Reichschancellery, the center of Hitler's government.

As we passed back through the Soviet checkpoint, I was haunted by the specters of those two destroyed churches, the great Cathedral Church and the American Church. They filled my whole horizon, blocking out all else. What must it be like to be a pastor in the East? What would I do if I were the pastor of the Cathedral Church or any other parish in East Berlin? Corrie ten Boom had said that to identify with suffering people, you must live and work alongside them. How could I, a pastor from Hollywood, stand alongside any one of the pastors in the East? How could I comprehend the depth of suffering they had experienced? First Hitler, then World War II, and now Communism. What could I offer these people?

My opportunity to find that out started when Dr. Siebens took us to a conference meeting of pastors from East and West Berlin at the Free University. The Free University, located in West Berlin, had been started in 1948 by professors and students who broke away from Humboldt University in the Eastern Sector to protest against the Communist regimented curriculum.

We met our interpreters, Elizabeth and Horst, and were warmly greeted by the pastors. Under discussion were the difficulties in coordinating students in East and West Germany, and in maintaining a united church in spite of the political division. Methods being used were student conferences, traveling youth leaders and student publications.

There was real danger in the East. It was not safe for the East pastors to take back any mimeographed material or notes. Names and statistics must be remembered because lists were dangerous. Methods of presentations were discussed, including specific words or phrases to use or to avoid so government informers could not latch on to something with which to threaten the Christian student movement.

I was humbled and awed by the terrific spirit, the joy of these men who were buying the right to meet and propagate the Gospel at great personal risk. During a break, Elizabeth, my interpreter, said to me, "Be careful. Even here there may be spies."

"Here?" I said in surprise. She nodded.

"There is tremendous pressure. Sometimes the only choices are to spy or to give up your work, your friends, maybe even your family and flee to the Western Zone. Are you going into the Eastern Sector?"

"We hope to."

"I wouldn't! You never know what may happen."

"What do you mean?"

"I was arrested three years ago because I had a list of names with me. I had done nothing! They kept me in prison for three weeks and told me I would be held for fifteen, twenty years. I never expected to get back again. I lost twenty-one pounds. Things are worse, much worse, now! People disappear and are never heard from again! The Russians are just releasing some people arrested in 1945. The people don't know why they were arrested then or why they all were released now."

This was our first meeting and we were working through interpreters, so rather than seeing and hearing the twenty-two men as individuals, the answers to our questions seemed to come to us from the group.

"Is the Church strong in the Eastern Zone?" I asked.

"Very strong," came the surprising answer.

"Strong spiritually?" I probed.

"Spiritually and numerically. The Church is stronger than before the Soviet occupation, stronger than before Hitler. The Evangelical Church thrives on persecution!"

"Is the Church free?" asked Warren.

"Paradoxically, the Church is free," came the again surprising reply. "The Church may hold meetings, conduct worship, be very free."

Our bewilderment was plain. The speaker continued.

"The Church is free, but the people are not. Their entire lives are regimented and controlled. Students are told who will go to school and where; workers are put into jobs based on the state's need, not on their training or interests. There is much insecurity. People are told what they must do for recreation, what books to read, when to attend demonstrations. Meetings are planned for Sunday morning.

"People must be in a group led by a Communist Party member and to be free from suspicion, they must each week make a confession of their 'sins' against the Party. Others may also point out their 'sins'. And anyone who stays in that group long enough loses their power to resist."

"Are you pastors in danger?" Warren asked.

"That's another paradox," answered a young man whom Elizabeth had pointed out as being an authority on youth in the Eastern Zone. "We enjoy a great deal of freedom."

"How do you account for that?" I asked.

The young man, with a strange look in his eyes, picked up a saucer and balanced it on one hand.

"There are two methods of attacking the Church," he answered. "One is attacking it directly as Hitler and the Nazis did," and his hand hit the saucer. "The other is to by-pass it completely," he said, his hand circling but not touching the saucer. "Ignore it, let it die on the vine as the people are regimented into the Party."

"What does that do to family life?" I asked.

"There is very little time left for family life! To avoid suspicion, every person must belong to the union, to the Party and to a social group. Again, it's the regimentation."

"Under this kind of system, your work with students seems pretty hopeless," said Warren. "Yet you seem so joyful."

The young pastor spoke again, slowly.

"Outward resistance is difficult for the students. Spiritual resistance is our hope. Compromises are made and often we feel we are doing no more than fighting a holding action, but it is in the realm of the Spirit that we place our hope. And the Party recognizes the student Christian movement as a threat, a block, a real resistance with which to reckon."

How would our students, how would we, function under these conditions, I wondered?

"How," I asked, "can American students help?"

"Send delegates to the Berlin Conferences," came the prompt reply. "Help us fight our sense of isolation. Send books or money for books. Support us with your prayers."

The next morning, Pastor Schröder picked us up promptly, got us moved into the Bonhoeffer House and took us to the conference room where Alfred was speaking to a group of youth pastors. Sunday had been full, but the next three days made it indeed look like it had been a day of rest. We had meetings, some of them in the Eastern Sector, with students, pastors and lay people. We went into the refugee centers and saw the overcrowded conditions, the disorientation and fear of the people. We learned that the Church was responsible not only for ministering to them, but also for supplying much of their food and clothing. Continually, we were receiving information, and forming an understanding of what it meant to be a believer here in this Island City.

Two meetings in particular impressed us. The first was with Bishop Otto Dibelius at the Bonhoeffer House. The second was with thirty-four East German pastors, former students of Dietrich Bonhoeffer, at the Protestant Evangelical Theological Seminary in West Berlin.

Bishop Otto Dibelius, head of the Evangelical Church in Berlin (East and West) and the Brandenburg District in the GDR—was a revered Christian statesman with a long record of standing against the principalities and powers of the world, both in Hitler's Third Reich and in the present confrontation with Marxist-Leninist totalitarianism. In the past year he had experienced particularly severe vilifications, abuse and threats from the East Zone Communist government. His people feared the Communists would find some way to arrest him. But fear seemed to be something he had left behind in his long life, amid need and persecution. He had been subjected to mockery, imprisonment, state-enforced limitations to his preaching and threats to his life. But with the inner resources he had amassed through faith, he had an imperturbable, Christian serenity.

Warren and I felt deeply honored that he took the time to come by the Bonhoeffer House and greet us. His straight-spined military bearing, grey hair, piercing eyes and aura of authority were at first intimidating. He saw the current struggle in terms of people, not political systems.

"Wherever people are, East or West, they are not the faceless automatons of a State, an economic system or political theory," he said. "Rather, they are souls for whom Christ died and they are precious in the sight of our Heavenly Father.

"When people ask the great, basic questions about life and history, the Church can only answer with the Gospel, for the Gospel is the only thing she has. Her answer must be Jesus Christ, our crucified and risen Lord. Only he can heal all the world's ills."

Bishop Dibelius emphasized the importance of Berlin. "Right now, Berlin is the only sizable place on earth where Christians of the East and West can still meet together for an exchange of experience and hope. The Church must continue to see herself as one entity in spite of political systems."

Listening to and learning from the Bishop, Warren and I understood why this man was known world-wide as a mighty stalwart of the faith. He was truly the embodiment of moral integrity.

Our meetings with the thirty-four Eastern Sector pastors were equally moving. All of them had studied under Dietrich Bonhoeffer, the young theologian hanged by Hitler as the war was ending. Led by Bonhoeffer's brother-in-law, Pastor Eberhard Bethge, we studied Bonhoeffer's book *Life Together.*[7]

In a discussion prior to the study, it slowly seeped into my consciousness who these men were. First, they were the backbone of the Confessing Church which rose in opposition to Hitler, and now, of the Church in the East Zone.

The discussion was about Eastern Zone Christian students who were being unjustly expelled from the universities. One student who had managed to get to the top with his complaint had been told his misconduct was in resisting the Free German Youth Movement, as the Communist youth group was called. The pastors knew there was no hope of getting these students reinstated, but if the matter was protested, they decided, it might dampen the tendency toward further expulsions.

The question was, who should make the contact and precisely what should be said? There was no question of anyone's availability to do the job, but only who would be the most effective. They knew that the person who confronted the authorities faced the possibility of one day simply disappearing.

Who would be the one?

I looked around the room. They pointed to one man.

"No, he doesn't think fast enough."

A second. "No, he has a short fuse, a temper. He will blow it."

Then every eye in the room was on Professor Johannes Hamel. I watched his face. He was serene, every little crinkle around his eyes relaxed, at peace with himself and everyone else.

"All right," he said. "If I am the one, I will do it."

I got a lump in my throat. I wanted to weep. These men did not hesitate to

---

[7] Dietrich Bonhoeffer, *Life Together* (New York: Harper, 1954).

speak up, to stand against the Communist government. They often paid a terrific price for the privilege of doing their jobs, of making their witness.

Watching Dr. Hamel, I thought, "There is the bravest, most remarkable human being I have ever seen. I want to talk with him." We sat together at lunch.

"Dr. Hamel," I said, "you are the bravest human being I have ever seen."

He shook his head as though I were stupid.

"This isn't courage. It isn't even remotely related to courage. When you put yourself in a position where God can use you, there is a Presence that comes into your life. You can do what you have to do. You are not afraid. It is as simple as that."

I felt like I had been slapped into another dimension of understanding. Here was a man who was in every sense of the word "free." He couldn't be intimidated; he couldn't be swayed; he couldn't be bought or sold. He was living in a prison world, but of all the people I have ever known, Dr. Johannes Hamel was the most truly free.

Another stalwart of the faith whom we met at the conference was Pastor Gloede. His wife had been raped repeatedly by the Soviet's Mongol troops when they invaded Berlin. His coat was in shreds, his shoes were broken, he looked like a tramp. But there was a glory in that man's face and a bond between him and his wife such as I have seldom seen.

"We don't have most of the things people feel they have to have in order to live," he told me. "We don't have butter, white bread, meat, cheese... many of what we thought were life's essentials... but we don't starve." He paused, lost in thought. "In losing what we thought essential, we have found what is really necessary." He stretched to his full height. "No man can take our freedom from us. Only God can do that."

And then there was our host, Pastor Schröder. He was reticent to talk about himself, but in bits and pieces we learned of his background and learned to respect him as a powerful leader and a master strategist.

This first visit to Berlin was clearly an introduction to a whole series of new relationships—relationships which would transform my life. Already I had a much deeper understanding of the meaning of Christian discipleship and of the vast dimensions of the life and ministry of the Christian Church. How many in our congregation—or any congregation—would continue attending church if doing so jeopardized their job, their children's education, their social life, perhaps even their family unity? And yet here, in the midst of those harsh circumstances, there were people living their faith with an integrity I had seldom seen.

Warren and I had a day to rest and absorb all we had seen and heard. Then it was on to the University of Göttingen where Uwe Hollm was pursuing his theological training. We had a grand and exciting reunion with our young giant. He was highly motivated, radiating energy and enthusiasm as he told us about his work. His integrity and clear vision stood out sharply and clearly. I sensed that Uwe was on his way to a place of strong leadership in the German church.

A serendipity for us was the discovery that Uwe's chosen life companion, his fiancée Gertrude Kroeger, was also in training for Christian ministry. As vigorous and vital as Uwe in her Christian life, I thought her in every way his equal, particularly in her potential for Christian leadership. She was a remarkably beautiful young woman with corn silk hair, deep blue eyes, a peaches-and-cream complexion and a figure to match. With her instantaneous smile and her vibrant personality, she captured Warren's and my hearts.

"You know a lot of what Jesus Christ has done for me, Walt," said Uwe, "but there's one major thing you don't know."

"What's that?"

Smiling, he looked at Gertrude.

A little embarrassed, she declared, "I would never have consented to marry Uwe had he not become a Christian."

I nodded, remembering how Colleen had been deeply attracted to Louie only after he gave his life to Christ.

"Having Christ in your marriage won't keep it trouble-free," I warned, "but it gives you the basis, the way to work through those troubles."

Uwe's and Gertrude's engagement warmed my heart. Then came more news in the same vein. Ralph, back in college and working part time as Deputation secretary, had been keeping Warren and me abreast of what was happening at home with long, newsy letters. In this week's letter there was a new subject.

"My heart is so deeply moved and grateful, and my joy so great that at times I think I'll burst. Love has unmistakably come into my life. There is a trust and a tenderness in my heart that I have never experienced before.

"The thought of Mary Barber brings out the very best in me. Walt, words won't describe how grateful I am and how I thank God for his generosity, for I feel that he is guiding me so clearly. I have seen so much dirt and pain in life that I'm thirsty for his goodness and love. And now to experience that with Mary! He showers upon us his approval."

Letter in hand, I leaned back in my chair, remembering the haunted, hate-filled young refugee I had met in 1947. It had taken two years before he had the courage to trust Christ with his life. Now, watching him grow and mature in his faith, I was seeing again and again how God honored that decision.

The next day Uwe and Gertrude went with us to visit Ellierode where Louie, Lardner and Carol had worked in 1950, building the home for orphaned boys. From there we went to Kassel, the site of our first encounters with Uwe. Seeing the boys living in the home at Ellierode, and seeing families living in homes whose foundations we had laid, reconfirmed the value of these work camp projects for Warren and me. So did the sight of Uwe, once again waving good-bye from the Kassel train station, this time with Gertrude by his side.

Warren and I were ready to go home. On our long return flight we reflected on all we had learned, deciding that World Deputation was going in the right direction. There was still an urgent need for teams of dedicated, trained young Christians to identify with people in need by earning the right to share their deep faith in Christ as the answer to pain, hate, alienation and indifference. We had explored the idea of establishing ties with students at foreign universities and decided it was more important to strengthen our outreach to foreign students studying at American universities.

We also knew we wanted to be involved in Berlin. Those Christians living their faith in the midst of persecution needed us as a link to the church worldwide. And we needed them to remind us what life looked like when it was being lived with complete trust in Christ.

Satisfied with our conclusions, I pulled down the airliner's window shade and we reclined our seats, hoping to catch up on some sleep.

But as soon as I closed my eyes, the interview in Geneva with Dr. Philippe Maury, head of the World Student Christian Federation, resurfaced. He had said students were turning to Communism because they felt that twentieth century Christian civilization didn't have answers for the world's great needs.

I thought about the 1950 CIMADE work camp and the three young refugees who had escaped from an East German prison camp and walked over 450 miles to find freedom. They'd wanted to know what my church was doing to break down the walls of separation and alienation that created Hispanic barrios and black ghettos.

Those young refugees' questions had simmered in my mind for over two years and now the European students' choice of Communism as more effective than Christianity turned that simmer into a full boil. What should I be doing to present Christ as the Answer wherever the need? Was I still making my life completely available to Christ? Was I serving him at the point of greatest need?

A possibility entered my mind. As I examined it carefully, a sense of peace invaded my being and put to rest all those nagging questions. For one of the few times in my life, I closed my eyes and slept peacefully on a plane.

CHAPTER FOURTEEN

THE POINT OF GREATEST NEED

My job was putting people to work in areas of hurt and need within the community. I returned from my trip knowing that I wanted, and needed, to expand what I had been doing to a much broader basis than one congregation. The problems in the barrios of East Los Angeles, in ghettos like Watts and in the rural slums such as those found in the Imperial Valley and the San Joaquin Valley were bigger than one church could handle alone.

Within a week of my return from Europe, Dr. Carroll L. Shuster, the newly installed Executive of the Los Angeles Presbytery, and the Reverend James Baird, Presbytery's Director of Missions—both men of great vision and compassion—came to call on me. (The L.A. Presbytery was at that time the overseeing body of all Presbyterian churches in Southern California.)

"Walt," began Dr. Shuster, "I'm sure you're aware that within our area nine churches have developed neighborhood houses or community centers in their parish area. These are almost all within poverty areas and are serving ethnic populations which are not necessarily Presbyterian or even Protestant."

"I think these congregations consider this an extension of the ministry of their own church by reaching out to those in deepest need," I answered. "But these individual churches often have tiny congregations, so the burden falls on the minister and a few volunteers. In every instance the budgets are woefully, pathetically inadequate for the ministry they want to accomplish."

The two nodded agreement.

"One of our prime objectives is to develop an inner city, urban ministry worthy of the people living in these areas," James Baird explained. "We're creating a Department of Social Work for the Presbytery."

"Everyone we talk to says you are the person to head up this new expanded ministry," Dr. Shuster continued.

I must have been in a daze, as I heard the exact job description I would have written for myself being offered to me. Then Dr. Shuster added quietly, "You know, Walt, the people in these areas need a ministry of reconciling love as surely as do the people in Europe."

I pulled myself together and, with a huge grin, answered.

"Gentlemen, you're an answer to prayer! I accept gladly." And so, providentially, a call was extended exactly when I was ready for it—God's perfect timing. The one condition upon which our Hollywood church had accepted my resignation was that I continue to serve on the World Deputation Committee and to work closely with Ralph and the teams.

On January 1, 1953, two short months after my return from Europe, I was installed to head this new ministry. That was the easiest job change I ever made. My family didn't have to move, the kids stayed in their same schools, we still attended the same church and had our local circle of friends. To make up for the ease of the change, James Baird immediately dropped a project of epic proportions in my lap.

His department had just completed a study indicating more than 500,000 people were living in "Islands of Need" in the urban areas of Southern California, and an additional 225,000 were in rural slums. Many in that second group were part of a stream of migrant workers who followed the harvests. But the developing trend was for them to become more and more settled in one place, forming large, rural slums fringing the urban areas. These slums represented—and still do—some of the most impoverished, deprived areas in the world.

Life in all of these Islands of Need, irrespective of ethnic or racial backgrounds, was characterized by common problems: congested, substandard housing often without indoor plumbing or running water; poverty compounded by large families and over fifty percent unemployment; ill health and poor access to medical care; illiteracy, with the average educational attainment around sixth grade, as opposed to twelfth grade for the county; cultural handicaps, often including language barriers; and a very high incidence of crime.

James Baird and I were discussing all this in my new office just a week or so after I started work.

"We have quite a challenge to respond to," I said.

"What we need," he mused, "is something dramatic. Something which would involve all our churches and the community as well."

"A moral and spiritual call to arms!"

"Yes! Exactly that! Did you hear about the congregation in Northern California that built a new church in one day?" he asked.

"Yes, what an accomplishment! With a mighty team effort they actually put it all together in a day."

"Let's do something even more dramatic," James urged. "Let's challenge all our churches and the city at large to join forces and build four top quality neighborhood houses to replace the really inadequate ones. Let's do it with donated material and labor. Let's do it in one day!"

"You've got to be out of your mind."

"But we need something dramatic!" he argued leaning forward in his chair, eyes shining. "Small dreams won't mobilize the kind of church and community resources we need to deal with these problems."

"It would be a very visual, concrete way to show those communities that we care," I said, slowly beginning to catch his excitement.

"Yes! We would be saying 'We care! We love you! The status quo is not good enough for you!' And doesn't this carry some of the same feeling as your Deputation teams, Walt? We'll be working alongside the people in these Islands of Need, earning the right to witness to our beliefs."

"Authentic Christians do care far more than is apparent," I said, my enthusiasm building. "They may not have the time to go on special missions, but in their neighborhoods and offices they are trying hard to make themselves available to Christ. If we enlist them, give them a handle to take hold of, we could accomplish real miracles of faith."

"That's the first step!" he responded quickly. "We've got to give our church members and the community that 'handle' to take hold of. And," he paused reflectively, "we've got to keep it Christ-centered, not let it turn into merely a social project."

"That's right," I agreed. "So our first step is not the 'handle', but surrounding this project in prayer and keeping it there. We need to start with the local communities and churches involved and make sure this becomes their dream, that new neighborhood centers fit their actual needs, not just our perceptions of their needs."

James leaned back in his chair, eyes still shining and a big grin on his face.

"Four neighborhood houses in a day. Not bad for your first assignment, is it?"

The next months were a whirlwind of activity. I met with the pastors and leaders of the existing neighborhood houses that would be replaced: Westminster Center in Bell Gardens, Cleland House in East Los Angeles, El Calvario Community Center in El Monte and La Casa de San Gabriel in San Gabriel. They were cautious at first. They wanted no pipe dreams to disappoint the people they served. But as they saw the commitment was firm, they enthusiastically became the core of my prayer and team support.

We did our homework carefully, documenting what we proposed to accomplish, how we proposed to do it and why. Seed money was one of the first needs. George Johns, a deeply committed Christian and vice president and general manager of the Robinson's Department Stores, headed up a blue ribbon fund-raising committee. In short order $150,000 was in hand, earmarked for the neighborhood houses. One of our first miracles!

We enlisted the support of all of our church congregations, then went into the community getting the endorsement of the city council, the mayor's office, the Welfare Planning Council, the county sheriff and, of course, the media. Reports began appearing on radio, TV and the newspapers explaining our goal of building four beautiful new neighborhood houses, not in one day, but concurrently over a few months' span by using largely volunteer labor and donated material. The stories invited public participation and support.

One of the publicity events I particularly enjoyed, given my early days as a motorcycle cop, was when Sheriff Eugene Biscaliuz publicly swore me in as a Deputy Sheriff and endorsed the program as a significant contribution to the county.

A specific item we still needed was blueprints. The prominent architectural firm of Daniel, Mann, Johnson and Mendenhall provided us with complete plans for all our facilities, including renderings and complete working drawings ready to use and all at no cost. That was our next miracle.

At precisely the right moment, precisely the right man volunteered to take those plans to completion. John Danis, a young builder specializing in concrete block construction—the type planned for the neighborhood houses— volunteered to be project superintendent. John wouldn't even accept gas money in spite of the fact that the projects were miles apart necessitating long hours of travel and many miles of wear and tear on the car of this already busy young builder.

And major contributions continued coming. The president of Portland Cement delivered, without cost, the concrete for all four projects on the day and hour needed. The steel needed for construction also came free of charge from fellow members of George Johns' San Marino church. Windows and window frames were sold to us at manufacturers' cost, less fifteen percent.

Volunteers came by the score. One of the highlights was when John Danis had volunteers on the roof and all around the Cleland House, each with a bucket of paint and a long-handled roller. At his signal, they dipped rollers into paint and within minutes the painting of the building was an accomplished fact.

Again and again, Ralph Hamburger's words when he had first brought the Deputation idea to Dr. Evans, Sr. echoed in my mind. "We don't need to worry about money. If God wants this, the money will come."

At the heart of each project was a board of management drawn from the local community and various sister churches, which provided prayer support, direction and volunteers. The people on boards of the neighborhood house, many of whom had little in material possessions, gave of their time, energy, love and money in sacrificial quantities that humbled me. Many had a quality in their faith that reminded me of the pastors in East Berlin.

Meanwhile, my involvement in Berlin was growing. Pastor Schröder and I had been corresponding and his April letter was heart-rending:

"The situation of our whole church youth work in the Eastern Zone is becoming more and more difficult. All the youth in our groups were declared enemies of the state and in many ways they were pressed to no longer attend our meetings.

"In the high schools our boys and girls were asked to defend their faith. And then they were required to make their decision. If they continued attending our youth groups, they were released from high school. For a lot of our young people, it is now the end of their school time and they have no possibility in the future to go to another school or university.

"Perhaps you can imagine what that means for our young people. We are thankful that most of them are going this difficult way, saying, 'We cannot deny our Lord and he is also the Lord of our future.' They are confessing with their lives that they are Christians. We are helping them as much as we can.

"In some cases in the last weeks, leaders of our church youth work were put in prison and we don't know why. The student pastor from Halle is already some weeks in prison. The deacon who is leading our work in the district of Saxonia is also in prison. Since their imprisonment, we've had no way to speak with them and we don't know where they are."

Schröder's letter continued. "The assault against the Christian youth groups and against this church work has started and we don't know what will happen in the future. But we see that the Lord has his confessing youth in the midst of this deep suffering. We are giving them spiritual and material help as well as we can. I am writing this to you because I know that not only are you interested in our situation, but you are taking care of us also in your prayers."

I also heard that Dr. Johannes Hamel, the pastor and professor chosen to confront the Eastern Zone authorities about their expulsion of Christian students from the universities, had had that meeting. Since then, no one had heard from him or knew where he was. Hearing about the disappearance of someone I had met and spent time with was like a physical blow. I took a couple of hours out and drove to the beach. Leaning against my car, watching the breakers roll in, I reflected on my time in Berlin, the people I had met there and the steadily worsening conditions. It would be so much easier for those pastors and students to acquiesce, to go with the system. Instead, they put their future, perhaps their lives, on the line. Pastor Hamel's words echoed in my mind.

"When you put yourself in a position where God can use you, there is a Presence that comes into your life. You can do what you have to do. You are not afraid. It is as simple as that."

I wondered if that would be true for me. The time would come when I would find out.

We had six international Deputation teams that summer of 1953. For the first time teams went to Korea, Japan and the French Camerouns, as well as to Europe. Home teams went to Alaska and the migrant farm workers' camps, while one worked with me in Los Angeles. Ralph led a camp in France, Harriet was on the team that went to Japan and her brother, Steve, was on the one that went to Korea. The five team members in Europe spent eight days in Berlin under Pastor Schröder's guidance.

"By far the highlight of our entire summer was our stay in Berlin," wrote Esther Kinoshita. "Staying at the Dietrich Bonhoeffer House, we felt we were at the crossroads of the international cold war. It provided us with a marvelous opportunity to observe the problems first hand."

"We all agreed," said Ted Nissen, "that Berlin and the work camp experiences were two of the highest points of our lives."

Less than eight months after we had set our goal and started our project, all four neighborhood houses were completed. John Danis had moved the projects along with an efficiency and precision I wouldn't have believed possible on even a highly paid project, let alone on one using contributions and volunteers.

James Baird was right. In a dramatic way we had focused the entire city's attention on these Islands of Need and shown the people there in a visual, loving manner that they were not forgotten. People did care. But the biggest challenge still lay ahead. With the houses in place, people and budgets were needed for reaching into the communities and helping to meet the great needs that existed there.

That was my job, the one for which I had been hired and for which I got good support. It was a job of finding and coordinating community, city, county and church resources not only for the four new neighborhood houses we had just completed, but for the older ones started by individual churches and now undergirded and supported by my department. I enjoyed it, enjoyed seeing people come together and problems at least eased. That's progress. But, the people whose lives were transformed through these programs is where my real interest has always been.

Take Smitty and Tex for example. When I first met them they were in a Juvenile Detention Camp because their gang had picked up a car that didn't belong to them. An officer in the Juvenile Bureau of the Los Angeles Police Department had told me about this gang. He considered them all high potential kids, but they were living in bad neighborhoods and were victims of impossible home situations.

"Walt," he said, "I believe that if someone would take a real, long range, personal interest in these kids and if we could get just a little parental support and community encouragement, something worthwhile could come out of it."

I did some intensive consultation with their parents, talked to some of the leaders in their community and then, to my delight, discovered there was a man in the community the gang members really seemed to like and respect. His name was "Pop" Holmes and he was a solid Christian with a world of wisdom and empathy.

So taking Pop with me, I drove up to the Forestry Juvenile Detention Camp to meet Smitty, Tex and the rest of their gang. I started the interview on a positive note.

"Smitty," I said, "You're a dumb stoop!"

"We're doin' all right," he said belligerently. "We ain't afraid!"

"You're in here aren't you? You know what's wrong with you guys?"

"I'm sure you're gonna tell me."

"Darn right. You claim you're the greatest. You say you can beat anybody in about any sport. The trouble is, you don't believe that. If you did, you'd be out of this place in short order and you'd be showing people a thing or two."

Smitty and Tex exchanged a long look. Then Smitty flexed his muscles, spit and said, "Tell ya' what we're gonna do. As of right now me and the guys are on good behavior. In six weeks we'll all be outa' here. Then what?"

Pop spoke up. "Walt and I will be waiting for you. I've got a place for you to meet in my church and I want to see if you guys can win the church league's football championship."

As we left, I heard Smitty say to Tex, "Maybe we will show people a thing or two."

Under Pop's leadership and with a lot of community support, the boys made incredible progress. They won the football championship and were well on their way to a city championship in the softball league. They were doing so well and I was busy with so many other things I lost touch with them.

Many weeks later I received a formal invitation to become a member of the Angels Boys' Club. Induction was to take place at the Hollywood Methodist Church where Dr. Glenn Randall Phillips was the pastor. When I arrived Dr. Phillips and I were seated in a pew, blindfolded and given twenty minutes to reflect on the importance of becoming a member of the Angels Boys Club. After what seemed an eternity of perfect quiet, we were led to the altar and asked to kneel.

"The power by which we live is faith in God," said a voice I recognized as that of Tex. "Will you, Dr. Phillips, and will you, Walt James, reaffirm your faith in God by repeating with me the Twenty-third Psalm?"

As we joined Tex, "The Lord is my shepherd, I shall not want...," I was speaking around a huge lump in my throat. Still blindfolded, we were led down a long isle, asked to climb up an iron ladder to the very top of the towering steeple, crawl through a small opening and again kneel.

"The inspiration by which we live our lives, day by day, is born of prayer," said Smitty's voice. "Will you, Dr. Phillips, and will you, Walt James, pray with me the Lord's Prayer?"

Voices around the rooms joined ours. Then a young hand pulled off our blindfolds and there kneeling round the Tower Room was the gang from the detention center, every one of them.

Pop Holmes had indeed proven quite an influence in these boys' lives. The authorities had no further trouble with that gang.

Word got around about our programs for kids. My telephone rang about 9:30 one night. It was the proprietor of a small malt shop in East L.A. A gang of rowdies was making his shop their gathering place and driving away his customers. When I arrived about an hour later, they were still there. I ordered a good thick chocolate malt and took my time enjoying it while I observed the boys, heard their topics of conversation and spotted their leaders. By the second night I knew most of their names and that they were ninth graders at Thomas Star King Junior High.

I visited the school the next day and got a run-down on each boy, then observed them on the playground. The following afternoon the vice principal called them all into his office. They had been there before and were prepared for the worst. He said, "This is Walt James. He's interested in sports and has something he wants to talk to you about." Then he left, closing the door behind him.

"Fellows, I hear that you have quite a softball team. Is that true? Are you that good?"

They did a real snow job. They said they could take on anybody, hands down.

"I'm organizing a softball league in your area. Would you be interested in signing aboard?"

"You bet!"

"There is a catch. You must have a coach, practice regularly and play according to the rules!"

They squirmed and looked at me with more than a little suspicion.

"You can choose your own coach, but Ben Alexander who plays Frank Smith on Dragnet is interested." I knew he was a hero of theirs.

"Wow!" was the response. "Could we really get him?"

Ben had been one of my finest volunteer leaders at summer camps and really wanted to get involved in some way with deviant kids. I'd already talked to him about this group.

"Why don't we call him now?" I asked, picking up the telephone and dialing. "Ben, I told you about a group of fellows who might be interested in a softball team. Would you like to talk to them?"

I handed the telephone to one of the guys. Even over a telephone, there was instant rapport. Ben took it from there, with me just checking in occasionally. Years later Ben told me that the Mustang Club was one of the great experiences of his life.

The neighborhood houses filled a variety of needs: tutoring and afternoon programs for all ages of kids; day camps in the summer; safe gathering places for teenagers; and classes in reading, health, cooking, sewing and English for teens and adults. Neighborhood boards worked with the directors to determine each community's needs. But some of the most important work didn't fall under any program heading. Chris Ruiz is one example.

One Saturday in the fall of 1954 we held a Play Day bringing together for the first time all the groups we served—around 600 kids from Watts, East L.A., Riverside and the rural areas. We wondered if we were setting up a war or some other form of ethnic confrontation. The sports and play time went well. I was to be the main speaker. I looked into the insolent, almost hostile faces and decided this was no place for speech-making by "Whitey."

"Hi gang!" I said and sat down.

Out of the crowd stepped a rugged, young Hispanic I hadn't seen before. He strummed a few notes on his guitar and the kids gathered to him like flies to molasses.

"Who's that guy?" I asked Tony Hernandez, a pastor and the executive director of the Cleland House.

"I don't really know. His name is Chris Ruiz. He just walked in one day. He loves kids and they love him. I'd like to put him on as a part-time staff person and train him."

"Do it! We'll find the money somewhere."

Chris took to neighborhood house work like a duck to water. But one day, deeply troubled, he poured his heart out to Tony. Chris had never known his parents. He'd been raised by grandparents who resented the responsibility and financial burden. Bitter at their resentment, Chris took it out on all those around him. By the time he was eleven, he had been in and out of juvenile hall many times. As he grew, he moved on to juvenile detention camps. He lied about his age and joined the U.S. Army Paratroopers, but was soon dishonorably discharged for infractions too numerous to mention.

"Every time I get a job, someone comes along who knows my record and I have to move on," Chris told Tony. "I love this work. I'm tired of running!"

"It doesn't have to be this way," Tony told Chris. Tony shared his faith in Christ, telling Chris that Christ offered him a new life, effective immediately. He used the verse, "If any one is in Christ, he is a new creation." (2 Corinthians 5:17 RSV)

"Christ forgives your sins, Chris, and you have a brand new start," said Tony. "Man, that's for me!"

Chris, his wife, Judy, and several of their friends started membership classes at Tony's church. A new life was starting for Chris and Judy.

But he was too entangled in his old one for it to just fade away.

A few weeks after the classes had been going, a blaring telephone at 2:00 in the morning interrupted my-all-too-short night's sleep. It was Tony Hernandez calling from Cleland House.

"Walt, we've got a problem. You'd better come on over."

It was Chris. Until he became a Christian, he had been secretary of the Young Communist League in East L.A. He still had most of their files. Now, as a Christian, he could not tolerate the League's manipulation and use of the young people in the area. But if he turned his information over to the authorities, he not only invited his own arrest, but quick and serious reprisal from the League or the gangs they controlled.

This was a new kind of problem for Chris, a moral decision he felt he must make and make now. He and Tony had been wrestling with it since early evening. I pondered Chris' dilemma, then with his permission, made a telephone call to an elder in my church, Maury Gouge. Maury was a top FBI man in our area.

"Maury," I said, rousing him also from a sound night's sleep, "I need you in your capacity as a Christian and an elder to come over to Cleland House now."

When Maury came, Chris poured out his story, beginning with his new life in Christ. Maury pondered, chin on chest, for a long time while the other three of us held our breath. Then, looking up, he pinned Chris with his gaze and seemed to be searching him to the very depths of his soul. Finally, he spoke.

"We have a long file on your activities, Chris. I can't expunge the records. But what I can do is write a complete report of all the information you have given me here tonight. You and I can sign that report and I'll put it in your file. I can't make any guarantees, but I believe if you commit no more offenses, you have nothing to fear from our agency."

Chris nodded slowly. "Thank you. That takes care of half my problem. Now I have to figure out how to avoid the League and the gangs' retaliation when they realize where your new information came from."

Maury grinned for the first time that night.

"I wouldn't worry about that, Chris. There shouldn't be any reprisal because there's been no betrayal. You didn't tell me anything the FBI doesn't already know."

Chris' mouth dropped open in amazement. Then slowly the significance of that dawned on him.

"Then I really can be free of my past!"

Chris and Judy dug into their new life with inspired dedication. Using the Presbytery's new scholarship program for training indigenous leadership from the inner city, they completed their undergraduate work, went on to get their masters in social work, and, years later, I got an embossed invitation from Chris to attend the granting of his doctorate in education.

That's one of my favorite stories, but it's not an unusual one. By being in the community, the neighborhood houses and their staff provided something that had been in very short supply...alternatives, opportunities and options. Most importantly, as in Tony's case, the dedicated Christians working there served as witnesses to the new life found in Christ.

Being the director of social work was an absorbing, demanding, frustrating and rewarding vocation. Not all of our programs took off with the same enthusiasm as those at Cleland House. In Watts we were having to rethink our entire strategy and start all over. But I was where I wanted to be, doing want I wanted to do, all by God's grace.

At the same time, my involvement in Berlin was growing with people from Pastor Schröder's and Hollywood's parishes, moving and working between the two as if we really were one. In retrospect, it was a honeymoon period, a time of deepening and strengthening ties, of forming bonds that would carry us into and beyond the crisis of August 13, 1961, when the Berlin Wall was erected, irrevocably splitting Berlin—and the world—into East and West and further isolating the Christians behind the Iron Curtain.

"I wish you could listen to the radio here in Berlin. It is quite something. I fiddled around on the dial the other night and got alternately the same political stories, but one voice said black was white, another said white was black, a third said white was gray, another that gray was black. It truly is a fight for the minds of men and Berlin is the immediate center of this ideological battle. Few people across the ocean can understand the issues that face the people of Berlin and the problems of living in a divided city and country."

These thoughts were expressed by Sam and Yolanda Entz, members of our Hollywood Church who, with their five-year-old daughter and three-year-old son, spent June 1954 to June 1955 working with teenagers in Berlin under Pastor Schröder's guidance. Their presence and their thoughts show the direction of much of our connection with Berlin during the mid- and late-fifties.

World Deputation's commitment was to identify with and stand alongside people in need earning the right to be Christ's reconciling agent. In Berlin that meant supporting fellow Christians living in the stress and tension of a city divided between East and West, a city becoming the focal point in the Cold War. Well-trained support people were one of the ways we did that. Every summer Deputation teams spent time in Berlin. In 1957 and 1958, teams whose members all spoke German worked in Pastor Schröder's summer camps.

In evaluating the teams Pastor Schröder said, "The Hollywood teams are a great, positive force on the whole, year-round program of the youth work in Berlin. You must always keep in mind that Berlin is an island of freedom within the sea of Communism. The contact is not only good for the young people who come to the camps from East and West, but it is also important for the two thousand or more lay youth leaders and the staff leaders for whom this cross fertilization is important. The work of the youth division in Berlin will go on without Hollywood, but Hollywood can make a significant and welcome contribution if it continues to see its way clear to be partners together in the work."

In 1959 Dick Spencer, one of our church members, did a Junior Year Abroad program working for Pastor Schröder at the Boje, a teen center in Berlin. Marguerite and I went in 1955 and I returned in 1959. In addition, we directed a host of Christians to Berlin for orientation, so they could be support people in their home churches.

German Christians also came to us to work and visit. By 1954 the U.S. Ecumenical Work Camp Committee was sending European students to work in our inner city and migrant ministry programs. Dr. George Winterhager, ecumenical adviser to Dr. Dibelius, the bishop of Berlin, spent time with us. Pastor Schröder was asked repeatedly to come as a speaker and Bible teacher, not just at our church, but all over Southern California.

To the occasional visitor like me from the U.S., life in West Germany, particularly in West Berlin, in the mid-fifties seemed like a kind of honeymoon period, a new birth of freedom for the German people. They worked energetically to rebuild their bombed-out cities and towns. Bomb craters disappeared. Mountains of rubble and destroyed buildings were gone almost as if by magic. Cities and industries were renewed. Public parks and gardens were restored. New office buildings, stores, apartment houses and hotels appeared almost overnight.

Lending greatly to this spirit of optimism was the Big Four Summit Conference in Geneva in 1955 where the heads of state for the U.S., Russia, England and France met together for the first time since the war to discuss disarmament. Marguerite and I arrived in Geneva one week after the conference and sensed an atmosphere of confidence and excitement for the future. People sensed an integrity, a deep sincerity and a quiet courage in this man who was our president, Dwight D. Eisenhower.

The thirty days in June and July that Marguerite and I spent in Europe gave me a sense of hope. Part of the time we traveled with Ralph and Mary, now married and taking the summer months off before Ralph started seminary the coming fall in New Jersey.

We saw Uwe and his fiancée, Gertrude, hard at work in their last year at the University of Göttingen.

In Berlin Pastor Schröder took us to meet young Christians from behind the Iron Curtain who were in West Berlin church camps for a few days. By affirming their faith, they often forfeited everything—jobs, education, coupons to buy food and clothing. To them the worst that could come to pass had already happened. They were dispossessed, their loved ones under pressure, missing or dead, and their cities were still in ruins. Yet they were dynamic, radiant, utterly free and unafraid. There was a transcendent, radical Presence at work in their lives.

We spent a week with J.B. Phillips and his wife, Vera, in their home in southern England. Our friendship had grown over the years and every summer a visit with J.B. was part of the Deputation teams' orientation. Just the year before he had come on a speaking tour to Hollywood and had stayed in our home. His reason for coming, detailed in his book *The Church Under the Cross*, gave me another insight into the effect of people living their lives as expendables in Christ's service. He wrote:

"It might not be out of place here to mention that what finally drew me to your great country was not natural curiosity (although I have plenty of that), not the kindly appreciative letters (though I have plenty of those), but the personal visits of several groups of young Christians who came to see me on their way to or from the work camps and rehabilitation centers of stricken postwar Europe. I felt I was meeting not merely fine, warm hearted youngsters ready to donate part of their vacation for the good of others, but living representatives of a new spirit rising in the Church. Here was no narrow vision, no parochial enthusiasm, no boasting of a local church's achievement; but a real concern for the whole scattered Family of God. I was very deeply moved by meeting year after year young people with such a vision of God's worldwide purpose. In the end, I felt compelled to visit the country and some of the churches which have produced such cheerful willingness to serve under the Cross."[8]

A letter from Pastor Schröder was waiting when we returned from Europe.

"I am so thankful for your visit to Berlin because it is so important to have brothers who know the difficulties and the blessings of the work here. You are really one of the full-timers in our youth work, even if you are not personally in this city. The Lord bless all your work."

In another letter Pastor Schröder wrote: "We have since the war received much help from the U.S. We have received food and clothing which has made the difference between life and death. However the most important thing is that America is sending Christian young people here as a living example of their love and concern for us."

By 1959 Deputation teams from our church had completed 111 assignments in Europe, the Orient and the United States. Many team members had chosen full time Christian vocations and were starting Deputation programs in their churches.

---

[8] J. B. Phillips, *The Church Under the Cross* (New York: Macmillan, 1956, Preface, p.V).

Wherever Deputation had gone, its goals remained the same: to live one's life completely available to Jesus Christ; to discover Christ as the basis for world brotherhood, and to make the walls that separate people transparent for Jesus Christ by identifying with those in pain and earning the right to be heard.

By 1959 Ralph had finished seminary and he and Mary were in Basel, Switzerland, where he was doing a year of graduate work at the University, including studying under Karl Barth. Uwe and Gertrude were married and working together in Tornesch, Schleswig-Holstein, he serving a pastor internship and she as a youth worker. Louie Evans had finished seminary, he and Coke had spent a year in Edinburgh, Scotland, where he had done graduate work, and now they were back in Southern California with their two young sons starting a church in the Bel Air area of Los Angeles.

But as the fifties drew to a close, it became increasingly clear to me that there was an opposite side to the optimism, the growth and the sense of hope we encountered both at home and in Europe. At home it was seen in the build-up of racial tensions as Blacks struggled to make equality a reality. In Eastern Europe it was seen in the repression of individual liberties by the Communists as they worked to bring about the ideal worker's state. Berlin, the hole in the Iron Curtain, provided a view of what was happening in the East.

The East German party members, wanting East Berlin to be a showcase for the West, were among the most fanatic Communists. They labored zealously to bring every aspect of a person's life under the Party's control, even creating ceremonies to replace the church's ceremonies for baptism, joining the church, marriage and burial. In the land which was the birthplace of the Protestant Reformation, the church was slowly being strangled. The State began severely limiting and sometimes forbidding its right to do charitable works, to minister to people in the armed services, to publish newsletters, to hold public meetings, to gather for conferences and to rebuild churches and parish homes destroyed in the war. The church tax, once collected by the State and given to the Church, was a thing of the past, leaving the Church without an established base of funding.

But the State's most intense focus was on raising up young people to be model socialists.

"Socialism calls for the new man with the best human qualities," declared Otto Grotewohl, prime minister of the German Democratic Republic in a speech on March 23, 1959.[9] "And these new men must be carefully brought

---

[9] "The Evangelical Church in Berlin and the Soviet-Zone of Germany" (Printed and produced by A.W. Hayn's Erben, Berlin West, 1959) pp. 8–9.

on, formed and educated with great patience but also with perseverance. The greatest and most intensive endeavor must be devoted to the young, oncoming generation."

Grotewohl went on to say that the Church was interfering with the "progressive development of our young people." It ended by declaring "Moral is therefore what serves the cause of socialism."

Dr. George W. Winterhager, Bishop Dibelius' assistant, delivered a lecture on January 25, 1959, at the University of Basel in Switzerland where Ralph was a student. In a letter, Ralph sent me the notes he took on that occasion:

"Since the end of World War II, for thirteen years, the new East German generation has not known anything but dialectical materialism and collectivism; youth grow up in isolation from the outside world and their hope is directed toward world Socialism. The East German government is vitally interested in the education of its youth and keeps sharp oversight that it is affected along the Communist line. Those young people who in 1945 were six or ten years of age are now nineteen and twenty-three years old. They are enamored of the Socialist state and of the new world which they are going to build.

"The old generation no longer can cope with the new developments; they flee to the West by the thousands. It is the young who remain. The young East German is conscious of the mission of a total world picture in which there is room only for the collectivism of the young worker. He has trust in his own capacity; he trusts in the slogans of his leadership, there can be no compromise at all, no inclination toward transcendence at all. The young East German is more versed in the doctrine of Marx and Lenin than many a young Russian Communist. He fights with almost messianic passion. He is required to give himself completely day and night, for the deities on this side."

Ralph's notes continued: "At the age of twelve to thirteen many young East Germans feel ready to give the pledge of allegiance to the Socialist State, promising to work for and, if need be, die for a better world; to work for peace; and to disbelieve any inclination that might point in the direction of a transcendental God. In 1959 eighty-five percent of the East German youth took part in the Jugendweihe, a Communist substitution for the church practice of confirmation (admittance to full church membership). The names of all who take the oath are inscribed in a book which ironically is called *The Book of Life.*

"The East German authorities forbid any gathering without a permit of more than ten people in any locality. At whatever church or place divine services were held in 1933, church services may be held today; but nothing new may be instituted—no new churches, no new services, no new groups—without the authorization of the East German government. This has led to the imprisonment of hundreds of people and untold hardship. Those who are caught are encountering untold hardships against which there is no lawful defense. It is a warfare about who will have the say over the future of the East German people."

I was torn by this paradox: On the one hand, the East German youth's idealistic belief in Communism, as described by George Winterhager; and on the other hand, the determined expressions of unqualified Christian commitment of Schröder's youth. Dr. Winterhager described the vulnerability of youth to the party line, but I had seen the contrasting realities of the depth and quality of life experienced by those Christians living and working behind the Iron Curtain.

I wanted to get back to Berlin and see first-hand what was happening to our brothers and sisters there. Ralph had gone to Berlin at Pastor Schröder's request on his way to Basel. Now his letter deepened my desire:

"I don't think that we even begin to have an idea how very desperate the struggle is which the Church is waging in the East Zone of Germany. The lines of demarcation have become so sharp that for many Christians who remained in the Zone for all these years, life has become virtually impossible. Consequently the exodus has markedly increased in recent months and the refugee camps are in such a state of overflowing and misery that even Pastor Schröder gets tears in his eyes when he speaks of it. In the East many Christians, for the sake of their faith and their witness, have been totally cut off from all possibilities for an education and must work as common laborers in factories.

"The Communist regime is copying the Church's creed and catechism line by line and substituting for it their own atheistic line. The consequences of this are disastrous. The struggle of conscience and mind among young people and parents alike, forced by circumstances mostly beyond their control, is tremendous.

"Pastor Schröder asked his leaders this morning, 'Do you and I have a share in this gigantic struggle? Can we be of positive help? Are we willing to identify ourselves with these frightful happenings in the East?'

"I think Pastor Schröder is asking the same question of us in Southern

California! Never forget that Berlin is the only place where the young people from the East Zone can have contact with young people and leaders from the West, where they can get the necessary encouragement to live another year under frightful pressure, where they can get perhaps an answer to the deepest questions of their hearts. I am not writing about this as someone who does not know what he is talking about, for I myself went through five years of fear and terror. I want to underline that the Church of Jesus Christ in Berlin and the East Zone is virtually and truly on the battle line."

How much the city itself was on the battle line was made clear by Soviet Premier Nikita Khrushchev's demand that the Western Powers withdraw from West Berlin by May 27, 1959, leaving it a free, demilitarized city. If they did not, Khrushchev threatened to sign a separate peace treaty with the East Germans which would give the Soviets control of all the access routes into Berlin. Berliners feared the German Communists even more than the Russians. The move was seen as a thinly veiled attempt to suck all of Berlin into the Russian Zone.

In April 1959 I was granted a six-week sabbatical leave for a twofold purpose: First, to study the social work of the Church in Europe, particularly in East and West Germany among the poor, the disadvantaged and the oppressed—my own area of specialization. Second, to strengthen the bonds of fellowship with the churches of Berlin by expressing the love and concern of our Southern California churches for them during these trying days.

This time my work was official by special arrangement between the Presbytery and the Synod of Berlin-Brandenburg in Germany.

My first stop was in Amsterdam where I visited with Ralph's parents and linked up with Ralph, who was taking a week away from his graduate studies to travel with me. We went to Tornesch to see Uwe and Gertrude Hollm.

Uwe has a way of looking at hard reality.

"I see a major defeat for the Church in the East," he said. "Up to now the parish community has maintained the position of 'no confirmation' for those youth who accept Jugendweihe, the Communist youth confirmation. Now a new policy has been adopted making it possible by the Church to do both."

"The 'adapt to survive' philosophy," I said.

"But it's impossible to do both. It is impossible to be a Christian and a Communist!" Uwe's voice rose.

"Our ultimate loyalty is to God," agreed Ralph quietly. "There can be no compromise."

"I'm afraid there are nowhere near as many convinced Christians in the East as we have been led to believe," Uwe continued. "I fear the Western Church has tended to overstress the heroism of the Eastern Church for propaganda purposes."

"This may be true," I answered slowly. "However, in my correspondence with Pastor Schröder and Bishop Dibelius, stress has not been laid on anyone's heroism or on great numbers, but that one holds in Jesus Christ an 'impregnable position.' This seems to be the Magna Charta of those who must survive, who must persevere, who must mature and flourish under a system that allows no room for the survival of the Christian Church."

"Under this system the numbers are less," said Ralph. "But those who persevere have a transcendent quality of life, an inner strength and courage out of all proportion to their normal stature as human beings."

Uwe agreed. "Those left are a highly dedicated minority within a system that allows very little room for the existence of the Church. You can't understand what living in the day-to-day pressure of an entire system determined to eradicate your faith can do."

There it was again: the dichotomy of belief about how Christians were surviving under Communism. In the days to come, I began to realize both sides were right.

Pastor Schröder met us at the airport. He had a full agenda laid out. With Ralph as my interpreter, we met with the leaders of the Church's ecumenical social work and visited neighborhood houses, homes for the aged, homes for displaced girls, hospitals and midnight missions for women and for men. We took part in meetings with the youth, youth pastors and leaders. One of the youth pastors described working in the East Zone, that part of Germany controlled by the Russians.

"The old, traditional Church structures are breaking down," he said. "Now the Church lives on an hour-to-hour basis. There are fewer and fewer theologically trained pastors since none are admitted from the West, but the number of lay preachers and Church workers is increasing. We trained pastors gather these people together for common study and planning. The situation is even harder for the lay people than the pastors because they have no official status."

"It's not easy for the pastors either," said Pastor Schröder, laying his hand briefly on the man's shoulder. "All Church officials are underpaid and must perform their duties in three or four different communities, often quite far apart. Almost none have automobiles and train connections are poor."

"Tell Walt what is happening to the young people," said Ralph.

"The State is doing its best to keep the pastors separated from the people, particularly the young people," said Pastor Schröder. "Dialectical materialism is taught in the schools, but no religious activities are permitted. Regardless of its physical condition, meetings must be held at the church or church house, not at a home, because the person would be suspected of subversion. Permits need to be secured for meetings of over ten people and it's almost impossible to get the permits. Special conferences may only be held on weekends, not during vacations. The night before a conference all the buses usually break down and need to be repaired. 'Ride bicycles or use some other means of transportation,' we are told. But the distances are often too great, so the conference can't be held."

"And what the Party is doing at Christmas is so divisive for families," said the East Zone pastor.

"The Party and now the government too," explained Pastor Schröder, "are trying to substitute secular holidays for all the Christian festivals. Christmas has been renamed the Feast of the Fir Trees or Feast of the Winter Solstice. Special trains aggregate at the beginning of the Christmas holidays to take the children to winter sports areas so they won't be home for Christmas."

"The same kind of pressure happens every Sunday," said the pastor. "Party officials schedule Sunday morning visits right during church with a farmer or worker to discuss how to improve their work. And of course, if you declare openly that you are a Christian, you'll probably lose your job. The State won't license Christian lawyers or engineers."

"Who's the man who directs the brass ensemble at your church?" Pastor Schröder asked.

"Erich?"

"Yes. Tell Walt about Erich."

"Erich directs our brass ensemble, a very important part of our church music. The Party decided it wanted to form a brass ensemble under Erich's direction. The catch is, it would practice Sunday mornings at eleven. Erich told them he had a commitment to his church at that hour, but he would practice with the group when he could. He was dismissed from his job as an accountant because he wasn't loyal to the Party and consequently was not one whose character would commend him for a place of trust and responsibility in his firm. He's been assigned a job as a street sweeper and since he had so much leisure for his music, his working hours were doubled. His pay is only a fraction of what he formerly earned."

"Tell Walt what happened to your daughter," Ralph prompted quietly.

For the first time this brave man's shoulders sagged and he looked haggard and worn.

"My daughter is nine and in third grade. Last Monday the teacher asked how many children attended Sunday School. She timidly raised her hand, the only one in the class to do so. The teacher commanded her to stand up. With the teacher leading, everyone pointed a finger directly at her and chanted, 'Stupid! Stupid! Stupid!'"

Slowly he straightened. "There is no guaranteed form of church life any longer, no lawful protection. When the party and the State don't succeed by indoctrination, they resort to ridicule, restrictions and harassment.

"We are no longer a fighting Church but a quiet, suffering one. The main point for the Christian layman is just to *be*. This is a Christian testimony in itself. Sometimes sharing can be done, but only on a person-to-person basis."

"You must feel very isolated," I said.

"That's why Berlin is so important," he responded. "Pastor Schröder and the other church officials can't go into the East Zone and it's getting harder for them to move freely in East Berlin. But at least for now, those of us in the Zone can come to East Berlin and then into West Berlin for a brief time of rest and fellowship. And his camps provide the same opportunity for the youth who need it even more than we do."

The day before I followed Pastor Schröder's itinerary into West Germany, I was received by Bishop Dibelius. Pastor Schröder and Ralph accompanied me.

Bishop Dibelius, harassed and persecuted first by the Nazis and now by the Marxist-Leninist regime, was highly respected both by friend and foe. He was an almost legendary figure, a warrior, a man of conviction and power.

He approached us with great warmth and humility. The thing that captured me first were his eyes—clear, deep brown, warm and alive, intelligent, penetrating and very kind. His voice was powerful and commanding. He spoke nearly perfect English. Every word was dynamic, powerful. His words were his arsenal.

Seeing the ever encircling noose of restrictions on his churches and staff in East Berlin and the Zone and anticipating the ultimate East-West separation of the churches under his jurisdiction, Bishop Dibelius was searching out means of communication that would not be cut off if East and West Berlin became inaccessible to each other. That had been a motivation behind Pastor Schröder's 1952 visit to the States and the invitation to us to visit Berlin. The team visits had strengthened the Bishop's conviction that Americans might provide one avenue of communication.

The Bishop dominated the discussion from the first. He probed to see if we truly understood the problems and difficulties of the local church, the local pastor and the local lay people. Did we understand the significance of Berlin, the one place where people from the Zone and from the West could meet? Did we understand the great dedication of the pastors in the East? Seventy-two percent of all the academically trained people and around seventy percent of the landed gentry and prosperous middle class had fled the East Zone. But only about one percent of the pastors in the Zone had left.

"Consequently, they enjoy a great trust among the people," said the Bishop. "The Evangelical pastors remain the same in a drastically changing world."

Did we understand the problem of reconstruction? There were over 300 churches in Berlin, only one of which was untouched by war's destruction. There were hundreds more churches in the East and so far, only one had been restored. The government would not issue permits. West Germans and Christians worldwide had been able to send in money or materials for reconstruction, but now that was considered an affront to socialism.

"How may we in America help you here in Berlin?" I asked.

"Formerly, the State had the financial responsibility for supporting the clergy," said the Bishop, "Now the Church must do it all. You in America can't pay the salaries, but in Berlin we can quietly provide the opportunity for fellowship, for training of workers, for medical care and help when their health breaks—and it does! Money can be used for these purposes.

"We are in the front line of the battle against Marxist atheism. Since it's neither wise nor safe to publish all of the factual information, you can help by conveying your impressions. It is important for people from other parts of the world to come to the Island City of Berlin to let the people in the East know that they are not alone; that they are not forgotten. They need to know that there are Christians in other parts of the world who know about them and who do really care about them, who still claim them as part of the worldwide community of believers." The Bishop paused.

"The Church will endure!" he continued. "It can endure this persecution for years. Yes, for three or four centuries, if it must. We must pray for a few more years of democracy when we may meet together and discuss these matters. And we must pray for the Marxist State."

Gracious, warm, with quiet dignity, he thanked us for coming and wished us well. I personally felt that we had been in the presence not only of one of the world's great statesmen, but also of one of the patriarchs, the saints of the Church.

"The Bishop was genuinely interested. He was impressed that Ralph and you had taken time and really gone into the situation here," said George Winterhager, who'd been in the conference. "Others come through with their preconceived notions and schedules." He paused, searching for a polite way of expressing his opinion on such visits. Finally, he just shrugged. "That does not seem to be the most appropriate method."

Pastor Schröder had arranged a power-packed exposure for me to "the other side of life," in Germany, to meet the people at the grass roots level who had suffered so much. The full impact of the need for a ministry of reconciliation was brought home to me in a powerful way in this visit to industrial West Germany.

Ralph needed to get back to Basel, so I was on my own in a place where almost no one spoke a language I could understand. With a dictionary and a great deal of gesticulating back and forth, I could get some partial ideas across, but only with a maximum of careful concentration and all-out effort. It was an exhausting business.

Fourteen years after its end, the Germans had not forgotten the war. In the industrial areas where life was grim, where they were so terribly bombed, where every home has pictures on the walls of loved ones who were lost—often wives and children—there was something beneath the surface even yet, even among the pastors.

On the top level, the fellowship of the Christian Community was at its best. Ideas could be exchanged and feelings shared. But I wanted to meet the pastors and members of the local churches as well.

I expressed an interest in actually seeing the men at work in a coal mine, to go deep down inside the earth and rub elbows with the men. Almost instantly it was arranged. At 6:00 a.m. the next day, Pastor Woreman would meet me for breakfast. At 6:30 we would leave for the mine.

I arrived at 6:00 a.m. for breakfast. Pastor Woreman came at 6:25, bolted his food, and we were off. He could speak no English, but he motioned me into the backseat of a Volkswagen. Another pastor was driving. He could speak no English either. The men carried on an animated conversation as we traveled some forty miles through the back country to a large mine. Once in a while I would try to edge in a question in my very best German.

"What town is this?

"Are we traveling North?"

Neither could understand.

We arrived at the mine and were joined by two other men. They shook my hand, muttered their names, and then swiftly and promptly forgot me. I tagged along. The mine superintendent who conducted the tour asked them in German if I spoke German.

"Nein."

It was a large mine, modern and well equipped. We stripped off every article of clothing—watches, eyeglasses, everything—and were provided with heavy underwear, heavy reinforced trousers and coat, a plastic helmet and a miner's lamp. We traveled the way the workers traveled, in rough iron cars attached to a train of some thirty other cars. They went banging and clanging through tunnels deep inside the earth. Twenty-five hundred men worked in that mine eight hours a day on their knees mining an average of nearly two tons per hour per man. It was hard, hazardous work.

I was fascinated by these rugged, dirty, hardworking men who worked steadily, unceasingly, and rhythmically like machines. They seldom spoke, only an 'Auf' which means 'Good Luck, come up well,' as we went by. They always said that. It was a world of anonymity. Everyone looked exactly alike down there, with the clothing, the plastic helmet, the miner's lamp peering at you through the darkness, and faces masked in coal dust until only the margin of the mouth, two distended nostrils and the eyes were seen.

I thought we had come to the end of the world when the men ahead of me started crawling through a hole not more than two feet high and two-and-a-half feet wide. With my gas mask strapped to my back, I had a hard time getting through that hole, especially when I discovered we had to crawl over the top of a moving conveyor belt which was carrying coal to a distant point where it was dumped into a long, swirling tunnel-like chute. Some of the chunks of coal on that belt were more than two feet in diameter and must have weighed one or two hundred pounds. We were squatting in a long tunnel three feet high, but fairly wide. My eyes adjusted, and there were the men digging, working on their knees silently and mechanically far into the recesses of the earth, scooping the coal onto the conveyor.

One by one, the men ahead of me crawled onto the conveyor with the coal and disappeared. No one said anything. I was left alone. There was nothing else to do but climb aboard the thing. I was carried further and further down this tiny corridor into the bowels of the earth. I was kneeling as low as I could. If I raised my head, my helmet crashed into the ceiling of the tunnel. Now and then I passed a grim miner dug into his little niche, but there was no sight of my companions. I traveled what seemed an endless way to me, probably 200 to 300 yards, several times the length of a football field. I became apprehensive. That belt had to dump its load soon. I watched, alert. Then it came—not six feet ahead—the great chunks of coal falling off the chute and plunging down into the cars ninety feet below. I leaped into space and landed on a narrow shelf beside the chute. I was completely alone. I couldn't go back. I waited. After awhile, one by one, the others came.

"You are a brave man to come here alone," the Superintendent said in perfect English.

The ice was broken. Once more the principle of identification, of coming alongside my brothers had worked. I had earned the right to speak.

The ride home was as warm, animated and conciliatory as the earlier ride had been frigid and isolated. I sat in the front seat of the car. The pastors spoke English and were warm and communicative. And so I learned as much as I could absorb about the mine, the men, the pastors and the social work they were doing for the miners.

Finally, I asked Pastor Woreman. "Did that incident at the mine really happen or did I imagine it?"

"It really happened," he said.

"But why? Why did your men deliberately do that to me? You are pastors, I'm a pastor. We are Christian brothers. Why?"

A pathetic, reluctant smile played on his face as he answered. "The last days were all-out war, indiscriminate bombing. Every day the American B-17s came.

Every night came the British Lancasters. Every day large areas of our city went up in flames, leaving rubble and debris. Every day several hundred of our people were buried—men, women, children, grandparents.

He continued, "The worst thing that happened was on the morning after a particularly bad night. There were fifteen hundred burials. We were feverishly, desperately working to complete the burials when a fighter plane came in at a low level, strafing the people, first in one direction, then in another. We had absolutely no defense. Our anti-aircraft were out, even our small arsenal was without ammunition. Our aircraft had been destroyed.

"The flyer came in too close and crashed. The pilot escaped, still alive. The crowd attacked him with shovels, crowbars, anything they could get their hands on. What happened to that pilot should never happen to any man. He was an 'American,' he was the enemy. We haven't been able to forget the horrors, the madness of the war."

Then he added simply, "You are an American."

No more such dramatic incidents occurred as I visited refugee camps, youth centers, girls' homes, mission centers, the German YMCAs, and Christian schools learning the full extent of the Church's social work in Western Germany. I knew my own work would benefit from what I was learning.

Overshadowing everyone's thoughts was the question of what Russia would do if the Western Powers didn't meet Premier Khrushchev's ultimatum to be out of Berlin by May 27. I had to be in Scotland on that day, but I wanted to go back to Berlin once more before I left.

Pastor Schröder's response to this latest threat was certainly not low-key. I arrived in Berlin on Friday, May 23. Saturday I went with him to the Free University where 1,300 young Christian Berliners had gathered for a field trip taking them through the heavily guarded East Zone corridor which linked Berlin to West Germany. They would spend the night in the concentration camp where Anne Frank died and on Sunday hold a memorial service of repentance for the crimes committed there. Pastor Schröder spoke to them briefly before they boarded the buses.

"Remember," he said, "as you listen to the speakers who were themselves prisoners in that very concentration camp, that our nation needs to face the horror of what was done in Germany's name. Remember too, that a new day of freedom has been born in which all people may walk with dignity and respect. That's what you are doing today. Walking with dignity and respect in the face of this latest threat."

He was answered with a roar of approval.

"And next Sunday we will continue that walk. We will gather for worship in the Reconciliation Church, split by the East and West sectors of Berlin. We will be a living testimony that there is no line of division between East and West as far as the Church is concerned. The body of Jesus Christ is one body! The faith of Jesus Christ is one faith!"

Singing and chanting, the youth and their pastors boarded the buses. I was once again struck by the exceptional job Pastor Schröder did in inspiring these kids to a real and living faith.

"Are you worried about them getting stopped in the corridor?" I asked as he waved the last person onto a bus.

"Not even the most fanatic Communist would arrest 1300 kids!" he said with a smile. "In this very time when people's hearts are faint, we must take a strong position regarding our faith for all to see as a witness."

We spent the day together and that evening he put me on a plane for England where I completed my trip by seeing J.B. Phillips and the social work the churches were doing in the industrial areas of England and Scotland.

Helped by a slight thaw in the Cold War, May 27 passed with nothing more ominous than low flying fighter jets screaming over the city repeatedly.

I returned to the U.S. charged up and inspired by the quality of faith I had seen. Being in touch with people whose faith was so dynamic and alive in the face of such tremendous pressure was exhilarating. I understood why there was such a dichotomy of feeling about how Christians were surviving under Communism. Uwe was right. The numbers were less. As he said, "Communism works." The control of all parts of a person's life paralyzed the will, poisoned the mind and distorted personal beliefs. The Communist Party had created suspicion, dread and fear which made both friends and family suspect. The individual was left utterly alone and solitary with only the Party to turn to for support and reward.

But as Uwe had also said, the Christians remaining were a highly dedicated minority. I had seen people living like lights shining in a dark world. How could I convey to people at home the depth of faith among people who paid such a high price for their beliefs? How could I convey to American Christians their own tremendous potential for the ultimate of all that life offers us? Bishop Dibelius' closing words to me echoed in my mind.

"I am told that sixty-six percent of your people are at worship every Sunday. Yet you have among the highest incidences of divorce, crime, and juvenile delinquency in the world. What is there in your faith, in the character of your people, that will stand against this militant atheism when your times of testing come?"

With no overt challenge to our faith, it was dangerously easily to slip into comfortable, complacent lives and ignore not only worsening social conditions in the States, but also Christ's claim on our own lives.

Thinking about those warm, radiant Christians in the East made me realize why these contacts with the East were such a reciprocal blessing. Those in the East were blessed by knowing that they were not forgotten, that their brothers and sisters in Christ remembered them and claimed them as part of the worldwide Christian community. And we were blessed by seeing the depth and integrity faith brought to a life irrevocably committed to Christ. We who faced no persecution were charged to live life at the same level as did these stalwart followers who had to sacrifice all.

How much we would need that mutual inspiration would be thrown into sharp focus in just two short years when the hole in the Iron Curtain would be abruptly and brutally sealed.

CHAPTER SIXTEEN

THE WALL

"The difficulties are increasing here in Berlin. Now the telephone cables between East and West Berlin have been cut. We have to call Dusseldorf or London and ask our friends there to transmit news into the East for us. West Berliners need an entry permit to enter East Berlin and these are often denied to 'undesirables' such as Bishop Dibelius.

"During the Kirchentag (all Church) rally, he was given an ultimatum. If he preached at St. Mary's, his preaching church in East Berlin, he would be arrested and imprisoned. You know how the Communists have attacked him personally because of his strong stand against them.

"He did return and preach. Thousands of people crowded in and around the church. Informers were there, protected by the police, recording names for reprisal. Many, many people crowded up to these informers, insisting that their names be included on the list even if they couldn't get into the church. The Bishop was not arrested or detained this time. I think the authorities were afraid of the crowd's reaction."

This letter from Pastor Schröder in late July 1961, was to the Berlin group, a loosely knit group of people, who'd all been to Berlin. We met once a month intent on finding ways to stay in touch with the Berliners through prayer and lending any support we could such as sending money or supplies and writing letters of encouragement. Pastor Schröder's letter continued.

"I hope that all of our friends from Southern California know that we have more than 1000 refugees a day already coming in the last weeks. It is terrible. The camps are overcrowded. That's the democracy in the East. The Church has now a tremendous work. You can soon make your own impression about this situation."

Just four months earlier in April, Pastor Schröder had again come to the States on a speaking tour. His program was planned to provide maximum coverage in our area as well as visits to other churches in the Mid-West and Eastern United States, including Bethany Presbyterian Church, Haddon Heights, New Jersey, which had recently installed Ralph Hamburger as pastor.

Pastor Schröder's mission was to acquaint people with the situation of the churches and our Christian brothers and sisters in the East. His enthusiastic presentation, his radiant spirit, his faith and his optimism, with that incorrigible sense of humor, stole the hearts of people wherever he went.

Perhaps Brother Schröder himself best summed up the mood of the trip: "I have the impression we are not only friends, but belonging to one family."

Our Berlin friends invited the Berlin group to bring a delegation to the Dietrich Bonhoeffer House the following October to meet with youth leaders and lay persons for a ten-day conference hosted by the Bishop. We would learn firsthand of the life of the Church, particularly in the East Zone, with time for conversation and small group discussions. Dr. Erich Andler, the headquarters chairman and the chairman of the Protestant youth council in East Berlin, with his youth leaders and staff, had enthusiastically entered into the plans to further "strengthen the ties of Christian community" between East and West.

Pastor Schröder was responsible for the arrangements. His letters, increasingly ominous, were warning of impending crisis.

"People in the East Zone are taking the Soviet threats against Berlin seriously. In July more than 30,000 found refuge in the West, nearly twice the previous monthly average. More than 11,000 refugees arrived in West Berlin in the first six days of August!"

Hearing this, I issued a summons to all who had ever participated with any team in Germany, especially in Berlin.

"Our friends in the East may be headed for a time of real testing, pain, persecution and suffering. More and more they are becoming isolated. We must rally to their support."

I requested a gathering to prayerfully search out a support system of some kind to show tangible, continuing evidence of our partnership in ministry with these Christians and their ministry in the GDR (German Democratic Republic).

Twenty-six people responded. Meeting Saturday, August 12, 1961, was unanimously agreed to come together on a regular basis to maintain through Pastor Schröder an open correspondence with our friends in the East and to:

(1) Pray through every detail of a program of support;

(2) Become faithful partners by attending and participating in this support group;

(3) Contribute regularly to funds forwarded monthly to Pastor Schröder for emergency needs in the East; and

(4) Be available to respond in any possible way to the needs of our Christian friends in Berlin and the East.

For want of a better name, we called ourselves the Berlin Fellowship Group, our members being largely the same ones who had been meeting informally for over two years. We collected and dispatched to Pastor Schröder that day a purse of $520. Ralph continued to be closely involved from Haddon Heights, New Jersey, where he was a pastor.

In the early morning hours of August 13, an hour and a half after midnight, acting on Soviet orders, East German police and military units backed by tanks began stringing barbed wire diagonally across the city, sealing off the Soviet Sector, and barring all access to West Berlin. Armed guards patrolled this new border which, in violation of the Four Power agreement that Berlin was independent, and part of neither East or West Germany, effectively incorporated East Berlin into the Soviet Sector, the GDR. The flood of refugees was dammed, families were separated, workers could not go to their jobs. In spite of the swelling cry of international outrage, within days the barbed wire was reinforced with brick walls.

"Only a little more than one week and this is what has happened," wrote Pastor Schröder. "It was and is a turbulent time. August 13 the East closed the border in Berlin and nobody from the East Sector or Zone was allowed to come to the West of Berlin. The tragedies you could see at the border are impossible to describe. So they stopped the stream of refugees and also the workers living in East and working West.

"For the West Berliner going East they have developed a special control system and have changed it daily. Today West Berliners have to have a special permit. It is inhuman if you have to go to the East and I have to do it for our youth work. For the East co-workers it is at the moment impossible to come to the West. The border is closed with two-meter walls and thorn wires. It is like war. Now it is important to prove the brotherhood for all our co-workers in the East, but it is growing more difficult from day to day. You know that the greater part of our Church area is in the East.

Schröder's concern was clear, "The question is about the conference in October. As of now nobody from the East will have a permit to such a conference and the main point was to have the East youth pastors and leaders to this conference. You know how interested I was and am in this conference and our Church leaders too, but quite a number of our Headquarters staff are in the Eastern Sector. Shall we wait to see what will happen, or should we arrange the conference with West Berlin youth pastors and leaders?"

For the first time since I had known him, I heard a note of despair and fatigue in Brother Schröder's words.

"This is a hard time for our work here. You know that I try to be realistic, very realistic. Since 1945, in spite of all difficulties, we have built this youth work with the help of our Lord, but now I don't know the way we have to go. I try to be realistic about the difficulties and to help and to counsel where I can. Sometimes I have the impression that we have the same situation in the Church now as with Hitler. It is a dangerous situation. It is the situation of fighting against atheism and often you are very alone. Ralph phoned some days ago and I was so glad to hear his voice, but I could not say much by phone.

"Please give my greetings to the Berlin Group. I hope all are aware of the fact that we have a time of verification here now. Lots of young people are suffering and we have to help by prayer and in practical ways. Medicine is difficult to get in the East, so I am like a beggar trying to get the medications and transfer them, so the need is met. There is so little help. Before the Wall I did not have to be in the front lines because I had co-workers there. Now I have to do all myself and it is not easy. The control is hard. The difficulties are hard and I have the impression very often that I am alone.

"But I know that Christ gives his Presence if we are obedient. The obedience to Jesus Christ is now the number one question."

With these drastically changed conditions, I wanted now more than ever to go to Berlin. What better time could there be for standing alongside and identifying with our fellow Christians? I wrote to Pastor Schröder.

"It is our desire to do all we can to strengthen the hands of the Church in Berlin and the Zone just at this time by prayer and fellowship. I know you will tell us frankly what would be most helpful. Our prayers are with you daily. The Berlin Group continues to meet and all send greetings."

Right after the Wall went up, some West Berliners could still cross into the East. That was stopped by the end of August. Brother Schröder wrote:

"The difficulties are growing. The Bishop is not allowed to go into the East Sector, and the members of the Church Headquarters from the East are not allowed to enter West Berlin. I have no permit to enter the East Sector. All permits are given by the East government and I am sure that no permit will be given to the youth pastor, so I am now separated from all my co-workers in the East. But, in spite of all separations, we will have a common work in the Church. It is similar like in the era of Hitler. It is all the same, nothing new for us.

"The Border is more closed than a border of the State, but the Lord is greater than any border."

Pastor Schröder described one means the East used to get rid of unwanted persons.

"The moderator of the council of the German Church, Dr. Kurt Scharf, lived in the East and had a permit to enter the West sectors of Berlin daily in order to fulfill his work in the church headquarters. On August 31 as he went back to the East, the officials of State confiscated his passport and permit refusing to let him go home. That's the easiest way to put away the inconvenient persons.

"The struggle is hard and we have to work out our own program because the Church there is called a non-peace-loving organization. This is real scorn. You know that we live in a very hard position and situation, but we trust in the help of our Lord if we are obedient. That's only a little bit about our own situation, and we are working with all strength concerning the October conference."

The ten day conference in October 1961 was to be based on a Bible study of I Timothy. All participants agreed to study the material before coming and to surround the conference with prayer. Ten of us were coming from the States.

Ralph and I left early so that we could visit with Uwe and Gertrude Hollm in Tornesch. Uwe had written to me in September:

"I was very happy when I heard that you and Ralph plan to visit. Gertrude and I need your fellowship. I don't know whether you heard that we had our third daughter—it was in April—a lovely child. In July when I was in Berlin, I got a telegram which told me that she—Katrin was her name—had suddenly died. Gertrude and I were wonderfully comforted by the Lord. It is a great experience for us to realize that the Word of God which we had to preach to others in similar cases, really gives strength. After the funeral Gertrude said to me, 'Return to the refugee camps. I don't need you as badly as they do. I have God.'

"I have two job offers to consider. You can imagine that I really want to talk things over with you. Very often I think 'What would Walt James do in my place?' You know, Walt, that you are in a certain way my spiritual father and that in critical times you have been a help to me."

Uwe greeted Ralph and me at the Hamburg Airport and took us to Tornesch where we saw his beautiful new church, parish house and parsonage. A home for the aged was still in process.

Uwe and Gertrude were struggling over their future. Uwe had been invited to teach in Africa and he had been asked to be the youth pastor of more than fifty churches in Holstein.

"But I don't think our job is finished here," said Gertrude. "We need to be obedient and loyal to a given task before God can use us elsewhere."

Uwe groaned.

"Most of my parish people are industrial workers and apprentices in industry. What I teach and preach has to be so basic that I sometimes feel frustrated," he said.

"Doesn't the Church need to find some answers on how to minister in exactly this kind of situation?" I asked. "Some real answers that can then be taught to others?"

The conversation turned to Berlin, but I sensed that they would stay in Tornesch.

Uwe had been in Berlin giving pastoral aid at the refugee centers as people poured in just before the Wall went up.

"History may be repeating itself, Walt," he said broodingly. "As Christianity was wiped out by Islam in Africa in the early centuries, so it may go in Eastern Europe under Communism. And there is a very real possibility that West Berlin may be swallowed up."

By 6:30 p.m. we were flying on to Berlin. Pastor Schröder gave us a warm reception and took us home for tea. Mrs. Schröder was trying not to betray the deep anxiety that every Berlin mother must be feeling at this time. As Pastor Schröder said, "There is real danger now."

The rest of the team arrived the next morning and we gathered at the Bonhoeffer House. The leaders of this October conference were Bishop Otto Dibelius, Dr. Kurt Scharf, Dr. George Winterhager and Alfred Schröder, our host and chief expediter. Dr. Scharf gave a welcome and orientation to our group and the West German youth pastors and leaders gathered with us.

"I am so glad that you have come," said Dr. Scharf. "It was a great event when Vice-President Lyndon Johnson came to Berlin on August 19! It was a great event when General Lucius Clay and the 1500 American troops came to reinforce the U.S. garrison! Now the Church is here too!"

Lean and vigorous with bushy brows and an iron jaw, Dr. Scharf was impressive. From the very outset of the Hitler times, he had been in the struggle between the Church and Nazism. He became both brother and pastor to pastors experiencing political pressures and dangers, and he, had served as pastor at the Sachsenhausen Concentration Camp, interceding countless times with the Gestapo. He was arrested seven times and ordered to cease preaching, writing or residing in Berlin.

After being released as a prisoner of war in 1945, Dr. Scharf was called by Bishop Dibelius to become the spiritual leader of the Brandenburg area at the Church headquarters in Berlin. In February 1961 he had been elected moderator by the Council of Evangelical Churches in Germany.

"Since August 13, things are completely changed," said Dr. Scharf. "In the past people came to Berlin to escape oppression or to 'experience the other world,' the world of freedom. That gave them the strength to return and be different from the Communist world.

"Why is the situation so terrible now? The government is endeavoring to break the moral stamina of the population. Families are completely separated, cut apart by the Wall. Party members, protected by the Wall, have begun tightening control in all phases of life because no one can flee anymore. Let me give you some examples:

"Listening to TV or radio from the West is illegal. By the direction of their antennas, offenders can be located. Groups of 'Free German Youth' go from street to street checking antennas. They force offenders to sign confessions saying, 'We know that the West lies and we are happy now to be freed from their propaganda.'

"Teachers in school must make spies out of the children, tricking them into telling what stations their parents are listening to.

"Recently an East German pastor had two teachers, members of his congregation, come to him. They wanted so much to take the Lord's Supper, but felt they couldn't because of their shame. They had tricked some of their young people.

"Farmers, whose families have owned their land for centuries, are dispossessed and the farms nationalized. Now they work as common field hands. Their spirits broken, they have no interest in the harvest.

"Young people are forced into the military. For ten years the Communists have been telling the young people, 'These Western warmongers are trying to set East German brothers against their West German brothers. They are the enemies of peace, preparing for atomic war!' Now the Communists are arming themselves and the young people are asking why. The answer, 'Atomic weapons in the hands of Socialists are weapons for peace! The West Germans are not your brothers if they consent to be trained in the West German army.'

"The youth are angry at being forced into the military and assigned to dangerous duties. The overwhelming majority of the population distrust the Communist state.

"In these chaotic times, pastors have the confidence of the population. They are the one thing that has not changed. This confidence was greatly increased by the elections last month on September 17. Because there was only one party and no choice, many pastors said, 'We will have nothing to do with such deception. It is a denial of humanity and of conscience.'

"In spite of intense pressure, over half of the pastors in the GDR did not vote. Many who did wrote 'NO' on the ballot. Those who didn't vote or who wrote 'no' are now subject to constant pressure and chicanery.

"Fellowship groups outside the Church have been closed down. There can be no more prayer circles in homes, team work in factories and Bible studies among various professions."

Dr. Scharf ended his chilling review by saying, "It is the unanimous opinion of the church leaders that if the twenty-two divisions of Russian troops in East Germany were removed, the Ulbricht regime would be overthrown within twenty-four hours. But the divisions will not be removed. Our advice to pastors in the East is to remove all longings for the West and to form and nourish cell groups for worship and fellowship."

Sunday afternoon we went to look at the Wall—the "Wall of Shame" the Berliners called it. It was shocking to see the Brandenburg Gate no longer a gate but a barrier, to see people on both sides waving to family members across the wire, to see bricked up homes incorporated into the wall, one with a flower memorial below a second story window where a woman had leaped to her death trying to escape. For me the most shocking of all was to see that "No Man's Land" actually incorporated as a line of demarcation between East and West, the great Reconciliation Church abandoned and destroyed, its front bricked closed.

Brother Schröder was standing with Ralph and me as we silently stared at the church.

"Horst and Heinz were co-workers in the Reconciliation Church and they are warm friends," said Pastor Schröder slowly. "They used to just live across the street from each other, but their street is the border separating the Russian sector from the American. Now they live in two separate worlds."

Pastor Schröder's Bible study on I Timothy, the focal point of the conference, started the next morning. The Apostle Paul's letter to Timothy, a young neophyte pastor charged with maintaining the church at Ephesus, proved particularly appropriate for illustrating the Church's and the individual Christian's role in responding to the Communist threat to faith.

Seldom have I known a man who commanded such wholehearted allegiance and respect for what he believed and taught. These Bible studies revealed much of the secret of his influence and power. Pastor Schröder, instinctively and perhaps subconsciously, walked in Dietrich Bonhoeffer's footsteps.

"Our job is not to try to knock down this Wall," he said. "Our job is to make it transparent for Jesus Christ. We do this through the bearing of our brother's burdens. And when we share his burden, we discover Jesus Christ. Christ is greater than any obstacle. He is pragmatic and realistic. He gives us simple commands and expects simple trust and obedience.

"This is my question for the Church in the East and the West, 'What are we doing? Sharpening our weapons? Developing methods?' Rather, we should be searching out the clear word of God. The only way to be effective is to make time for a half hour of Bible study and meditation at the beginning of each day, in order to see what God has to say to you, to know the truth of the Gospel for this day."

The shape of what made this man so effective began to emerge as he taught us. First was his consistent, prayerful, daily searching out of biblical guidelines and spiritual priorities. "What is God's command, God's plan for this day? We find this plan," Schröder emphasized, "through daily Bible study and meditation and through simple faith, simple obedience and simple trust. "The real answer is that something results, not by our efforts but by Jesus."

Second was his emphasis on spiritual community. "We are belonging together," was one of his favorite expressions. "To be effective we must work within the Church, because together we are links of the body of Christ." Bonhoeffer said, "Christ coming from my own heart may be weaker than coming from the lips of another! Today, I am sure! Tomorrow, I am not!"

Third, Pastor Schröder knew without a doubt that the call of Jesus Christ is not a dream, but a very realistic thing involving the details of how to deal with all situations. As an example, he used the pastors in the East.

"In the East, some ministers try to compromise with the political system," he said. "They have no weight or influence. They are not respected by the officials or the people. But those who have not compromised are respected even by their enemies because they look to Jesus Christ and not to the people or State they have to work with."

Finally, Schröder's living faith was versatile and open to the new realities and the new priorities of a drastically changing scene. He reported that "In the East a pastor had said, 'There are no more possibilities here. Should I go to another parish?' That is a great temptation, but he is there by God's command. He stays. Then quite another new type of ministry develops. People come by night. Personal contacts are made. Relationships develop. These personal relationships and contacts may be more important than the sermon on Sunday. This is the way we have to meet now. Not in groups, but the original way of Christians, by helping the individual!"

His was always "the little way," finding the loopholes that made it possible to survive and to succeed in a system that "allowed no room for the Church or the Gospel of Jesus Christ." He had a persistence that knew no limits. Again and again he would say, "Our Lord is greater than any walls! Any obstacles! Look always at the positive things about a man and about a situation and find "the little way!"

It dawned on me that Brother Schröder's method was the same one we used in Deputation: Prayer, finding the Biblical guidelines and then applying what we learned in helping our brother, all within the context of the Christian community.

The tension in the city surrounded us. From time to time in the mornings we could hear rocket fire, machine gun fire and even cannon fire. Ernst, one of the conference participants, lived fifty yards from the border of the Zone. He said that almost every day they could hear the sound of firing. Sometimes they actually heard the cries of the wounded.

Every night another small group would attempt to escape. Some succeeded. The night before we arrived a bus crashed through the barbed wire and nine German boys escaped. The next night four came over in a boat.

The People's Police discouraged aid from the West any way they could. Some East German boys appeared on a housetop, calling for help. Neighbors called the Fire Department who spread nets; whereupon the supposed "escapees" bombarded them with sacks of red paint which burst and showered the firemen. Another time, some young men appeared by a wire section of the

Wall crying for help. When four West Germans responded, two were shot by those asking to be rescued.

Our days in Berlin were not flooded with mountains of detail or propaganda, but rather with firsthand exposure to the persons and the realities in the life of the Church, both East and West. Always the message was the same, "It is good that you have come just at this time."

George Winterhager told us that since May 1959 a plan had been in place in case the border should be closed. A thirteen-man Council was now functioning in East Berlin, replacing the leaders who could no longer cross the border.

"East Germany is the land of the Protestant Reformation," he said, "the land of Luther. We have strong people there."

Bishop Dibelius spoke to us one evening. "It is a special joy that you are here on the spot at this time! It is good that here East and West could come together. When the situation in the East looks discouraging to you, remember that the primary thing is not what a Church does in a totalitarian system. The primary thing is that the Church exists in a totalitarian society!

"What can you do to help? Individual letters are a strengthening force. 'We think of you. We pray for you.' There should be nothing political. Tell us nothing on Communism. Just write in a personal way. It will be contagious. People will tell each other, 'There are people in the West who think of us! Who pray for us! Who pray for us all the time!'

"You can provide sustaining help, materially, morally and spiritually for this Island City of Berlin. When you support the Christian witness of the Church in West Berlin, you make us your envoys to the East."

The Bishop ended by saying, "That you examine the situation on this spot is of mutual help, not just for you, but for us. It is a positive reassurance and a positive evidence that our brethren are concerned and continue to support the work of Berlin."

As the days of this 1961 Berlin conference progressed, I realized that these veterans, these old campaigners of the Hitler times and the Confessing Church—Bishop Dibelius, Dr. Scharf, Pastor Schröder and Dr. Winterhager— were ideally gifted and prepared for this East-West confrontation. They were profoundly sensitive to the world-wide implications of this socialistic and atheistic system which, like Nazism, was willing to use force without compromise.

"Once more," said Pastor Schröder, "The right of the church to fulfill her mission, to evangelize, to grow, to go out and proclaim the Gospel to all men, must be purchased at a great price."

Stories of persecution in the East Zone kept coming. Some young East Berlin Christians were on the coast of the Baltic Sea at a camp. The youth wrote a letter to the ship captain as a joke, 'May we stop at Denmark on our return?' The captain reported it to the police. The police came to the camp, checked luggage and found a poem reflecting negatively on President Ulbricht. All twelve people were put in prison. The public prosecutor asked for five years' imprisonment for the two leaders. Almost the entire parish came to court pleading that the letter was a joke, but the leaders were condemned to eight years in a reformatory, and the others to three months to one year in prison. The prosecutor apologized to the judge for not realizing the seriousness of the crime and asking for a stiffer sentence.

A second story came from a small city near Berlin. On a Sunday afternoon some kids on motorbikes were downtown looking in shop windows. Police came with half-tracks, surrounded the area, and picked up the kids. For days no one knew where they were. A mother asking at the police station about her son was told, "It's none of your business!" Some finally returned, but the others were pressed into the People's Army.

A week after the conference started, a small group of us decided to see if we could go into East Berlin. Theoretically, anyone other than West Berliners could enter, and we knew that some West Germans had gone back and forth. Checkpoint Charlie, the border station manned on one side by U.S. troops, was the only point of entry for us.

Under Ralph's leadership we boldly approached the checkpoint requesting permission to enter East Berlin. We were surprised to learn that we were the first foreign civilians to pass through.

The U.S. soldier on duty said, "We have no diplomatic relations with the so-called GDR. Sign your names, addresses and telephone numbers here. If you don't come back by midnight, we will notify your relatives."

I thought he was pulling our leg. Moments later I wasn't so sure.

Checkpoint Charlie consisted of a series of parallel concrete barriers alternately extending from opposite sides of the street, set so that a vehicle could, by weaving back and forth, pass through at about one mile per hour.

Our hosts on the other side were neither friendly nor hospitable. In fact they were, without exception, convincingly mean and ugly! We were stopped dead in our tracks because a group couldn't pass beyond this point. The guards, armed with "burp" machine guns and bayonets, blocked our path shoulder to shoulder. Immediately to our left was a prison with men peering fearfully from behind bars. One overweight elderly man was being taken into custody as we stood there.

Ralph, veteran of the Dutch underground, courageously entered the headquarters, housed in the same building as the jail. After what seemed like hours—actually only fifteen or twenty minutes—he reappeared, and looking neither to the right or left, walked past the guards and on into East Berlin.

I was next. I spoke no German, and if I had, I probably wouldn't have admitted it. Each of us carried only our passports and four D Marks, about one dollar—nothing more. I was also detained for a period and asked many questions, all in German. I didn't have to appear dumb. I was dumb! If I'd had any hair, it would have been standing on end! I realized the complete vulnerability of being confronted by authority which had no respect for human dignity or human rights. It was terrifying.

"When you put yourself in a position where God can use you, there is a Presence that comes into your life. You can do what you need to do. You're not afraid."

Dr. Hamel's words, spoken to me in 1952 before he confronted the East Berlin officials and disappeared, filled my mind. For the first time in my life those words were real to me in experience. I was no longer afraid and have never been again.

Finally, I was dismissed and permitted to pass down Alexander Platz and on into East Berlin, closely followed by a policeman, machine gun at the ready, and a guard dog pacing beside him. I felt as if people with binoculars were peering at me out of every window.

I made my way to the church offices, our arranged meeting place. Ralph was there with Dr. Erich Andler, the top-ranking church official in the East since Bishop Dibelius and Dr. Scharf had been denied entrance. It was for Dr. Andler and his youth pastors that our conference had originally been planned. Eventually, the other three team members arrived. It was a highly emotional, soul searching time as we met with Dr. Andler and shared the feelings aroused by personally experiencing the hostile, suspicion-laden atmosphere that our fellow Christians lived with daily.

"Is it dangerous for you to have us here?" I asked.

"We cannot live our lives in fear!" was his stalwart answer. "The work of the Church and the Kingdom must go on."

We learned from Dr. Andler that the Berlin and Brandenburg Synod was holding its meeting just at that time. He said it wouldn't be wise for all five of us to go, so Leonard Picker and Ralph Zorn got the honor.

Ralph Hamburger, Dr. Carroll Shuster and I stayed and talked to Dr. Andler.

"Ever since August 13 people have felt like they are in a prison," he said. "We pastors must convince the church people that this new border is permanent. One of our most important jobs is to counsel young people, particularly regarding military service. We have printed a small pocket Testament for military personnel. We advise the Christians in the military to join together and form a fellowship within the armed services. Since we can have no access to the military, the problem is how to help them do that. These young people look to the church for truth."

"Is your preaching restricted?" asked Ralph.

"We can preach with some measure of freedom as long as it's not political. There are spies in the worship services. We must be very careful, because new laws have been passed which can instantly and severely restrict the personal freedom of any individuals who might be problems."

"We've heard," said Ralph, "that church attendance is up?"

"Yes. Since August 13, church is the one place where people can come and hear the truth and where they can feel a homey atmosphere. The young people ask questions with absolute confidence in the pastors or church workers. A new trust in God is emerging."

"What can we do to help?" asked Dr. Shuster

"Just love us and pray!" said Dr. Andler. "Keep in contact! It is good that you have come today!"

We sensed the warmth of the man and his loneliness. He was from West Berlin, where his family remained. Years before he had voluntarily taken residence in the East, a true act of identifying with those in need and under oppression. The sun was setting, throwing the room into shadow as we prayed together. It was heart wrenching to walk away and leave him behind.

"Remember, we love you," I said, my voice gruff with emotion.

"Should we leave separately?" asked Ralph, concerned with endangering him and his work.

"No, no!" he said, impatient with such restrictions, but at the same time walking to the window and glancing apprehensively through the curtains.

"We'll leave in two groups," said Ralph quietly.

Dr. Shuster spoke with great feeling as the two of us left. "We can go back to our homes and freedom. We leave this wonderful man here alone to face a very uncertain future!"

As we walked toward the Brandenburg Gate, it seemed to me that there were more new buildings and well-stocked stores than I had seen two years before. The few people we saw were less shabbily dressed and there were some children playing on the streets. People walked freely, as did we.

At the Brandenburg Gate we were cautioned by a scowling policeman to get back across the street and onto the curb in a hurry. We did! Soldiers patrolling with machine guns checked our money. No East marks could go West.

When we returned to enter Checkpoint Charlie, the control officers on the East side were surprisingly courteous and friendly. They gave us a list of places in the East where money could be exchanged, meals bought and purchases made. We could carry a camera, they said, but could not photograph soldiers or military equipment.

What I considered the greatest serendipity of all and the crowning realization of all our dreams for the 1961 Berlin Conference was the discovery that the Synod of Berlin and Brandenburg (of which Bishop Dibelius was the chief officer and Dr. Scharf the moderator, even though they were barred by the GDR from attending) was at that very time in session in East Berlin. When we gathered again at the Bonhoeffer House late that evening, I was eager to hear Ralph Zorn and Leonard Picker tell about their time with the commissioners at the Synod.

"Some of the commissioners had actually walked for several days to get there because they had no automobiles or the money to ride a train," Leonard reported. "I wonder if I would do that? They depended on fellow ministers and Christian families for food and shelter en route."

"This is a desolate time for them," Pastor Schröder reminded us. "But it is also the first time since August 13 that travel restrictions have been eased enough for them to meet at all."

"When the commissioners saw two American brothers come in, they wept!" Leonard continued, his voice choking up. "They said, 'We didn't realize that anyone knew or cared what was happening to us.'

"I felt so helpless to do anything for them," he said. "But I know our being there meant a lot."

"And it will mean a lot to many others," Pastor Schröder added, "because you have spoken with 'Christian multipliers' in the East. They will be telling about the visit of American brothers throughout the East."

"We've been hearing stories of family tragedies caused by the Wall," said Ralph Zorn. "In fact, Leonard became involved firsthand today when we met an East Berlin pastor and his wife at the conference. She was in West Berlin visiting friends with their eleven-year-old son on August 12. She woke up on August 13 to discover herself and her son cut off from home, husband, family and parish.

"She knew she must take her place by her husband's side, but what about their son? Should she take him back to spend the rest of his life in a prison world, devoid of freedom and subject to persecution? Or should she leave him in the West, perhaps not to see him again? She left him in the West! It's been nearly two months since then and she has had no word of him. She was desperate to know what was happening. Was he being housed and fed? How, and by whom? She and her husband were devastated, beside themselves, in tears.

"Then Leonard went, as only Leonard can," Ralph Zorn said, smiling, "and put his arms about her and said, 'Don't worry, dear. We'll find your son for you. If he's not already cared for, we'll see that he's placed in a fine Christian home. We'll see to it that he is housed, cared for and properly educated. Tomorrow we will come again, so that you may know all about it.'"

That was quite a commitment. But Leonard, a new-born Hebrew Christian, a top executive of the United Artists Studios in Hollywood and a man of tremendous love and compassion, did exactly what he said he would do. Through Pastor Schröder, he found the boy, who was living with a doctor and his family. Having an extra person had created a money problem for the family, so Leonard gave them money and guaranteed that support on a monthly basis. The next day Leonard took two more team members, Bob Young and Dave Crawford, and with their pockets loaded with items hard to find in the East (coffee, chocolate bars and ball-point pens) they braved the border crossing again.

Understandably, the pastor and his wife were overwhelmed by Leonard's actions and the speed with which he carried them out.

The next day we went to West Berlin's Marienfelde refugee center. The flood of refugees which had been pouring in since August 13 had been effectively stemmed. Nevertheless, there were still escapes from the East. Marienfelde at this time accommodated less than 300 persons. Before August 13 there had been from 2,000 to 5,000 people there. Some of the escapees were older people and families, but most were young people between ages seventeen to twenty-five. Three girls to whom we talked had found maps of the sewers and waded through them from the East, sometimes in sewage up to their necks. One family group of father, mother, small child, grandfather and grandmother made their ways over the wires on boards. With only seven minutes to get across between changes of the guards, they made it in five.

Some cut the barbed wire; others tunneled under the barriers; some swam the Havel River which was patrolled by heavily- armed speed boats. Two boys buried themselves in the coal tender of a train, and many jumped from buildings and roofs, all at the risk of their lives.

Suddenly it hit me as never before. In one night, 40,000 workers, troops and People's Police had effectively closed a border of twenty-two miles across the middle of a city of between three and four million people, separating them into two entirely different worlds. One was a world of freedom and opportunity, the other a prison world. It became clear to me what a tremendously vital and crucial task these leaders of the church had taken upon themselves: the task of maintaining the unity and integrity of the Church, and of obeying the mandate of Jesus Christ to claim this broken, decimated, wounded world as the Kingdom of our Lord and Savior, Jesus Christ. To our amazement, they wanted us as partners in this task.

Pastor Schröder's Bible studies, centered in 1 Timothy, built the foundation for this partnership in ministry, a partnership and a brotherhood in which we were to share more than we could possibly realize at the time.

"Brotherhood among Christians means responsibility. It is a permanent task," he said. "This brotherhood is more dynamic, more spiritual than any other fellowship we see in this world. This brotherhood must be renewed day-by-day! It is not an easy thing.

"Sometimes I like to push the brother away because he makes difficulties for me. He thinks another way. He has a different theological system. We have to see that our brother is also a creature of God and that Jesus Christ was crucified for this brother personally. Between you and your brother always stands Jesus Christ!

"The strength of the brotherhood comes from the Gospel," Schröder emphasized. "The Gospel, not your own ideas, is the basis for the brotherhood. You must train yourself in the Gospel. You cannot say one valid word to your brother, if you have not this training!

"In order for the Gospel to make the brotherhood, you have to pay a high price: obedience to God. You are asked to say 'Yes' to this obedience! A living obedience! A positive reaction! Absolutely, 'Yes! I will do it!'

"Even if you cannot see the results," he continued, "trust the Word of Christ. Jesus Christ is the only existing hope! Our church life must be an example of this fact, a very extreme example. In the Gospel are answers. Answers! We must stay in this training of the Gospel; otherwise we are not sure of our answer! The Living Christ! This man who makes us an example. This one who is the Savior of all men: rich and poor, dark and light.

"We have to obey the orders of Jesus Christ. All I can do is to remind you of the orders of Jesus Christ and you can remind me. That is enough. Be obedient to the orders of Jesus Christ. This work which we have to do is not of ourselves; it has been entrusted to us by Jesus Christ.

"Sometimes we hesitate to pass on Christ's orders and teachings to others because we are not sure of these orders ourselves. Christian fellowship must have in its midst the orders and teachings coming from Jesus Christ. We must follow him, walk in his footsteps. It sounds extreme; It should be! In all the world the trend is to normalize Christian teachings, to water down the truth of the Gospel, to dilute it.

"All appeals, all exhortations must come from the Gospel itself, not from me, in order to be effective. Teaching otherwise means compromise. It is as possible to compromise with the system of democracy in the West as with Communism in the East. Our task is to live as soldiers of Jesus Christ in the very strong battle of today. Fight the great fight of faith!

"Trust the Gospel first, then you can trust the Gospel more than you can trust yourself. It is important that you can trust the brotherhood in all moments; that you can trust the brother to stay in the same brotherhood, not only in the sympathetic situations, but at all times! No vacations!

Alfred concluded with this reminder: "In this way we have the brotherhood of Jesus Christ, even when oceans are separating us, even though we are not together daily, for this brotherhood of Jesus Christ is broader and wider than we think. If it is true that Jesus Christ is Lord, then we should see that distances mean nothing because he is Lord everywhere."

It was not that Alfred Schröder was some sort of spiritual giant, a special hero of the faith, or even a creative genius at Bible study. He would be incredulous and unbelieving if anyone spoke of him as such. It was simply that he took the Gospel seriously in his life, for all of his life. He believed and put into practice, through all of the challenges and experiences of his daily living, what the Scriptures had taught. And he admonished others to do the same. He really did look to Jesus Christ for results, not to himself. In his own inimitable brand of English, he got his points across.

After much discussion, we decided that this brotherhood would be based on intercessory prayer, Bible study, letters and visits.

"Guard against your prayers becoming routine or systematic," warned Pastor Schröder. "We must keep each other informed and have clear ideas of what we are praying for: eight kids in prison, a high school boy in the East who can no longer attend school, theological students being pressed to go into the army. And send us concrete news so that we might have a prayer fellowship together!

"But please pray without looking for 'success'. We are called to be obedient in prayer. The success is in the hands of the Lord. We have evidence here already that he will do it!"

A result of this Bible study was to bring us into a deeper understanding of one of Brother Schröder's favorite themes, "We are belonging together."

We would stay in touch through letters and tapes.

"In writing letters to people in the East, think about every sentence! Be very positive, write nothing political. Be imaginative. Stick in refills for pens, a watch, chewing gum,...," he reminded us.

On the final day of the conference, some of us went for one last look at the devastated Reconciliation Church just East of the Wall.

At one place along the East side, a row of apartment buildings had apparently been evacuated, bricked up tight and made a part of the Wall.

There had been a number of escapes along this stretch of the Wall. East Berliners would climb up on the roof, or find an upper-floor open window, and by some sort of mysterious prior arrangement would leap out into a fireman's net or some other device to escape into the West.

While we were there, a canvas-topped truck pulled over very close to a high building just down the street from us. A little man smoking a cigarette and wearing a leather apron, part of a crew evacuating an apartment, leaned casually out of a fourth story window. Abruptly he tossed away the cigarette, put his legs over the sill and leaped out, falling onto the canvas top of the truck. The truck came roaring in our direction. In the upper stories the People's Police promptly appeared and began hurling gas bombs at the truck. We found ourselves in the midst of the attack! With Bob Young of our U.S. group running backwards while taking colored slides of the whole sequence, we quickly made our escape.

Pastor Schröder saw us off at the airport.

Seared into my memory was the sight of the Reconciliation Church, abandoned and destroyed in that No Man's Land between East and West. But...But...the great tower of that church still stood, a majestic and a mighty reminder that with God there are no walls—East and West are ever and always one in Jesus Christ; one Body, one Life, one Spirit.

I thought about Brother Schröder's attitude: "We should learn to be thankful for these difficulties. They keep the church alive. Just as the Church was thinking, 'Now we can relax,' we have had to develop new methods to show that the body of Christ is a living one, that these walls are no separation for the body of Christ."

But how would individual Christians living behind that Wall, behind the Iron Curtain, be able to maintain a sense of unity, of being part of the body, when even the most simple expression of faith could cause harsh repercussions? Bishop Dibelius and Pastor Schröder seemed to think that we could help. Remembering the joy with which we were received in East Berlin, I knew that all of us connected with Berlin were eager to see if there were some way we could help make that Wall of Shame "transparent for Jesus Christ."

Opposite page: 1961 Berlin team—(left to right) Ralph Hamburger, Ralph Zorn, Pastor Schröder, Leonard Picker, Darrell Meyers, Bob Hoag, Dick Langford, Bob Young and Walt James.
Top: The Reconciliation Church behind the Wall in East Berlin. The sign says, "The Wall must come down."
Left: The Brandenburg Gate, once a major thoroughfare, blocked by the Wall.

CHAPTER SEVENTEEN

THE CHALLENGE OF THE SIXTIES

With the passing of time, there did indeed develop a relationship with these sisters and brothers in the East, a relationship so compelling, so binding as to become irresistible.

But our relationship with these people didn't come quickly or easily. Ideologically, the Marxist East German government was dedicated to the eradication of Christianity. Practically, the government distrusted the Church and its orientation toward the West, its insistence on maintaining institutional unity with the Church in West Germany, and it's refusal to recognize the new national boundaries. Because of this distrust and suspicion, contact with Christians from the West could be hazardous to East German Christians already in a precarious position.

Pastor Schröder described this tension in an April 1962 letter: "It is quite impossible to describe all the new difficulties in connection with the fact that all young men have to do their service in the People's Army. This would be a normal situation if this were a normal state. But in this atheistic, system service in the army is combined with atheistic education. The oath they have to take is so extreme that it is quite impossible to take it seriously. It is like an inflation of an oath. I think we have to give real Christian and biblical answers to our youth. We now have about twenty youth leaders in prison. We try to help them, but it is difficult. This is the minimum task of the Church today. If we are not obedient in these minimum tasks, all of the big programs will not fit and help. Thank you for your prayers and intercessions. You may be sure this is a very important work you are doing for us."

Ralph, and I, and the other Berlin Fellowship members did stay in close touch with Berlin. On November 13, just weeks after we returned from our October 1961 trip, Bishop Dibelius was in Los Angeles speaking to 3,000 people at an ecumenical day of prayer for the Christians behind the Iron and the Bamboo Curtains. Leonard Picker, the team member who had made the dramatic commitment to the pastor and his wife in East Berlin concerning their son's care and well-being, introduced the Bishop.

Tragically, Leonard died only ten days after he made that introduction. The Berlin Fellowship Group was ready to assume Leonard's commitment, but we heard from Pastor Schröder that the boy's family had decided, in spite of the pressure applied to Christian young people, that he should be with them in the East. Deputation teams in Berlin and visits between our linked parishes of Southern California and Berlin filled 1962 and 1963. In October 1962, a year after our team had been in Berlin, Pastor Schröder came to the U.S. on a month-long speaking tour. The impact of this man, who spoke with an aura of the power of God, was immense on our people.

In November that same year Ralph went to the Netherlands on family matters and visited with Pastor Schröder, with some of the pastors in East Berlin, and with Uwe Hollm. Both Pastor Schröder and Uwe wanted Ralph to come and work with them. The offers were tempting, but just as in 1961 Uwe knew he needed to stay with his work in the parish, Ralph knew that his work at Haddon Heights Church in New Jersey was not yet finished.

About that time Ralph sent me a document, formulated the previous spring by the Church in East Germany, entitled "Freedom and the Ministry of the Church: Ten Articles." In it was laid out the Church's role in a society dedicated to the Church's eradication. I was awed and humbied at how these people were not only maintaining their own integrity and identity as Christians, but were also advocating a strong role for the Body of Christ as an agent for peace and reconciliation within this hostile environment. A few excerpts demonstrate the spirit of the document:

"Jesus Christ sent his church into the world to proclaim the reconciliation of God to all men and to bear witness to the will of God in all areas of life. Whoever accepts God's word is not exposed to a pressing restraint, but moves toward a wonderful freedom. Whoever withholds himself from God remains under his judgment. It is God's will that we preach his word confidently without fearing or pleasing men. The church may trust the power which is inherent in God's word.

"We fall prey to unbelief by imagining that the word of God should gain for us influence or prestige.

"We act in disobedience when we stand silently by while justice is being abused or destroyed because of political or economic interests, and when we do not stand up for our neighbors who are being deprived of their rights and threatened in their humanity, to suffer with them.

"...Christians must be servants of reconciliation in the world. This ministry obliges us to seek peace also in temporal affairs. Even if we get caught between the battle lines of a peaceless world, we take pains at every station to be agents of reconciliation and to bring peace by apt decision and action. We don't give way to hate or to the urge for revenge because they contradict the reconciling will of God."

Powerful words, I thought, applying to Christians surrounded by the materialism of the West as well as to those living under Marxism in the East.

The Berlin Fellowship Group continued to send Pastor Schröder monthly support which he used in the East for medical care, theological books, Christian literature, food and transportation for pastors and laymen. He continued to send us taped Bible studies and we exchanged specific requests for prayer.

In March 1963, Alfred's letter contained good news.

"And now I think I have to report that the leading conference of our Church has called me to become one of the co-workers in our church headquarters. Eighteen years ago, just after the end of the war, I started the youth work of our Church in the midst of the ruins of houses and the ruins of men. The Lord was in the midst of this work, in the midst of the hunger, the illness, the troubles. He confessed himself in this work, done only with Bible study and prayer, the same as he is doing behind the Wall now."

It was hard to imagine the youth work in Berlin without Pastor Schröder as its leader, even though I knew at headquarters its oversight would still be his responsibility. In my life-time I have known few leaders of youth who have had as many as 5,000 active youth participants at one time. Alfred Schröder had 45,000 in twenty districts, East and West; also thousands of adult volunteers he had trained who were working under the most taxing and challenging circumstances. A devoted and effective student of Bonhoeffer, he was a simple man of faith and integrity who daily gave his life for what he believed and taught. Thousands of young Christians gladly laid their lives and destinies on the line to follow in his footsteps. He is the most remarkable and effective of all the youth leaders I have ever known.

The pressure from the GDR intensified. "I should not say much in a letter," wrote Pastor Schröder in July. "One of the boys in jail, age 22, is having difficulties with his eye. Another, age 19, is losing his hair. Sometimes I think our help is only a drop of water on a hot stone, but it is more. Since I'm working in the headquarters, I realize that the burden of our responsibility is growing, and how much help and counseling we have to give."

In October the autobahn, West Berlin's link to West Germany, was blockaded for a period of days, an example of the continued harassment, said Pastor

Schröder.

But then in December 1963, just before Christmas, the East German government began issuing permits allowing West Berliners to go into East Berlin. This lasted about two weeks.

"It's hard to understand what has happened," wrote Pastor Schröder. "For East Berlin it was like an invasion. I was there several times."

There were other bright spots.

"We could see a wonder of prayer last month. After August 13, 1961 we had a number of youth leaders from East Berlin in jail. Among them were two condemned to nine years. Since that time we have had, in different parts of West Berlin, regular weekly meetings of intercessory prayer groups. The two were released from jail, allowed to come home and, a new wonder, they started again to lead their youth groups. Two years in jail instead of nine!"

But by January 1964, the Wall was again closed and pressure intensified.

"The connection with the East is growing more and more difficult. We have to find new ways of communication. The best way is the personal one, when someone from abroad with good understanding of the situation is here," said Pastor Schröder.

That was our hope and our prayer, to be that someone from abroad who could stand alongside our brothers and sisters under persecution. The Berlin Fellowship Group had again been invited by Bishop Dibelius to participate in a Berlin Institute in April 1964, meeting with West Berlin pastors for prayer and Bible study, and quietly in small groups visiting with East Berlin Christians. The Berlin Fellowship was a small, unstructured group because that kept more avenues open than a formal, official group might have. Nevertheless, we did operate through our denominational structure and the invitations from the Church in Germany always came through our church headquarters in Los Angeles.

In preparation for the institute, our friends in Berlin, we on the West Coast, and Ralph and two of his fellow pastors in New Jersey began a common Bible study on Colossians.

The disciplines we had found so effective in Deputation we continued in the Berlin group. The first was study: find the biblical guidelines, get educated about where we're going and study the language. The second was prayer: surround the event with personal and corporate prayer. The third discipline for Deputation was field work: find a place in our own community to be agents of reconciliation. Most of our lives already included that kind of involvement. So the third discipline took a little different twist and became the discipline of availability: taking the time out of already full schedules to be available to our sisters and brothers in the East.

Twelve of us, five laymen and seven pastors, were going to this Institute scheduled for the week beginning Sunday, April 5. Leaving April 1, we stopped first in New York and then in Geneva for orientation meetings with denominational and ecumenical leaders, and arrived in Berlin on Saturday night. Pastor Schröder took us to the Bonhoeffer House. The next morning, dividing into groups, we worshipped in three West Berlin churches. Bible studies and meetings started on Monday morning.

On two of the mornings, studies were led by Americans now working full-time for the Church in Berlin—Ralph Zorn and Ted Schapp.

Ralph Zorn had worked with Pastor Schröder after the war. I had met him when he was part of the team in 1961. Ted had been a pastor in Encino when Pastor Schröder spoke there in October 1962. Deeply moved by Schröder's spirit and message, and by my stories of our work, Ted packed up with his wife Lorraine and their three young children and, with a German uncle's help, by July 1963 was living in Berlin, attending the Free University and the German Evangelical seminary. When we arrived in April 1964 Ted had just been assigned to the Berlin Nikolassee Church and was working with the remaining refugees at a nearby camp. He served as one of our interpreters in East Berlin.

Dr. Kurt Scharf, moderator of the council of the Evangelical Church in Germany, gave us a report on current conditions:.

"I would like to connect directly with our get-together in 1961. In those days the total situation was tremendously tense. However, in the last two years, there has come about a recognizable liberalization of the whole situation in East Germany.

"There exists a freer discussion of the various questions, not only in printed church papers, but also in the public magazines and newspapers. Nevertheless, it is just as obvious that the goal of the government is to destroy the church and faith. The government no longer fights with the same rude means, through public law suits and long imprisonment, but seeks to mar the life of the church by administrative obstructions and by personal intimidation."

On Tuesday afternoon, dividing into groups of four so we would be less conspicuous, we ventured through Checkpoint Charlie and into East Berlin.

Since it was not wise to carry any written directions, we had all memorized different addresses and went from home to home visiting pastors and church members. It was a rainy, cold day, but the receptions we got were warm and wonderful. All people in the East, but particularly Christians, were so cut off from contact with the West that our visits were a real event.

My group met with Pastor Schelling and sixteen young people, all about fourteen years old, who had just finished confirmation classes. They were a radiant group of kids bubbling with energy and enthusiasm. Pastor Schelling was obviously proud of them.

"For these kids to join the church is a major decision," he told us. "It very well may mean that they have forfeited the right to college or vocational training. Christians choose not to be Communist Party members, so they lose the privileges that party members have."

The next day he and about forty members of his church were taking the teens on an outing to Wittenberg, where the home of Martin Luther, father of the Protestant Reformation, is located.

"I'd love to go with them!" I said to Ralph as he, Ted Schapp and I trudged back to West Berlin through the rain.

"I wonder if it would be possible to get a one-day visa into the East Zone," Ralph said thoughtfully.

"Very few foreigners have," said Ted.

Five of us decided to give it a try, and to our amazement, we got the visas.

Pastor Schelling was overwhelmed when five Americans showed up the next morning. Five members of his congregation generously gave us their seats on the bus and we were off on the ninety mile trip to Wittenberg. It was a memorable adventure and a real inspiration to have so much time to talk with these people. I heard then from the teens' parents what I would hear again and again through the years. They could tolerate what the Communist system did to them, but it was heartbreaking to see so many opportunities denied to their children.

Visiting with Pastor Schelling, I found that he knew one of the teenagers in the class was a spy, but welcomed him along with the rest.

For me the highlight of the day was when we all gathered in the Castle Church in Wittenberg, where Martin Luther is interred. Joining hands, we sang one of Luther's powerful hymns, "A Mighty Fortress Is Our God." I closed in prayer.

That evening both Dr. Scharf and Pastor Schröder were more than surprised that we had been permitted to go to Wittenberg.

"This is unheard of," said Dr. Scharf. "Please know that this kind of being together greatly strengthens the Christians in East Germany."

"We are grateful that you took advantage of the opportunity," said Pastor Schröder.

Beep Roberts, a layman from Ted Schapp's former church in Encino, told us about his group's experiences.

"When I was president of the Presbytery's United Presbyterian Men's Club, I started wearing our symbol, the Ichthus—a fish pin in my lapel. We were at Pastor Merkel's Bible study in East Berlin with some of his members and some men from the East Zone. One of the men from the Zone asked me about my pin and I told him that the Greek letters forming Ichthus stand for 'Jesus Christ, God's Son, Savior.'

"He looked at my pin for a long time, then finally said, 'Could I have that pin? I can't go home and tell people what I've been doing here. That's illegal. But if I had that pin and they asked me where I got it, I could explain its meaning and tell them that I received it from American Christians when we were having prayer and Bible study together in East Berlin.'"

Beep paused in thought. "A pin I wear as a matter of course, he's going to wear to declare his faith."

Dan Towler, a Methodist pastor and our first Black participant, spoke up. "Pastor Merkel says that if you're a neutral Christian, you're not really a Christian at all. By the way, Beep, how many of those pins do you just happen to have?"

"About 170," he said with a grin.

By the time we left, Beep didn't even have a pin left to wear home.

We ended our stay on Sunday by attending churches in East Berlin, the only legal places where the Word of God could be proclaimed, and the only place where more than ten people could gather without a special permit.

As we left, Ralph, as he often did, summed up the experience for me.

"Conventional Christianity in the East has become an impossibility. But danger and problems here do have the positive effect of forcing people to become very clear about their personal position and mission." He mused a moment. "We go to help ease their isolation, and we come back shaken out of our complacency."

Following the institute, Dan Towler and I went to see Uwe and Trude at the laymen's academy in Rissen where they had been about two years training lay leaders for the work of the Church. Then we went on to Amsterdam to see Ralph's parents.

While there, I received a letter from Louie Evans who had recently become senior pastor at a church in La Jolla, California. He asked me to join his staff as the minister of visitation and mission. I cabled back a quick refusal, remembering as I did so how his dad had pursued me for a similar position at the Hollywood church way back in 1946.

I called Louie when I got home.

"Walt, the La Jolla church is really serious about developing a program of social outreach. We need you here."

Praying through Louie's request, I realized that I was ready for a change. In my own mind, the extension of the church's ministry into the total community was a real priority. With Marguerite's enthusiastic agreement, I accepted the La Jolla church's invitation to join its pastoral team.

Since Louie was as much in favor of the Berlin Fellowship as I was, I knew that the change of locations wouldn't affect my involvement. I left my Presbytery job in L.A. at the end of July, Marguerite and I took a month off, and by September 1, 1964 we were in La Jolla.

Brother Schröder and I kept in touch. "Thank you for the week in Berlin and also for the fellowship together," he wrote. "It was a gift for me and also for our work here. I heard from East Berlin how thankful they have been for this visit and service. This cannot be expressed by words. I only can hope that the experiences you and the men had in the East may be worthwhile for your work too."

The rest of 1964 and 1965 passed with a continuing exchange of letters and people. Young people from California worked in Pastor Schröder's summer camps and Deputation team members helped in the Berlin summer youth programs. My secretary from Los Angeles, Joann Shira, a long-time Berlin Fellowship member, spent October, November and part of December 1964 working with Pastor Schröder.

"Walt, my life will never be the same again," she said.

In April 1965, the Berlin Fellowship sent Darell Guder, a pastor, to work with Uwe.

Trying to be Christ's reconciling agent, trying to stand along-side people in need, was not a concept limited to Europe. It was a principle of daily life for many people I knew. America in the 1960s desperately needed people with the commitment to find a spiritual basis for world brotherhood. Drugs among the youth, alienation over the Viet Nam War and deepening racial tension were some of the severe problems facing the nation. I could give many examples of the wonderful things that happened in the midst of these problems because of people's personal commitments to making their lives available to Christ, but I'll stick to just one!

When I was called in the early 1950s to develop and strengthen the Los Angeles Presbytery's work in the Islands of Need, Watts—a community of some 59,000 Blacks in south Los Angeles—was recognized as having explosive social ills. Our model in the inner city was to find the local leadership, usually in a neighborhood church, and to bring in well-trained Christian leaders to help them develop a program. That didn't work in Watts. What did work was to encourage and truly support the people at the grass roots level to develop their own programs under the indigenous leadership of the Blacks themselves. Our role was to identify with them all the way, to become partners in their own effort.

The people in Watts responded to this challenge with a will. They formed the Westminster Neighborhood Association, Inc. (WNAI) with their own board of management, largely Christians from the area. Their decision was not to invest in buildings and grounds, but to house the operation in four federally funded, low cost housing units. They used the oldest, least pretentious unit as headquarters so that all would feel free to come.

The groundwork was done carefully, taking plenty of time for the people to fully participate. An adequate budget was put together with funds largely coming from the Presbytery, but supplemented by United Way and other community sources. A staff person from my office was assigned to work with the WNAI board.

In August 1965 Watts exploded into five days of riots, caused by the rage and pent-up frustration of years of sub-standard housing, inadequate education and health care, lack of job opportunities, police harassment and blatant discrimination. It was the start of inner city riots which swept the country for three long, hot summers.

The burning, destruction and looting that took place in Watts was not indiscriminate. Most of the buildings marked "Blood" or "Soul Brother," meaning they were owned by Blacks or by people respected and trusted by the Blacks, were spared. The rioters themselves threw a cordon around the WNAI buildings and put people on the roofs with hoses to protect them from fires. Not so much as a lead pencil was lost. I imagine the rioters had no idea they were protecting a program developed by Christians of all races who wanted to identify with their brothers in need. They just knew they were protecting something important to them.

The Watts riot took place a year after I had moved to La Jolla. There I received a call from Archie Hardwick, the WNAI director, asking for immediate help. Accompanied by my new friend, Bill Gibbs, we drove through military and police roadblocks and through smouldering ruins to the WNAI offices. Archie told us that the people who were suffering the most were the Watts residents. They were terribly threatened by the violence, the burning and the looting. It was like a war. People dependent on Social Security or Welfare checks had no money because no mail was being delivered. No markets were standing, much less open. Many people were without food, clothing or shelter. Rallying a network of churches and church people, we soon had supplies gathered and delivered to Archie and his WNAI people. In a place as tense and volatile as Watts, Jesus Christ was our basis for brotherhood.

In my job at that time in San Diego (the city of which La Jolla is a part) I worked through the area churches to develop a model program for the denomination called Greater Parish Ministry (GPM), an outreach to the Blacks, Hispanics, Indians and the poor in the "less-chance" areas. The best possible person we could find to be GPM's first director was Ralph Hamburger! He agreed and by September 1965 he, Mary and baby daughter Rachel were in San Diego. I was thrilled to once again have them close and to be working on a regular basis with Ralph.

In April I had a letter from Pastor Schröder, updating me on Berlin. "You know through newspapers that we had a critical week in Berlin. In the East were maneuvers with parts of the army from the Soviet Union, jets and special noise. People became nervous and we learned once more the insecurity of this city. Six hours a day the autobahn was closed and we had miles of waiting cars and trucks.

"In spite of all this, we have now a new visiting period for West Berlin people to East Berlin. This is helpful. The personal living contact with brothers on the other side is necessary to continue the work of the church."

In any ministry there are problems. When that ministry goes back and forth across an ocean and involves different languages and cultures, it takes the grace of God, patience, skill and volumes of correspondence to keep it going. But the warmth of the relationships, the growth we experienced, the commitment from both sides to be available to Jesus Christ in whatever way he wanted to use us, more than compensated for any problems.

Having seen the joy with which our visits were received in East Berlin, Ralph, Dan Towler and I were eager to see if we could extend those visits into East Germany. We told Dr. Scharf and Pastor Schröder of our desire to travel in the Zone and meet with Christians as soon as it was expedient to do so.

When Dr. Kurt Scharf succeeded Bishop Dibelius as Bishop of Berlin in 1966, he decided the time was right to take us up on that offer.

CHAPTER EIGHTEEN

MIRACLES OF FAITH IN MARXIST LANDS

"...We want to prove ourselves genuine ministers of God whatever we have to go through...Our sole defense, our only weapon, is a life of integrity, whether we meet honor or dishonor, praise or blame...We are penniless, and yet in reality we have everything worth having." (2 Corinthians 6:2-10)

Meeting separately but simultaneously in East and West Berlin, the Regional Synod of the German Evangelical Protestant Church on February 15, 1966, united in unanimously electing Dr. Kurt Scharf as its bishop, succeeding the retiring Bishop Otto Dibelius, now in his late eighties. Bishop Scharf called Pastor Schröder to be his right hand-man with responsibilities for pastoral care—a job for which he was well qualified since he knew so many pastors personally inasmuch as they had started in his youth work.

I was elated when I heard from Pastor Schröder soon after the election that at that time there seemed to be no major restrictions on foreigners traveling in East Germany. He and Bishop Scharf welcomed Ralph's, Dan's and my willingness to go there and see if we could make contact with local churches.

From Pastor Schröder's earliest visits to the States, and from our first visits to Berlin, I had had the feeling we were being tried and tested for the day when we might be needed to go where these stalwarts of the faith could no longer go. But now that the day had come and our traveling into the East seemed a possibility, there were concerns. Although it was never said in so many words, our Berlin friends had some doubts about sending Americans into the GDR. Would we be able to handle the pressures, the constraints on freedom and the lack of personal power inherent in traveling in that regime? Did we have the discretion to be inconspicuous?

I too was concerned about travel arrangements in East Germany. Would we be able to get visas? Would Christians living under oppression want to take the risk of meeting with us? How would we make contact with them?

I responded to Brother Schröder by writing, "The heart of our trip to Europe this July will be to renew our relationship with you and with the work of the Church in Berlin and East Germany. We've been carefully planning.... We look forward to a summit conference with you to talk about the program of the Berlin Fellowship Group. We want to look into the future together to see what our relationships should be."

In May, after six months of preparation, a team of women from Los Angeles traveled to Berlin for a Women's Institute. They stopped to see Uwe and Trude's work in Hamburg-Rissen, then went on to Berlin for a program arranged by Frau Dr. Seeber and Pastor Ted Schapp. The women visited church schools, slum areas, youth centers, church hospitals, orphanages, and homes for the aged; also, they attended women's meetings. They went into East Berlin to meet with pastor's wives and heard their stories of discrimination against their children, of being charged twice as much for groceries, of ordering church material that never got delivered, and of other forms of persecution.

"The women's team is back home," I wrote to Pastor Schröder in June. "Last Saturday we met in Laguna Beach and had a most enthusiastic, heart-warming report from each member of the team. We are grateful that each time someone from here goes to Berlin and is exposed to the life and fellowship of the church in that part of the world, their lives are changed. It's evident when they return."

On July 7, 1966, Roz and Dan Towler, Marguerite and I left for Germany, going first to Hamburg-Rissen for a three-day visit with Uwe and Trude.

"Don't try taking anything illegal into the East, Walt," Uwe said grimly. "I tried to smuggle insulin in because there are thousands of Christian diabetics in the GDR who can't get it. They aren't 'good citizens.' I got caught and all the insulin was confiscated. That'll be on my record forever."

Uwe had been offered a position with the Lutheran Church in England. Trude and he were seriously considering it because the press of work would be less strenuous, giving him more time with his two young daughters and baby son, Jan.

In Berlin Ralph joined Dan and me for three days of orientation and visiting with our friends before we left.

Pastor Schröder told us, "In East Berlin we have seen what an event it is when Christians from so far away as California visit. Your visits strengthen them, give them new hope, new power to live as Christians on the other side. The Christians in the GDR (Russian Zone) are even more isolated than those in East Berlin. East German pastors say, 'The material help is not the same as the spiritual help. We need the personal contact and the opportunity to pray together because we can no longer pray alone.'"

"Recently, it has become possible for Church leaders from West Germany to get visas to visit with their counterparts in the East," said Bishop Scharf. "But that's only on the top levels and there's a limit to the number of those visits we can have. We don't want your visits to be official, connected with the church headquarters. We hope you can make contact with the individual parishes which are still quite isolated."

"Only small groups can go," said Pastor Schröder. "You may feel that that is not really getting the job done, but what you do are signs, a witness that we are belonging together, that we know that they are there!"

Ralph, Dan and I started early the next morning in Ted Schapp's square-back Volkswagen, loaded with luggage and such hard-to-get items in the East as chocolate, coffee and even cartons of cigarettes. Roz and Marguerite were going to Italy for the week and would meet us in Munich.

Crossing Checkpoint Charlie was again a memorable experience. We still were not sure we'd be issued visas. (Until 1966 getting a visa had been pretty much impossible because the authorities were so nervous about the "negative influence" of Westerners.) We parked in a special lot and went through passport control. Then a gate was opened and we drove into the next parking lot, walked into the Reiseburo and gave them the route Bishop Scharf had laid out for us, requesting accommodations in each town—Wittenberg, Weimar, Eisenach, Karl-Marx-Stadt, Dresden, and Eisenhüttenstadt. With little hesitation they issued vouchers for hotels in each place even including the latest time of day we were to arrive. We exchanged our money, the rate being about one-quarter of the dollar's value. It was a complicated procedure and each step cost us more money.

All this, and still no visas. But at the police station next door they were issued politely, with instructions that we were to stick strictly to our schedule. Any deviation would be considered an offense.

Driving decorously, we at last set off for Wittenberg only to be stopped at the edge of East Berlin. All of our papers were inspected again before we were permitted to continue.

The first place we stopped in Wittenberg was at our hotel, where, once again, all our paperwork had to be inspected. The clerk took our passports and vouchers and held them until we left the next morning. That procedure was repeated at each hotel.

We wanted to see the Luther House, which contained the most complete collection of Martin Luther artifacts in the world. As we walked up, the custodian opened the door.

"Are you Mr. Towler, Mr. Hamburger and Mr. James?" he asked.

We were completely nonplused. Communication with East Germany was limited and had to be circumspect. We had memorized names and addresses for each stop because Bishop Scharf didn't even want us carrying a list. As far as we knew, no one knew we were coming.

The curator, Professor Dr. Oscar Thulin, a very distinguished theologian and scholar, greeted us warmly and invited us to tour the Luther House and then to come to the Castle Church. When we got there, we found several individuals waiting, eager to meet us and hear news of the West. During our conversation, I mentioned that I was surprised that the Luther House and Castle Church were in such good condition since I knew the State wouldn't renovate churches.

"That's not always true," said Dr. Thulin. "If the church has a historic and cultural value, the State may put a great deal of money into it. However, it is very selective, interested only in cultural development. Nothing is ever done for religious reasons. These old cathedrals, beautiful as they are, are a real drain on a parish to maintain. We aren't allowed to build any new churches or religious centers at all, not even in the new residential areas where they're really needed. Any re-modeling done on old churches has to stay within the same foundation."

Talking with these people who couldn't even invite us into their homes, who couldn't meet outside the church without a permit, which probably would not be issued, I was impressed and humbled by their serenity, by their deep, abiding commitment to their faith.

"When can you come again?" they asked.

We were greeted by name at each of our stops. In Weimar and Eisenach, just as in Wittenberg, doors opened as we were about to knock. Since telephones were tapped and letters were read, I'm still not sure how it happened. But I didn't ask. We learned quickly not to ask questions, just to accept what happened and take things as they came.

In Karl-Marx-Stadt we had been told to be sure and meet Dr. Theo Lehmann, a youth pastor there. Theo had caused quite a stir a few years before with his doctoral thesis. A lover and devotee of jazz music and Negro spirituals, he had been fascinated to learn this music had its roots in the church. His thesis was on the history and theology of the Negro spiritual.

The state authorities, in the process of "de-Stalinizing" the country, were throwing out the songs used by Stalin to unite and encourage workers and were substituting Negro spirituals. They saw these as perfect propaganda stressing the plight of a people enslaved by a capitalist system. Completely missing the theology in Theo's paper, the authorities encouraged the nation-wide publication and distribution of his thesis. The music and its theology won the hearts of the people, causing quite a stir and some very red faces with its Christian impact.

When Dan, Ralph and I came to meet the Lehmanns, the state authorities had just left. They had told Theo and his wife Elke that rumors were circulating about their being immorally involved with the kids in their youth groups. That was just the beginning of the harassment that followed Theo and his family for his entire career. Then, as always, the rumors were completely discredited by the kids themselves.

Theo was too successful. He had started services for the young people in his congregation and kids from all over the city were coming. Pastors from other congregations were asking him to come and speak to their youth.

We asked Theo what was different about his services. "Well, for one thing, I have no long, black robe," he replied with a smile. "I'm coming to the young people as a normal citizen. And we don't sing songs that the young people can't understand. We have songs from our times. We have new songs because my answer to God's message must be my own, not the answer of my forefathers."

We asked him about the repressive measures of the State. He gave a surprising answer, but one we would hear again through the years.

"The problem is not the State," he said. "The problem is internal. People didn't read the Bible before Communism, so they certainly don't read it now. They aren't passing it on to their children. That's one of the reasons why I tell Bible stories in my services. People don't read the Bible, but sitting in church, they hear its stories."

In Dresden we met the Bishop of Saxony, Dr. Gottfried Noth. From him we learned more about the life of the Church in East Germany, about the adjustments it had to make in a socialistic system that limited and controlled it, left it without its traditional methods of support and was dedicated to its eradication. One clear example was the State's refusal to let Church members engage in outreach visits in the vast apartment complexes going up to house 40,000 to 60,000 people on the outskirts of most cities.

"I've been negotiating with the State for fifteen years to try to get compensation for the destroyed churches in Dresden," said Bishop Noth. "In the twenty-two years since the end of the war, we've only been able to build ten new churches and those were in the outlying areas, the smaller communities.

"We are developing outreach programs for the apartment dwellers, but we must be very careful because even to ask someone their religion is against the law. But we must do this outreach because the needs are so great. The people in the apartments don't know each other, often they're separated from their extended family, the husband and wife both work, the kids are in day care. So the family life is being destroyed."

I had heard that Professor Johannes Hamel—who had been imprisoned in 1952 because he spoke up against the expulsion of Christian students from East Zone universities—had been released and was now in this area. Bishop Noth confirmed that.

"Is he still active?" I asked. "Does he still speak out?"

Bishop Noth thumped himself on the chest and said, "He is as I!"

As with all the people we met, after just a few hours of visiting with Bishop Noth we felt like old friends. We loved these cheerful saints with their ability to live their faith at a level that often put us Western Christians to shame. As we went on to Eisenhüttenstadt, we discovered another miracle of faith.

Eisenhüttenstadt, the "Iron City" was designed to be a utopian Marxist city, a prototype for the GDR's new industrial cities in which there would be no churches, was built using beautiful architecture, with artistic mosaics and arty propaganda productions on entire buildings. But the Church still owned some land strategically located in the center of the city. And one highly dedicated young pastor, Heinz Bräuer, became convinced that God wanted a church in Eisenhüttenstadt. He managed to secure a twenty-six seat gospel wagon from a mission group and to get it delivered and parked on the church property. A big sign went up alongside the wagon which said "Protestant Evangelical Church." Three large, deep-toned church bells, found somewhere, were displayed prominently in front of the bus and rung to announce all services being offered.

Since freedom of worship is guaranteed in the GDR, as long as it's inside the four walls of a church, Pastor Bräuer hadn't broken any laws. But he couldn't invite anyone to church. That was illegal. He went around the neighborhood saying, "I am a pastor and there is a worship service if you are a Christian."

Eventually, so many people were coming to the church wagon that he couldn't hold enough services to seat them all. A tent seating 160 people next appeared on the property, but it too was soon outgrown.

Sensitive to the fact that public opinion was highly in his favor, the city administration granted permission to replace the tent with two large, creosote-covered army barracks. One became the place of worship, the other held the Sunday classes, manse and offices.

The barracks were so unsightly, that the authorities themselves were embarrassed and granted permission to landscape the premises. One part of the landscaping was a rock garden the exact size of the barracks used for worship. One Sunday morning, as if by magic, the barracks had been lifted and placed atop the rock garden, the exterior had been stuccoed white and a cross had been placed high near the entrance. The same three church bells were in front, summoning the people to worship.

We met Pastor Bräuer and toured his barracks church now complete with pews and a pulpit. He was eager for news instead of propaganda about the West, and was also eager to share with us about his work.

"I wouldn't trade places with any pastor in the world," he said. "I have a thriving congregation, mostly of families in their late twenties with two or three children. We have cottage congregations in every neighborhood of this city which was not supposed to have a church. And we are still growing!"

But even here amidst a growing congregation, Pastor Bräuer seemed lonely when we left and he too asked, "When can you return?"

At lunch in the hotel, Dan Towler, full of enthusiasm from our meeting with Pastor Bräuer, decided to bless our meal out loud.

"Dan," said Ralph, looking strained, "this is really not the right place to do that kind of thing. Those men over there, the ones in uniforms? They're Russian soldiers."

Ralph, having grown up under oppression and tyranny, was much more sensitive than Dan and I to the similar atmosphere in the GDR, to the military presence and to the power of the system. All three of us had chafed under the strictly controlled travel schedule with no possibility of changing plans, the inability to freely meet and talk with people, the aura of mistrust even at first among fellow Christians. Ralph was a bit amused at Dan's and my amazement when we discovered our hotel rooms were sometimes bugged and our luggage searched.

Americans, with their sense of fair play and assumption of human rights, would have to be carefully trained before coming here so as not to endanger the people they visited or themselves. But the pleasure of our brothers and sisters at seeing us, their sadness at our leaving, and the challenge we felt to live our own faith at their level reconfirmed our basic commitment to stand along-side these people in need.

From Eisenhüttenstadt we returned to West Berlin committed to making trips into the East part of the Berlin Fellowship program. We had our summit conference with Bishop Scharf and Pastor Schröder. They asked us questions and debriefed us. We told them whom we'd met, passing on what information we'd gathered and relating how we were received and welcomed in each place we visited.

"I'm impressed with what you have accomplished," said Bishop Scharf. "I would like to have these visits on a regular basis. Maybe twice a year? I will make sure the bishops in the East know about these visits, but you understand that you'll always have to go as tourists in order to go where you want to go."

"Yes," said Ralph. "We are very comfortable having this as a grassroots movement, nothing official."

"We are thankful to get these impressive, firsthand experiences," said Pastor Schröder. "The Lord is doing with you and through you his work. This is a Christian fact."

Before we had to leave he and I visited a while. He felt he was needed in the headquarters, but admitted that administration was not his favorite position. He often felt lonely, with people always looking to him for counsel and decisions, and sometimes resenting his continual emphasis on finding spiritual guidelines. We had developed a bond that let us advise and help, mutually encourage and strengthen each other even when we were far apart. This relationship was one of God's gifts to each of us.

In September of 1966, just a month after we'd returned to the States, Pastor Schröder's wife, Elizabeth, ill for many years, passed away. Their daughter Annelene was with us in La Jolla when Elizabeth began to fail. We managed to get her home in time to have a last week with her mother.

Brother Schröder wrote in October. "All has been a testimony of the victory of our Lord and I can be thankful in tears. I could report a moving story about the living work of our Lord and the truth of his words. Thank you for your prayers at the very moment of the funeral. The strength of our belonging together has been demonstrated in these days."

Ralph's, Dan's and my enthusiastic report to the Berlin Fellowship Group of our trip into the GDR and Bishop Scharf's request for two teams the following year, were the incentive the group needed to commit to the visitation plan. One hitch that Ralph and I hadn't anticipated was that both Pastor Schröder and the Bishop felt strongly that someone who had been involved for years and who knew the people and the situation should be on each team. That meant Ralph or me. We had planned on spreading the leadership around, but realized that would come over time.

A team of four led by Ralph left for Berlin in April 1967. They first visited the Hollms and J.B. Phillips in London, spent one night in Amsterdam visiting Ralph's parents, then went on to Berlin.

After two days of orientation meetings with Pastor Schröder and Bishop Scharf, the four went into East Berlin for the first Berlin Fellowship Conference in the GDR. About sixty ministers and laymen from East Berlin and many parts of East Germany attended the meeting at St. Stephen's Center, the church's social services center for housing the aged and helping the handicapped.

A Bible study on Isaiah, prayer, speakers on specific subjects and group discussions were the order of the five-day conference. There was general amazement that Americans were so interested in church life in East Germany. Ralph and the other team members were impressed with the fortitude and general cheerfulness of the participants.

"I thank God for Communism," said Pastor Bräuer, the man who had started a church with the gospel wagon in Eisenhüttenstadt. "Communism has placed the accents so clearly around what it means to be a Christian. In a hundred years of preaching we haven't succeeded in doing that. Now we're learning how to consciously live in the State, but not to accept its ideology."

"We can be thankful for the Wall because we again have more young people," said Dr. Appel, the director of a Church social ministries training center. "They can't flee to the West anymore, so they are making themselves available to the life of the Church. The Christian student association in Dresden is the largest with over 400 students. The one in Leipzig is just about as big. Both meet weekly for Bible studies, then divide into smaller covenant groups for discussion. Of course, all of this must take place within the church, never in private homes even for the small meetings."

There was general agreement that people who for years hadn't come to church were now coming. Bridges were being built.

"Why now?" asked Ralph.

"People are regaining their courage," said Pastor Bräuer. "They're seeing through the propaganda of the State.

"But it is very difficult to see through it when there is no news from the outside," he continued. "I came to Berlin convinced that West Germany was about to invade East Germany because that's what we've been hearing. It's only from the four of you that I've learned differently."

Another person spoke up. "I feel that for once I've been able to come out of my ghetto and get some new perspective. This meeting has stimulated me. What's important, too, is that we've been meeting each other and sharing about our churches and our situations. We really haven't done that before."

Germans often felt that Americans were babes when it came to theology, and perhaps we were. But one area where we really helped them was in group prayer. Some of the most moving moments of the conference came during prayer time when the four team members prayed audibly for others, modeling how to support another's prayer and how to share personal concerns. Just as Uwe had been profoundly effected by open prayer in 1950, so were these people—deeply committed Christians all—experiencing a new level of sharing and of supporting one another. By the last amen, tears were streaming down many faces.

"I've never heard anyone pray for me before," said Pastor Scharnweber from Rostock.

Ralph was asked to preach in an East Berlin church on the Sunday morning of the conference. He was kidded about the American accent his German had acquired and complimented on the theological content of his sermon. Conference participants asked for copies.

After the East Berlin conference, our team went to Wittenberg, Dresden, Eisenhüttenstadt and Rostock, visiting in many of the participants' churches and seeing friends from the previous year's trip.

It was a shock for the three first-time team members to travel in the GDR. Staying in St. Stephen's Center, just over the Wall from freedom and joining in fellowship with other GDR Christians had blurred for us the edges of this totalitarian state. From Ralph the team members learned, as Dan and I had, that a quiet, non-confrontational strength was needed to deal with the constant surveillance, the endless red tape, the wary officials. Occasionally, one could break through an official's mask to the human being inside. That was hard, though, because officials had other officials watching them.

The team met Pastor Friedhelm Merchel and his wife Edelgard in Dresden. Pastor Merchel was the director of the Church's city mission which ministered to circus people, Gypsies and others too marginal to matter to the Marxists. The Merchels had once lived in West Germany but chose to live and serve in the East.

In Rostock the team met with Pastor Scharnweber whom we had met at the conference, and with members of his congregation. Here in northern Germany by the Baltic Sea the Christians of Rostock were amazed that Americans would come so far. Pastor Scharnweber introduced the four of us to Pastor Rathke and told us the incredible story of Pastor Rathke's circus wagon church:

Heavily damaged by the bombings of World War II, Rostock needed a new church in a strategic, unchurched area. But new churches were not permitted. To build a new church was impossible. When young Pastor Rathke was appointed to Rostock, he learned that the Church owned some land in the area needing a new church. Somewhere, he found an old horse-drawn circus wagon. It was dingy, decrepit and obsolete. Somehow he managed to get it transported to the Church's land.

Unlike Pastor Bräuer's gospel wagon, this circus wagon was not usable in its present condition. Only some hard manual labor could make it so. But labor was such a valuable commodity that permission from the local authorities was required for anyone to give it even on a volunteer basis. This was particularly the case for a church project which wasn't on any priority list.

Pensioners (or retired people) gave generously of their time, and with their efforts the circus wagon was beautifully refurbished, inside and out. Pastor Rathke even managed to find thirty-five seats, an altar and other appropriate furnishings. The result was a tiny but attractive church sanctuary which obeyed the law regarding worship within the four walls of a church.

Like Pastor Bräuer's gospel wagon, the circus wagon was filled many times over each Sabbath until ultimately the authorities were forced to let a church be built.

Our team met in Pastor Rathke's church with members of his and Pastor Scharnweber's congregations.

"It's not possible to put into words what this visit means to us," a medical doctor told Ralph. "Can the four of you come again?"

Those sentiments were heard at each place the team visited.

The four of us returned to West Berlin and were debriefed by Bishop Scharf and Pastor Schröder.

"Much more contact with people was possible than when Walt, Dan and I had gone into the Soviet Sector on our previous trip," Ralph told them. "This time we met people at the conference who invited us to visit Christians in the East. There's a great need to be discrete, but people seemed to feel the fellowship is worth the risk."

"It is decidedly important for you to come," said Bishop Scharf. "Right now your visits are the most important thing we have in the GDR. We must repeat this."

"You can see how important it is to always have someone who has gone before with the team," said Pastor Schröder. "Having someone who knows the current situation and who can make the necessary contacts greatly simplifies matters."

The next team, again led by Ralph, went seven months later in November of 1967. The same schedule was followed: two days first in West Berlin, then a conference at the St. Stephen's Center in East Berlin and a week of traveling in the GDR. Pastor Schröder and Bishop Scharf emphasized how circumspect the team members needed to be in the East.

"The relationship between Church and State has not been this tense since 1953," said Pastor Schröder.

"Why is that?" asked Ralph.

"The Synod of the Church held its meeting in East Germany for the first time this year," he said. "Now the Reformation Celebration is about to start in Wittenberg. I think world attention makes the GDR authorities more nervous."

"Make no mention that you attended a conference in East Berlin while you're in the GDR," warned Bishop Scharf. "Don't mention your contacts with the Church in West Berlin. West Berlin is a real sore point to the GDR government because East Germany would have developed quite differently politically if the Berlin escape valve hadn't existed. Many of the skilled laborers and 80 percent of the college and university trained people fled to the West through Berlin."

"Make no mention of anything organizational. Bring no official greetings from your congregation to large groups," said Pastor Schröder. "If you're asked, say you are Christians visiting the Reformation places, seeing the beauty and progress of the land and also seeing some friends."

This eight member team was the largest we had sent and because it had members from different geographical areas, had not been able to prepare together, as had past teams. Members of the team felt some lack of cohesiveness among themselves. Some felt the orientation was incomplete. There was also some tension between the pastors' desires for theological discussions and the laymen's for more sharing time. We were experiencing growing pains.

In spite of this, team members and GDR participants were appreciative of the conference and the time together. The visits into East German parishes received glowing evaluations.

"Other congregations are jealous when they hear of our visits with you," said Pastor Bräuer. "You'll find virtually unlimited opportunities for fellowship in the future."

"You are like fresh troops coming to renew our courage," said another pastor.

Bishop Noth in Dresden said, "The joy which you Americans bring with you is real, and you are real. You are children of God whom we gladly welcome here. Your visitations are tremendously important for us. I tell people often of your existence and how you manage to come here and how regularly you do it. This is a real service, the kind we can use greatly on the part of the ecumenical Church. Come back soon."

To my delight, Goldie McCue, the English Bible teacher who had inspired me to become a real student long ago at Ohio Wesleyan University, was a participant on this team.

"Young in spite of her age," is how fellow team member Alice Young, who had been on the Women's Team a year before, described Goldie. Goldie's account of the trip made plain to me once again how reciprocal our relationship with the East was.

"This sense of oneness across the barriers of language, nationality and denomination was indescribably meaningful. Never have I felt a deeper sense of welcome and of 'at homeness.' It was a new dimension of fellowship, not to be compared with any other experience I have ever had. To meet such Christians day after day, to be a guest at their table, to move with growing empathy into their daily, costly choice of loyalty to Christ rather than a modern Caesar provides an opportunity that defies evaluation. My memory cherishes words of warm welcome, hearty handclasps and pictures of a dozen or more white handkerchiefs waved through the misty rain by those who had traveled miles just to set us on our way."

Even with the glowing evaluations, the growing pains were evident in this part of the trip too. Eight American team members plus Ted Schapp, the American pastor now living and serving in West Berlin, were too many to descend on an area at once. That many people needed to be divided into two groups.

"Let's have no U.S. invasion," said one GDR pastor. "One car is better."

Pastor Schröder came to La Jolla soon after the team returned, not on a speaking tour this time, but simply to rest. His heavy workload and his grief at his wife's death had tired him to the point where he really needed some rest and relaxation. Even so, he wanted to see Ralph's and my work, and his insights and observations were helpful.

Student riots were a huge concern and problem in Berlin as both student and race riots were in the U.S. Pastor Schröder and Bishop Scharf were heavily involved as mediators between authorities and the students. In La Jolla and the wider San Diego community Ralph and I were involved as mediators between communities who thought there were no racial tensions and the minority people who disagreed almost to the point of violence. We found that being agents of reconciliation in the Black-White confrontation involved the same principle as it did in the work camps or in East Germany—identifying with people in need.

"What are your dreams?" we asked when we came together in small groups with minorities. "How can we become partners in making these dreams come true?"

In La Jolla those questions brought the Black, Hispanic and White community members together, creating a community center in the heart of that affluent community which ministered to the housing, education and day-care needs of low-income, minority people.

Always we tried working in such a way so as to enable the people themselves to bring about the changes needed. Usually that involved a lot of dialogue, getting the differing groups together to air differences, bridge gaps and try to begin seeing each other as human beings.

Brother Schröder's letter in January reflected my own feelings.

"Students of the left disturbed the Christmas services and the New Year's services. We met with them to help them find positive answers. It is difficult and dangerous, but I think this is the genuine work of the Church."

These often violent manifestations of unrest were the background as the Berlin Fellowship Group formed the spring team for 1968. We recruited and trained Christians who would be able to answer sensitively the questions we knew our friends in the East would ask about the Black-White confrontation, student riots and American involvement in Vietnam. I was asked to lead the team. Casper Glenn, who had been unable to go on the fall team, was now available to go. Casper, a Black pastor at the Bel-Vue Presbyterian Church in Los Angeles, was a friend of Dr. Martin Luther King, Jr.

Two days before I was to leave, the Rev. Dr. King was assassinated on April 4. At Mrs. King's request, Casper flew to be with the family. I was in New York on the day of the funeral. There and across the nation every store was closed, every TV channel showed nothing but the funeral all day. The outpouring of shock and sympathy, culminating in the passage of the Civil Rights Act, was one of the greatest tributes ever paid a private citizen by our nation.

I spent three days with Uwe, Gertrude and their three children, who were now in London. (My visit with J.B. Phillips had to be by phone since he was in bed with a bad case of the flu.) One thing Uwe particularly liked about working for the Lutheran Church in England was that it involved him in the ecumenical movement.

"The job is too much administration, Walt," he said. "I miss the parish work. But still, to me, the miracle of the new community of Christians, in spite of all differences of churches and societies, becomes more and more the fundamental experience of my life. I wouldn't know how to serve as a minister nowadays if I didn't have this very deep knowledge that there is a real church, a community of saints, right across all borders and divisions which unites men and women within and by the love of Christ. To bring to light this unity and to witness this communion is something worthwhile to live and to strive for."

This love of Christ across all borders and divisions had first become real to Uwe in the persons of that 1950 Kassel work camp team—Ralph, Harriet, Duke and John. Their commitment to let God use them, to be his agents of reconciliation, was directly responsible for the direction Uwe's life had taken. Louie and Colleen Evans' commitment to those same principles had brought them to Berlin and been the start of our partnership there. As I've said before, we can't trace all the rippling effects of that first team, but the ones we can are heart-warming.

Students were rioting and Molotov cocktails were being thrown in Berlin even as I landed. April 1968 was a very tense time and Bishop Scharf and Pastor Schröder were important and strategic to the situation.

I had come a few days before the rest of the team arrived in Berlin, so I was able to go with Ted Schapp out to see a student demonstration. To me, it was uncanny how much these students' speeches sounded like the ones I'd been hearing in the inter-racial dialogues where I had recently been involved in community efforts to keep hot-spots of unrest and tension in San Diego from bursting into angry flames, as in the Watts riots earlier.

While I was awaiting the arrival of the team, Ted also introduced me to Bärbel Eccardt, a Berlin parish worker. The previous November Pastor Schröder had invited Bärbel to meet the team and, seeing her interest, had assigned her to Ted's church. The two of them were now responsible for planning and organizing the team visits, working closely with Pastor Merkel in East Berlin.

I was intrigued by this slender, thoughtful woman and from Ted learned some of her story. Bärbel was a young nurse in Berlin at the end of the war and lived through it all: the euphoria of saving victims trapped in bombed buildings, the despair of losing patients because of dwindling medical supplies and then the horror of defeat, suffering the worst the invading army could inflict. For eight years afterward she was an invalid. A slight woman, she gained weight until she weighed more than 200 pounds. She was completely incapacitated, physically, emotionally and spiritually. Every form of medication, every kind of therapy was used but to no avail. The day came when in the futility of despair, Bärbel made a fateful decision.

She said, "Either Jesus Christ can help me and heal me, or I am undone."

She became a transformed person, needing no medication or therapy.

"She's a flaming evangel, an inexhaustible instrument of love and peace," said Ted.

The rest of the team arrived on Wednesday and we met that evening at Pastor Schröder's home to be briefed by him.

"You must approach the East with the utmost care and caution. Things are delicate in the East now and the authorities are suspicious of all foreigners, particularly visitors from the West. The GDR is extremely defensive and threatened because of the liberalization in Czechoslovakia and Poland."

Learning from the growing pains of the previous team, not wanting to be an American invasion, we split into two teams, one going north and the other south. Casper Glenn, Ted Schapp and I went south. Ralph Zorn, a U.S. fraternal worker, led the team going north. Part of the time they were joined by our newest fraternal worker, Joyce Evans, who had just arrived in Berlin. A young woman from La Jolla, Joyce had recently graduated from college with a major in German. A year earlier Joyce had hesitantly shared with me her "pipe dream" of spending a year working in Berlin.

Casper Glenn was the man of the hour. It was providential that he hadn't been able to go with the team six months ago and could be here now. Dr. King, the apostle of non-violence as the Germans called him, was really a hero in East Germany and our friends wanted to know all about him—his leadership, the response to it, the reaction in America to his death. They'd all watched the funeral via satellite television. They wanted to know why we had poverty and segregation in the U.S. Why did Dr. King have to die to convince Christians that men are brothers? Why was the church segregated? What would happen to the civil rights struggle now? Would it follow the non-violent approach of Dr. King or the revolutionary tactics of the Black Panthers and Eldridge Cleaver?

This trip showed the fine organizational skills of Ted, Bärbel and Pastor Merkel and set the format for years to come. After our orientation in West Berlin, we started with a weekend conference at a city in the GDR, then traveled to small villages during the week to visit congregations, and the next weekend had a second, city conference. These conferences were attended by groups made up of five or six people each who joined with similar groups of representatives from as many as twelve different parishes. On this trip, the southern team went to eleven different cities and towns, was with twenty different groups and saw over eight hundred people. The districts represented fairly well covered the whole of southeastern Germany. And the other team was having similar experiences in the north.

We'd been told the atmosphere was tense. It was. We were stopped by the police many times and politely asked to see our passports. The hotels were the worst we'd ever been assigned. All the meetings were in the boondocks, out of the way of observation.

We got lost trying to find our first conference meeting near Plauen and arrived there an hour-and-a-half late. When we finally walked in, never having seen these people before, all sixty of them—in English, in four-part harmony—sang, "You're late, you're late, you're late you bums, you're late!" Amidst waves of laughter, it felt like old-home week.

The singing, the warmth, the love, the manifest deep dependence of each individual upon the nourishment and strength of the group life, the radiant quality of the young and old all attested that theirs was a "world within a world." The deepest revelation of their inner spirit came when Casper led our Sunday morning service, at their request, in singing Dr. King's hymn, "We Shall Overcome." Hands crossed right over left, forming a circle around the sanctuary. Faces, many with tears falling, reflected both infinite pain and infinite hope.

"Does the liberalization in Czechoslovakia offer you hope?" I asked.

They shook their heads. Their new constitution had less guarantees for the church's freedom than the old. The GDR was the most extreme and inflexible of all Russia's satellites.

The questions we encountered during the week concerned racial tension and Vietnam. The questions were sympathetic, not hostile, but really showed the slant and bias of the information received through the State media. Always the response to our conversations was, "Well, this is certainly different from the way we've been hearing it."

At Karl-Marx-Stadt the Church superintendent had brought together about twenty people to spend the afternoon with us.

"We'll squeeze you like an orange," he said.

They did. Sober and realistic, they made us think as they were thinking about the critical priorities confronting them and us, too.

"You're free, rich. How do you account for this racial tension? The poverty? The crime? How is your materialism different from ours? Is the Church really winning the battle in America? Why must Martin Luther King crusade against segregation in a country where sixty-six percent of the people are reportedly regular church attenders?"

We met with Dr. Theo Lehmann again, the youth pastor who had written the book on Negro spirituals and who used spirituals, jazz band and gospel music in his youth services. The authorities had ordered him to discontinue his monthly worship services, which were drawing 1,200 to 1,800 teenagers. He was disregarding the orders and nothing had happened so far.

At Dresden we were met by Pastor Mieth and Pastor Merchel for our next three-day conference. They got us going early in the morning and kept us going until late at night. The same questions kept coming. Always, Casper was the key man. He gave simple, direct, honest answers. He was factual and compelling. The participants said over and over again, "We only hear one side here. We've never heard this side before."

Because this was such a tense time world-wide, we discussed these critical issues in depth. But the heart of our time together was prayer, fellowship and our common Bible study. And always, always, wherever we were, the question was, "When can you return?"

On our way back to Berlin we stopped in Magdeburg to meet Bishop Dr. Werner Krusche in the hope of finding through him a contact person for that area.

"How about me?" he asked.

I realized Bishop Krusche was another one of those stalwarts of the faith who had come to Christian maturity through the Confessing Church and its opposition to Hitler. In 1954 at the request of the Church, he'd come from West Germany with his wife and first child to be a pastor in Dresden.

He said, "I might never really have known God had I not come back to the GDR."

The Bishop helped us understand the current situation.

"The Church leaders who took over after the calamity of the war had a decidedly critical attitude towards the State because of their experience under Hitler's dictatorship," he said. "That attitude confirmed the Marxist rulers in their ideological stand toward the Church. In their eyes the Church was allied with and dependent upon conservative, nationalist, capitalist and anti-Communist powers, and represented a disruptive influence in the development of a new social order."

"How should the Church have reacted?"

"We should have realized sooner that Marxist atheism is at least in part a product of disappointment in a Church that didn't stay with the poor and weak, but with the mighty and powerful. Perhaps as we Christians demonstrate that belief in Jesus Christ is not an ideology but a way of life, following our crucified and risen Lord, the State will see that we have answers that atheism can't provide to the basic questions of life .

"But now we're paying the price for our critical attitude," he said sighing. "These are hard times."

In our debriefing period back in West Berlin with Bishop Scharf and

Brother Schröder, I aired some disturbing impressions I'd gathered through our travels.

"When I was here two years ago, church leaders were exuding confidence, saying the Church could still do its work under Communism," I said. "Now they are tired, worn and weary. The talk now is, 'We must find ways to break out of the ghetto—the ghetto we have made for ourselves by retreating within the church walls and the walls of our homes, the ghetto the State has imposed on us.'

"I feel a degree of hopelessness that I've never before sensed. Am I wrong?"

"No, no, you are not wrong," said the Bishop. "The firm, inexorable, persistent pressure upon the Church by the State at every point is taking its toll. The new constitution has us all depressed. It is so general that it can be interpreted any way the local authorities choose. Our freedom is less guaranteed now than before."

"There are still signs of new life," I said, "in the new patterns and forms of worship, the cottage congregations, and work with the youth, the transients and the alcoholics."

"God is still showing his sovereign power, " said Pastor Schröder, "but some of his instruments are tired. They've now faced over twenty years of militant, atheistic opposition. That is why the team visits are so important. You are like an infusion of fresh blood."

"Yes," I said reflectively, "it was definitely some sort of infusion when Beep Roberts kissed that staid, old German pastor right smack on top of his shiny, bald head. I thought the roof was going to blow right off the church." (Beep was the one who had passed out all the Ichthus [fish symbol] pins when he was with Ralph Zorn's group in 1964.)

I waited a day after the team left and then, with Bishop Scharf, his wife and Pastor Schröder, flew back to California. They were going to the U.S. on a speaking tour of Southern California and to attend the Presbyterian Church's General Assembly in Minneapolis.

"The Bishop and his wife won the hearts of all who met them," I wrote to Pastor Schröder after they'd returned to Berlin.

"The Bishop was overwhelmed," he replied. "He will never forget these days and the cordial belonging together he has seen and felt. He is speaking with great respect and is full of thankfulness for what he has seen. I have never seen him so moved. And this means a lot. You will see continued a very strong support for our work in the Berlin Fellowship."

Brother Schröder also had good personal news to pass on. On June 15 he and Erika Stenzel were married in a small family ceremony presided over by Bishop Scharf.

But news from the East was not good. The Prague Spring of 1967 was over, the liberalization in Czechoslovakia crushed in August by an invasion of East European troops led by Russia. I thought of the Czech Christians traveling in East Germany we had met just months before and wondered what had happened to them.

At Pastor Schröder's urgent request, another team led by Ralph was sent in October 1968. Ralph felt Ted and Bärbel had done a good job in balancing the requests for repeat visits and also in getting the two teams into new areas.

Both teams learned that youth work in the church was being drastically limited. Bishops were told that the standard two-week camps could now be no longer than a week, including travel time. Retreat centers were declared unsanitary and closed. Buses were canceled. In Bishop Noth's area of Saxony, 4,000 students had applied for camp and only a 1000 were permitted to attend.

Christian students, particularly pastor's children, were singled out in their last two years of high school and cut off from further education.

"Kids in school are discouraged from thinking for themselves," said one pastor. "They become experts in running their lives on two rails, not revealing their thoughts, just coughing back to the State what it wants to hear. Only those who toe the line are advanced."

In spite of this, Theo Lehmann in Karl-Marx-Stadt and Pastor Vödisch in Plauen said their youth gatherings were large and growing. Other areas reported the same.

"I have experienced three miracles in my life," Pastor Vödisch told Ralph. "The reconstruction of St. Mark's Church in Plauen, the large youth gatherings in my church and the encounters with the Berlin Fellowship teams."

Ralph met with Bishop Krusche, now our contact in Magdeburg.

"The laymen are the real missionaries in our country," he told Ralph. "They bear witness to Christ by living their everyday life in a socialist environment. As soon as a man or woman discloses that he or she is a Christian, he will be closely observed in the work place or wherever he is to see if what he pretends to believe coincides with what he lives. When a Christian acts differently from what others expect him to do, when they are astonished or angry with him, he gets questioned.

"'Why are you doing that? Why do you keep straight to the truth and provoke unnecessary difficulties? Why are you so uncooperative and won't put down more hours than we really worked?'

"If one is ruled by the love of Christ, this becomes evident socially," he said.

From the laymen and pastors in Bishop Krusche's district, Ralph heard stories about how evident Christ was in the Bishop's life.

"Three farmers and their wives were put on stage at a public hearing to justify why they wouldn't voluntarily join the collective," a pastor told Ralph. "The audience was packed with bused-in spectators hostile to the farmers.

"These men and their wives were sitting there looking like scared rabbits. Then here came Bishop Krusche striding through the auditorium and up onto the stage. He pulled out a chair and just sat down with them. The authorities were acting inhumanely. He told them so, and after some fussing, the meeting was called off!"

One of the reasons our visits were so important was that they brought the Christians in the GDR together, something that seldom seemed to happen in those days without the stimulus of our visits. As we learned from them the quality and depth of a life totally committed to Christ, they learned from us relational tools such as praying aloud and sharing their experiences of faith.

"It is a very difficult time for Christians in East Germany," Ralph reported back to the Berlin Fellowship Group. "Pressure is again overt, with arrests and imprisonment becoming common. Be very careful when you write to our friends in the East. Say nothing political and don't refer to the Berlin Fellowship or to anything organizational by name. Remember at home, too, that we keep a very low profile with no publicity about where we go or what we do."

In the spring of 1969 Darrell Guder, the young pastor who had worked at Hamburg-Rissen with Uwe and who now was a youth pastor in Hollywood, led a team to Berlin and the East. It was the first time neither Ralph or I had gone and we were pleased with the reports and with the new, young leadership developing within the Berlin Fellowship. While maintaining my contacts and friendships in Berlin and the East, my desire was to back out of the day-to-day leadership of the Berlin Fellowship, to be more of a consultant allowing new leadership room to grow. The time was right for me to do that.

"The team had good contacts and experiences in the East," wrote Pastor

Schröder. "The Bishop said how thankful he is for this kind of work. This Christian contact with the West is growing more and more important."

"Darrell has grown and matured," I wrote to Brother Schröder. "He has a new understanding of the significance and importance of this relationship. He says that he feels this is a part of his life and something he will be devoted to through his entire ministry."

Early in 1969 the churches in the GDR, under government pressure, had created a new church federation which in effect separated them from the churches in West Germany. After the separation, the government continued making any contact with West Germany difficult.

This separation left the West Berlin Church stranded between two political blocks with its own status uncertain. There was a strong desire from the West Berlin Christians that a team meet with them. The fall visit was planned to include a conference in West Berlin before the teams went into the East.

A letter from Uwe Hollm gave me a new reason for looking forward to my Berlin visits. He had received two calls to new jobs, one of which was to become the general secretary of the Berlin Mission Society headquartered in Berlin.

"You can imagine that we didn't find it very easy to find out what the right way would be for us," he wrote. "Now we have decided to accept the call to Berlin and—as it should be after a good decision—I am happy and relieved and looking forward to the move to Berlin West by October 1, 1969.

"I shall have a threefold task to perform: 1) to look after missionaries and nurses in Africa, Asia and the Mideast; 2) to keep close contact with East Berlin and GDR churches; and 3) to seek ways to integrate the work of the Society into the West German Churches. The Berlin office is a real ministry and is related to the direct proclamation of the gospel. I must preach and speak very often which will urge me to read, listen, think and pray. That's at least what I hope.

"Gertrude and the family are very keen on going to Berlin. Sometimes I feel a little bit like a Gypsy, but so were Abraham and Paul himself. Our home is where God wants us to be. I feel he wants us to be in Berlin.

"One of the nicest thoughts in this connection is the hope that we might see you and other members of the Berlin Fellowship more often. Your names are as well known in West as in East Berlin."

I wrote back, "Berlin will have an entirely new appeal to us now because you are also there and we can be co-workers."

Uwe commented on the Black-White confrontation in the United States.

"One really wonders what God has in mind with your country. Sometimes I think of the biblical word about the sins of the fathers which reach into the second and third generation. On the other hand, one might say that God has picked out America first to tackle this problem because he thinks that this country might have the courage and faith to deal with it properly. Within the next generation most of our countries will have that problem as well."

"Believe me, things are tense and we are having our problems," I answered, "not only in the national church, but here in Southern California as well. Sometimes I'm not so sure how much difference there is between the East and the West. We're all being challenged to a greater degree of responsibility and commitment and directly driven to our knees in a quest for greater wisdom, understanding and judgment.

"I, too, like to believe that God has chosen to challenge the Church in America to a place of special responsibility, maybe because America is so vulnerable in terms of the way we've used our freedom, our wealth, and the way we've misused so many of our brothers, Black, White and Brown. We're searching for real solutions from a Christian point of view. To be a minister of reconciliation in these days demands all the grace, wisdom and strength that we have and more. Our real reliance must be in the fact that God does his important work through limited human beings like ourselves."

Since 1965, Ralph had been the director of Greater Parish Ministry, our denomination's outreach program to the poor, disenfranchised and alienated in the San Diego area. He was doing an excellent job, but he felt that at this point in our nation's history the program should be headed by a minority person. He felt this so strongly that he recruited Casper Glenn, the Black pastor who had gone on the 1968 spring team, and then yielded his position to him. Casper had been a strategic person in the maelstrom of the Watts revolt and was well prepared to give effective leadership in San Diego.

It was a step of faith for Ralph and Mary since he resigned before having a call to a new position. It was a step that eventually led to his life work, his consuming passion for ministering to people in Eastern Europe.

The small group movement was in full bloom in the States and our German friends wanted to learn about it. We recruited team members for the fall 1969 team who had special skills in that area. I was asked to be team leader.

The theme of the conferences in the East and West was "The Future of the Church," and special regard was given to how small group work fit into that.

Ardys Heise, a communications specialist with the University of California, led the small group part of the conference for the twenty participants meeting in the Bonhoeffer House in West Berlin. The Germans hadn't experienced anything like this intimate, personal sharing in groups and we were all surprised at the easy openness with which the groups got involved in very essential problems. The enthusiasm carried through our week in West Berlin. As team member Lonnie Wormley— the Black pastor who had developed the interracial ministry in La Jolla—said, "The most rewarding part is that the groups plan to continue meeting after we leave."

Our conference schedule had been so full that by Sunday morning I still had not had time to call Uwe and Trude. Our group came into church a little late and it was jammed, so we all squeezed into a back pew. As the service progressed, I suddenly realized why Pastor Schröder had been so insistent we come to this particular service. It was Uwe's installation service as secretary general of the Berlin Mission Society. The chancel was filled with distinguished leaders of the Church, all in full regalia.

Looking out over the congregation as he spoke in response to his installation charge, Uwe somehow spotted me. Interrupting his speech, switching momentarily from German to English he said, "You know, Walt, nobody would have dreamed when we first met twenty years ago that we would be here today under these circumstances, would they?"

Only the love and grace of God could have transformed that arrogant, brash, young giant—that Nazi youth leader—into this mature Christian pastor now charged with responsibility for the churches in the GDR and for mission outreach to Africa, Asia and the Middle East. Pastor Schröder said our job was to work for Jesus Christ and maybe, if we were fortunate, a few times in our life we would see the fruits of that work. This was one of those times for me.

The conference in East Berlin also involved small group work. There were seventy participants, most from East Berlin and the GDR, many friends from our previous visits. It was exciting to also discover people from Poland, Hungary and Czechoslovakia participating and asking to know the theme of the next one as soon as possible so they could prepare for it.

By adding six American fraternal workers from West Berlin, we were able to form three teams for our week in the GDR.

The southeast team and the southwest team discovered the same warmth and fellowship, the grace under unremitting pressure, that so moved and inspired me each time I was in the GDR. The sharing of life experiences in small groups usually deepened this fellowship, although in some places the intimacy of it was more than the Germans were ready for.

As always, they were hungry for news from the West. Dianna Pohlman, our youngest team member and a music major about to enter seminary, reported that teenagers were startled to find that Americans, whom the State propaganda painted as evil warmongers, shared similar concerns about war, peace and the environment.

Dave Willis—a seminary professor and Reformation scholar who spoke fluent German—Ralph Zorn and Ted Schapp—both Berlin fraternal workers—and I went to a pastor's and laymen's conference in Greifswald where the theme again was "The Future of the Church."

Delving into that theme, we began to make some remarkable discoveries. Our problems, East and West, were almost identical: materialism, secularism and how to reach young people, to name a few. East or West, the Church needed to be involved as a positive force within society and it failed as a Church when it wasn't. The biggest difference was that we in the West were freer to do something about our problems.

But lovingly, our brothers and sisters at that conference left us with a very sobering thought. "We don't know who's in the greater danger," they said, "you or us. We know what our enemy is. We're not sure you do."

Soon after I returned home, I wrote to Uwe. "I shall never be able to adequately express what it meant to me to be with you on the occasion of your installation. I think God has important work for us in the future and I am looking forward to these possibilities with real anticipation."

From 1970 on, the format of the Berlin Fellowship visits changed. Bishop Scharf was concerned that the twice a year visits didn't allow ample time for preparation by the teams and that such frequency might cause problems in the GDR. The Berlin Fellowship had the same misgivings. Spring teams continued to be large and kept the format of intense training at home, orientation and visits in West Berlin and dividing into small groups for travel in the East. In the fall a group started coming to Berlin and meeting with key people East and West, finding out their needs and interests and then recruiting the spring team to meet those needs. Ralph and I stayed in touch, often taking those fall trips, but really encouraging the developing leadership in the group both at home and in Berlin.

We've maintained our policy of no publicity through the years to protect the people we visit. Even so, occasionally someone in the GDR who had been an enthusiastic participant one spring would never again meet with a team because of pressure from the authorities. Given these experiences and our continuing commitment to keep a low profile, we won't talk about any teams beyond 1969.

But what we discovered in the East was a community, a generation of men and women who were truly liberated, emancipated from the tyranny of both fear and despotism. There were no spiritual heroes, no spiritual giants, but there were men and women of all ages who couldn't be intimidated, who couldn't be bought or sold, who couldn't be influenced by force or desire for power or status. They faced threats, harassments, pressure, even at times imprisonment, and they realized in experience the sustaining Presence, the Power of Christ. They had an inner freedom best expressed by Professor Hamel in 1952 when he said, "A Presence comes into your life and you can do what you need to do. You're not afraid. It's as simple as that."

It has been my pleasure to watch the new leadership developing in the U.S., in Berlin and in the GDR to see young people coming to Christian maturity with a firm belief in a community of saints that transcends national borders and denominational boundaries.

For the Berlin Fellowship, for World Deputation and for the people touched and changed by their experiences in these groups, the guiding purpose through the years has remained to show Jesus Christ as the only spiritual basis for world brotherhood and to make all the walls that separate people from people, brothers and sisters from each other, transparent through him.

CHAPTER NINETEEN

So Great a Cloud of Witnesses

Therefore, since we are surrounded by so great a cloud of witnesses, let us also lay aside every weight, and sin which clings so closely, and let us run with perseverance the race that is set before us. (Hebrews 12:1 RSV)

"Things have changed dramatically! It's as if someone has turned a page in human history." It was the spring of 1987 and we were in Berlin talking to Uwe Hollm, now leader of the theological department of the Church Headquarters.

"It's a new day," Uwe continued. "This past is history. The ideological warfare, the terrorism, the atmosphere of coercion—they are being replaced by a new atmosphere of hope for the future. It's all due to the influence of one man, Mikhail Gorbachev."

Dan and Roz Towler, Marguerite and I were once again in Berlin, once again visiting with Uwe before we headed East. Slightly greying and a grandfather now, Uwe, after eleven years of distinguished service as Secretary General of the Berlin Mission Society, had been elected to his new position in 1980.

"The real question," said Uwe, "is will the hard-liners let him live?"

As we traveled in the GDR with our dear friend Bärbel Eccardt as interpreter, we saw that Uwe was right. People were more relaxed, less cautious, more willing to speak freely. There was hope that the pressures would become less and there could be a little more of what a free world would call a normal life.

Paradoxically, the Church was in a state of flux. The years of restrictions and hindrances of every kind had taken their toll. Church attendance was declining, particularly among the youth. The financial burden of maintaining antiquated churches as required by the State, some of which were even designated museums and not places of worship, was oppressive.

On the other hand, for some time now the State authorities had been coming to the bishops and pastors for help.

In Dresden we met with Bishop Hempel, the Bishop of Saxony following Bishop Noth's death.

He said, "Officials come to me saying, 'The Church is the only institution in the whole country that people respect.' Christians are the only people they respect because they don't lie, they tell the truth, they are honest, they have a kind of joy, an inner peace, a sense of humor and a zest for life that others simply don't have."

Pastors could now make house calls and some religious broadcasts on both television and radio were permitted.

"What about the young people?" I asked Bishop Hempel, knowing that from the earliest days of Marxist domination, the youth had been subjected to the most intensive indoctrination. This generation had lived their whole life under the socialist system.

"We have just received the results of a study done in a thousand parishes," he said. "The results are uniformly the same. Young people want nothing to do with the Bible. They hate all institutions: the State, the government, the Church, even marriage and the family. They want peace, nuclear disarmament and environmental protection, and they want it right now.

"But they need the Church," he said with a gentle smile. "They need the legality it can give them. For example, the city authorities came to me a few months ago and told me that a youth demonstration demanding change was being planned, a mass demonstration of probably some 3,000 young people. It was pro-glasnost and very threatening to the authorities, who refused to issue a permit for it. The response of the police would be to rough up the demonstrators, to make mass arrests and to use violence if needed.

"I sought out the leaders of the rally, explained what the authorities had told me and suggested an alternative plan. Legally, all three thousand demonstrators could come to The Church of the Holy Cross here in Dresden as my guests. I would have the authorities present, they could make their points in a far more significant way. They agreed. The plan worked. Not 3,000 but 5,000 came and there was no violence."

With a beautiful smile on his face, Bishop Hempel said to me, "I found myself giving leadership to something that I couldn't support."

For the most part, these weren't Church youth, but the Bishop had contributed to their cause and had won both their respect and their abiding affection. As Christians in the East had been doing for so long, he met them at the point of their deepest need and stood alongside them earning the right to be heard. He had truly been Christ's reconciling agent.

In Karl-Marx-Stadt we met with Theo and Elke Lehmann. He was grey around the temples and seven times a grandfather, but still he was drawing youth by the thousands. Considered the Billy Graham of the East Germans,

Theo traveled the country preaching to youth congregations, always needing the largest church in the city to hold the numbers which flocked in. The harassment hadn't lessened. Right before we came, Elke had been interrogated for four hours by the police because she made a rolling stop at a stop sign on a deserted, country road.

"What you heard about the youth in the Saxony area is correct," said Theo. "But the youth of the GDR are desperately hungry for real answers, for the truth of the Gospel. They may not go to a church, but they'll go into the woods, hundreds at a time, for their own worship service where they gather around the Lord's table for holy communion. This is of course unsanctioned by the Church, but this is where they say they feel God's presence. They aren't rejecting the Gospel or Christ, they are rejecting traditional forms of worship.

"One thing is certain. When the Gospel of the living Christ is preached, where a living faith is practiced, there will always be a living Church."

All of our friends whom we visited on this trip—Uwe, Theo, Pastor Schröder and Bishop Scharf, both now retired, (See note at end of Chapter.) Bishop Hempel and Bishop Krusche—agreed that the Church's problems couldn't be blamed on the system under which it lived and operated.

Bishop Krusche said, "The real danger for the Church is not from theoretical atheism, but from atheism in practice, the way of life in which God, even if not verbally disavowed, actually plays no part. That way of life is not practiced by Marxists alone. Real dangers to the Church never come from the outside, but always from the inside."

That struck home. I had often pondered to what extent the Church in America was shaped by the materialism, the racism, the militarism and the nationalism of our society. How often were we the salt, the leaven, the shining lights Christ called us to be and how often were we a pale reflection of our culture? Were we bound or were we free?

I remembered Pastor Schröder's words, "A neutral Christian is of no value."

Pastor Schröder was retired, but still in touch with youth pastors across Germany and still deeply concerned for young people.

"Where will young people get the rules for life in this modern world?" he asked. "If they only imitate the rules of others, they are lost. The task of the Church today is to give this generation the right rules for a right life. Not the changing rules of the world, but the biblical rules that stay for all time."

In bits and pieces, not yet with any great clarity, that's what we saw happening in 1987. Responsible Church leaders, seeing the high potential and idealism of these young people, were providing the rules, the umbrella under which they could coalesce. The Church was the only place where protest groups could legally meet. Here the pastors could bring them into contact with the authorities and quietly provide the direction and guidance so desperately needed. These young people, just as surely as the young people who went on the Deputation teams, were seeking a vision of peace, reconciliation and human rights.

"They had been struggling to find a way to bring about change," said Ralph who now traveled extensively in all of Eastern Europe for World Vision. "They found a nest within the Church. The pastors and members enlarged their perspective by bringing in Christian elements not there before. They discovered in these leaders a whole, new context and became aware that the way to reach their goals wasn't by confrontation, but by dialogue and responsible action."

What the Church was experiencing in 1987 was the restlessness that led to November 9, 1989, when the Berlin Wall came tumbling down. This was an event so incredible that literally no one, anywhere, believed it could happen in our life-time, or without a confrontation of the two superpowers costing millions of lives and resulting in the destruction of civilization as we know it. Yet it did happen and it happened overnight, just as in 1961 the Wall went up overnight. And it happened by non-violent means.

It has been a young people's movement. They bided their time; then, when the time was right, they came out of the churches and into the streets, thousands of them, not with rocks or guns, but with lighted candles. Their quiet approach took hold and permeated the East German society, becoming a pivotal point in the collapse of the government and the dawn of a new era.

The cradle of this revolution was the St. Nikolai Lutheran Church in Leipzig, one of the churches in Bishop Hempel's district of Saxony. Since 1982 people had been meeting there with Pastor Christian Fuehrer on Monday nights to pray for disarmament and peace. As economic conditions worsened and discontent with the government increased, the Monday night attendance grew from a few dozen to hundreds, then to thousands.

A crisis point was reached on Monday, October 9, 1989, during the Communist anniversary celebrations. Police had used violence against the protesters, and Communist party officials, fearful of the reaction if people gathered, brought in a thousand party members and filled up all the pews in St. Nikolai

Church to keep out the regulars. They did, but the party members themselves were moved by Pastor Fuehrer's service and thanked him as they left.

Kept outside the church, the church regulars swelled to a crowd of 70,000 and marched peacefully through the center of town. The following Monday, the number gathering at St. Nikolai soared past 120,000 and the next Monday past 300,000. The movement spread throughout East Germany, the hard-line government crumbled and the reforms began.

The future is still uncertain because freedom is not free or easy. It takes endurance, hard work and the patience not to settle for easy answers and quick solutions.

This bloodless revolution became a signal to the youth of other nations until in just a few short months the entire structure of Eastern Europe has been changed.

I see this as a clear demonstration of how God not only honors but also relies on those who make themselves available to him. That small minority of people who had learned to live their faith in a society dedicated to their eradication, who had learned to live without power by relying on the strength of the Gospel and on the strength of their personal relationship with Christ, stayed where God needed them. Because of that, just as the Confessing Church which rose in opposition to Hitler became the backbone of the Church in the GDR, the Church in the GDR became the cradle of the national protest movement which transformed the nation.

"They aren't heroes," said Ralph. "They're just ahead of us in their pilgrimage. They aren't aware of how advanced they are in their faith. They're pioneers. Their convictions were hammered out under painful duress, formed at hard cost.

"The world needs to hear the message from the Christians in the East, because it has a tendency to follow the path of least resistance, to move in the direction of self-destruction and meaninglessness."

Hearing that message is what I've been doing on each of my twenty-one trips to Berlin, the GDR and, as time went by, other East European countries. This journey of discovery began in 1950 when that first Deputation team sought a spiritual basis for world brotherhood. We developed the steps: find Christ's guidelines through intensive Bible study within a covenant group; commit to corporate and individual prayer, and find ways to become involved identifying with those in need and earning the right to be Christ's reconciling agents.

Person to person it worked beyond our wildest dreams and when followed faithfully, it still works today.

Immersed in Berlin and the East, we became aware that, along with person to person involvement, we needed to be involved with the corporate Body of Christ—the Church. We became one part of the Body reaching out and strengthening another part of the Body under oppression and in turn being strengthened and blessed far beyond anything that we gave. What an experience this has been for these decades to have followed the lives of these "so great a cloud of witnesses," to have observed and experienced with them how God used and honored their lives as they made themselves wholly available in loving service to him. How privileged I am to have been closely related in some small way with those who have been living their lives daily and triumphantly under inhuman stress. Clearly life for them became a transcending process, for they were daily driven into the waiting arms of God.

What have these experiences of yesterday to say to the generations of today and tomorrow? What have we learned on this journey of discovery that answers the fundamental longings of the human heart?

The first and most basic principle of life is that God is God, he is faithful and absolutely to be trusted with our lives. As Ralph says, "All of life is on shaky ground if we don't believe in a God we can trust. We accept that premise at first intellectually and eventually it becomes real to us emotionally."

The second is that God's greatest and best and ultimate revelation of himself is Jesus Christ, his own Son and our Lord. He is and remains the Light of the world.

The third is that human nature has built within it a nostalgia for God that nothing else can satisfy. Materialism, be it of the East or West, is no answer to the human spirit. Without Christ at its center, the whole fabric of life begins to unravel and come apart. Drug addiction, alcoholism, family disintegration, corruption in government and business, destruction of the environment—we see it all in the Western World and Ralph reports the same is true in Eastern Europe.

"We have lost from our perspective what we were put on earth for," said Ralph, "to be in tune with, to cooperate with the heartbeat of God."

The fourth principle is that God has a unique way of honoring the most ordinary of people if they yield themselves wholly and unreservedly in loving service to Jesus Christ.

"Guaranteed," said Ralph, "that God will do his marvelous, precious work through each one of us in a very distinctive and a very beautiful way if our hearts are open to him. That takes learning. That takes walking with him. That takes succeeding at one time and that takes failing at another time. But God will have no other person to do that job. It is only on this pilgrimage, only by such trial and error, this hanging on that we find Life with a capital 'L'."

Finally, in this process of life, we have learned that we need each other. One can't live this life in Christ in a vacuum. As Pastor Schröder said again and again, "We are belonging together." That's why our visits were so important to Christians living in isolation behind the Iron Curtain. That's why we gained so much by being part of this world-wide community of believers. That's why each individual needs to be part of a Christian community.

Bishop Krusche said, "One can endure quite well in East Germany, even without compromising, if one is a member of a support group, a circle of friends who trust each other, who can speak freely without fear, who turn to each other for the strength to carry on and cope."

He was describing an authentic Christian community, one based on living out the Gospel of Jesus Christ in daily life. Wherever people see this kind of a community, they are drawn to it just as Ralph was drawn to the First Presbyterian Church of Hollywood by the light of God's love shining through the young people there.

The challenge of our times is to be the authentic Christian community, to be the Church and to be explicit about God.

Once in a while we see the world at a pivotal point. It was such a time at the conclusion of World War II, with the new threat of the atomic bomb, when Albert Einstein said, "We must find a spiritual basis for world brotherhood...." The building of the Berlin Wall, cleaving the world into two armed and hostile camps poised on the brink of nuclear war, was another such time.

We're at such a pivotal point again. The Wall is down, but ethnic clashes all over the Soviet Union, inexperienced, untrained political leadership in Eastern Europe and—world-wide—drugs, the environmental crisis and widening economic disparities have our world in a state of turmoil.

At this time in history we desperately need a spiritual basis for world brotherhood—person to person, neighborhood to neighborhood, community to community, nation to nation—just as surely as did the post-World War II world. This time in history desperately needs people willing to find the disenfranchised and the alienated; to find the points of greatest need and to come alongside; to earn the right to be Christ's reconciling agent; and to be the leaven, the candle, the light in a dark world. There is an urgency to the moment lest we lose this window of opportunity.

This kind of involvement calls us into the heart of Life, Life at its most rewarding and deepest, at its most painful and productive level. It calls us into close, intimate association with God as revealed in his son, Jesus Christ. It is a glory like no other, to be in some small way part of this "so great a cloud of witnesses."

(Note: Bishop Scharf, born October 21, 1902 died suddenly March 28, 1990 and was buried at St. Mary's Church in E. Berlin April 5, 1990).

1964—Dan Towler prepares to photograph Alfred Schröder, his wife, Elizabeth and daughter, Annelene.

1987 visit to East and West Germany. Left to right: Rev. Dan Towler, Marguerite James, Helga Krusche, Bärbel Eccardt, Roz Towler, Walt James and Bishop Werner Krusche.

Left: 1967—Uwe, Gertrude and Jan Hollm in London.
Below: 1987—Jan, Gertrude and Uwe Hollm.

Top: 1985—Bishop Krusche and Ralph Hamburger visit at World Vision Headquarters in Monrovia, California. Center: 1987—(left to right) Pastor Schröder, Ralph Hamburger and Walt James.

At left: Bärbel Eccardt, Bishop Kurt Scharf, Rev. Dan Towler.

The Reverend Dr. Walter E. James

THE AUTHOR

The last thing I ever thought I'd be was a minister. I have a natural appetite for adventure and I intended to always be where the action was. So I became a motorcycle cop in Ohio. Not much of a cop, for those were early, somewhat primitive days of law enforcement, but I wore a uniform and I carried a gun. And I rode a motorcycle faster than it was ever intended to go.

Then one night I had to arrest some young boys who had "borrowed" a Cadillac convertible and gone joy-riding. As I put an eleven-year-old into a dark, dingy, foul-smelling county jail, I looked down into his fear-filled eyes, as big as saucers, and something happened deep down inside me.

"I'll never do this again!" I thought. "I'm going to keep them out of jail, not put them in it."

I gave up my job and entered Ohio Wesleyan University, majoring in Physical Education. Football, gymnastics, wrestling and track—I reveled in them all.

"Sports!" I thought. "This is the way to get to kids!"

Two other forces began working in my life at Ohio Wesleyan—Christ, and a tiny, ninety-pound English teacher named Goldie McCue. When my life began coming apart academically, socially and financially, I challenged my Christian roommate, Bob Brinkman, to a prayer vigil.

"Bob," I said, "I'm going to find out if Jesus Christ is for real or not. We'll get down on our knees and pray until I get an answer."

Long hours later, nothing had happened. There was no great revelation, no transforming light. Nothing.

Bob finally said quietly, "Walt, this verse keeps going through my mind. 'By this may men know that you are my disciples, that you have love one for another.'"

When he said that, something clicked inside me. I prayed quietly.

"God, I've blown it. I'm a failure and I don't think I've ever loved anyone but myself. Revelation or no, from now on I'm going to be your man—lock, stock and barrel. I'm no minister, but maybe you can teach me to love people the way You do. I'm not much, but all that I am and all that I have belongs to you. I want to see what you will do with a man my size!"

That was the beginning. Starting with a scholarship that eased my financial burden, from that day to this, life for me has become a succession of miracles.

Then there was Miss McCue. She stopped me after class one day.

"Mr. James, you could be a real student if you wanted to. Is there anything I can do to help you?"

She really cared! She really believed in me! I was not going to let her down. I began to hit the books and started making A's. I liked it! English Bible and Physical Education became my double majors. What a combination!

After graduation, with the help of a scholarship, I started Yale Divinity School in New Haven, Connecticut. I started taking classes from Tracy Redding, a nationally recognized authority on group dynamics, at that time a new field of study in the social sciences.

As a project I began working with tough gang groups. These kids loved sports as much or even more than I did. Name athletes were their heroes and could, I realized, become dominant influences in their lives. This knowledge, this experience, became the first ingredient in what would become one of the major aspects of my life's work. I thought I'd found a key to keeping kids out of trouble.

Then I met Phil Giglio.

Phil was really gifted, with a high IQ and a truly great athletic talent. He was also the leader of a gang of dead-end kids, from the New Haven waterfront, called the Angels. Angels they were not! A police record was a prerequisite for membership. I'd asked for the toughest, roughest gang around, and boy, did I get it!

Phil had an uncanny way of working me over. He knew my every move, my every strategy, even before I did. He would say to his gang, "Now dis guy is trying to convert us. Now today, dis will be da strag-ed-y," and he would tell them what I would do. And I did! Not once, but many times over. It was downright embarrassing. Every night I would pray that God would teach me to really love those kids the way he did, to understand and care about them. I guess he did, because I couldn't give up on them, particularly on Phil.

Finally, I got an idea. If I could just get him away from the gang for forty-eight hours, maybe something could happen. So I invited him to go to Cambridge with me for the Yale-Harvard football game. I asked his high school principal if I could borrow him for a day or two.

"Take him and keep him!" was her comment.

"Now dis is da big push!" Phil told his buddies. "Dis is da coupe da tat!" And he told them what I would do. And I did.

By the end of the second day, the game was over and I knew I'd blown it with Phil. It was a real heartbreaker. I couldn't penetrate his defenses. I'd done everything in my power, but I couldn't reach him. Heading back to New Haven, feeling low and defeated, I suddenly noticed we were driving by Trinity Church in Boston. The chapel was open for meditation and prayer. If ever anyone needed to pray, I did. I stopped the car and excused myself to Phil.

"Oh, sure. Go ahead," he said. Candles were lighted; organ music was being played. Kneeling, I literally became lost in the wonderful sense of the nearness, the power, the Presence of God. I came to my senses with no idea how long I had been there. I had loosed Phil on the city of Boston. Anything could have happened by now! I turned to get up and there, kneeling beside me, tears streaming down his face, was Phil.

Then it hit me. Deep down inside this hardened, tough, two-fisted kid was a hunger so great only God Himself could satisfy it. If ever I was going to reach Phil Giglio and countless others like him, I was going to have to learn how to make Jesus Christ real to them in experience.

This was a turning point in my understanding. Sports were not enough. Famous athletes were not enough. They might be the means, but Christ was the Way. And I wasn't prepared for that. I transferred to United Theological Seminary in Dayton, Ohio to train for the ministry, taking with me my long-time friend, a fellow Ohio Wesleyan University graduate and now my bride, Marguerite Bolyard James.

One Christmas vacation, I attended a student volunteer convention in Indianapolis, Indiana. We had a number of famous people as our speakers. One of these men said, in describing his own pilgrimage in life, that the world has yet to see the result of any single life wholly dedicated in the service of Jesus Christ.

What would God do with any given life if it were wholly dedicated in the service of Jesus Christ? A voice deep inside me said, "I want to be that man. I want to make that experiment, to find out what life can really hold at its very best."

My appetite for adventure developed into a quest: to test out in the crucible of experience the heights, depths, width and breadth of the real meaning of life at its very best—the life of Faith in the arenas of greatest challenge. I wanted to put to the test the claims of Jesus Christ in the midst of the painful realities of the disadvantaged and the disinherited; amidst the hurt, the pain and the alienation of which Jesus spoke when he said:

"I was hungry and you gave me no food, I was thirsty and you gave me no drink,...naked and you did not clothe me, sick and in prison and you did not visit me." (Matt. 25:42-43 RSV)

Making myself as available to God as I knew how and searching out his answers to pain and alienation became the focus of my life.

A love of athletics and an ability to motivate people seemed to be tools God gave me to work with. It just seemed natural to combine kids' enthusiasm for sports with Christian leadership. While still at Dayton, working through the churches, I searched out inspired pastors and lay people, gave them training in group work and got them together with kids, forming after-school clubs usually centered around sports.

It really worked. It was Jesus Christ who made the difference. In New Haven, Dayton, Oakland, Hollywood and San Diego, wherever I've been, the results have been the same.

In Hollywood I headed community work for the YMCA from 1940 to 1946. Again, I worked with gang groups, this time the Zoot Suiters. The Probation Department, the Police Department, principals and parents all referred kids to our Y clubs which were led by dedicated, inspired Christians. Wherever a kid was in trouble, somehow his name came to me and I got him plugged into a club.

The County Sheriff's Department and the Los Angeles Police Juvenile Bureau credited our Boys Clubs with reducing juvenile arrests in the Hollywood community by as much as ninety percent.

An ordained minister myself, I always worked through the churches. That's how I met Dr. Louis Evans, Sr., Senior Pastor of First Presbyterian Church of Hollywood, a dynamic preacher and a remarkable man of great vision and compassion. His church sponsored thirteen of these Boys Clubs.

"Walt," he said one day, "what this church needs to do is to flex its muscles. Our people are overfed and under-exercised. We want to put our people to work in the community, extend our ministry into a weekday activities program. Do you know an ordained person who could give leadership to this program?"

I mentioned a few names.

"I'll be frank with you Walt. Would you do it?"

"My ordination was in the Methodist Church!" I protested. "And anyway, my career is with the YMCA."

Dr. Evans was persistent, but I felt solid, secure and rewarded in the work I was doing. What he was suggesting would mean a radical change in my life. But he wouldn't give up! After a few months of parlaying over this, he said to me, "Walt, I want an honest answer."

"What do you mean, an honest answer?"

"You haven't prayed about this, have you?"

"No, I guess I haven't. But that's a fair request. I'll do it and give you an honest answer."

Taking only my Bible, I drove up the coast beyond Malibu, rented a motel room and, like Jacob of old, I wrestled with God.

"I won't leave here, God," I said, "until I know what you want me to do."

When he told me, I didn't like it. But never were the skies so blue, the flowers so fragrant, the trees so green...my heart so at peace. I was willing to change jobs.

So in 1946 I was installed as the Minister of Weekday Activities at the First Presbyterian Church of Hollywood. I was there to put people to work for God, to help them find and be Christ's answers to pain and alienation. That has remained the basis of my ministry and a primary motivation for all that I have done wherever I have since served.